Blake Wentworth studies Tamil and Sanskrit literatures, with a specialization in medieval Tamil literature and the religious literatures of south India. He has taught Sanskrit and Tamil at the University of Chicago and Yale University, and Tamil at the University of California, Berkeley. He is the translator of Sundara Ramaswamy's mid-century Tamil classic, *Oru Puliyamarattin Kathai.*

Youth

The Balakandam of Kampan's Ramayana

TRANSLATED BY

BLAKE WENTWORTH

SPEAKING
TIGER

SPEAKING TIGER BOOKS LLP
125-A, Ground Floor, Shahpur Jat
New Delhi—110049

First published in India by Speaking Tiger Books 2022

ISBN: 978-93-5447-000-4
eISBN: 978-93-5447-005-9

10 9 8 7 6 5 4 3 2 1

Typeset in Palatino by SŪRYA, New Delhi
Printed at Chaman Enterprises, New Delhi

மாயாவுக்கு

for Maya

Contents

Kampan's Ramayana

An Introduction

The Ramayana of the late 12th-century Tamil poet Kampan is the supreme achievement of classical Tamil literature. In its narrative scope, conceptual depth, and poetic virtuosity, this grand poem reveals itself as a work of genius.[1] No appreciation of South Asian literature can be complete without it.[2] We begin with a brief account of the Ramayana tradition that Kampan inherited, and his relationship to the Sanskrit poet Valmiki. Next, we turn to the traditional Tamil poetics that shaped Kampan's verses, and the contexts in which he worked: political, religious, and geographical. We end with some remarks on legends associated with the poet, and a brief account of the history of his text's reception.

The Ramayana Tradition

Since the last centuries prior to the Common Era, the epic tale of Rama has inspired new tellings in the literary, plastic and performing arts, which were produced everywhere Indian culture exerted influence.[3] In its magnitude, significance, and the vast space across which it circulated, premodern India knew nothing comparable to this tale. Kampan's Ramayana is one of the most remarkable of these retellings. The text is commonly called *Kamparamayanam* after its author, but Kampan himself titled it *Ramavataram*, 'The Avatar Rama'.[4] It is the first version of the Ramayana to embrace Rama's identity as an avatar, or unique earthly descent, of Vishnu, the supreme being knowable to his devotees through bhakti: the ideal of loving, intimate devotion that was first expressed in south India. Bhakti was well established by Kampan's time, but the sheer scale of his work—somewhere between 10,500 and 12,000 verses comprising six books—gave bhakti an unprecedented vehicle.[5] This one text makes Kampan the most prolific of Tamil authors, and this immensity, taken together with the complexity of his poetic idiom, accounts in large part for the fact that *Kamparamayanam* remains remarkably understudied in Western scholarship.[6] It is a lifework, both for its author and for those who return to it time and again.

With Rama's avatar, the earth gains a perfect embodiment of power who arrives to rid it of a seemingly imperishable antagonist. Rama is a potently liminal being, transcending both mortal humanity and the omniscient, immortal divine.[7] The reason for his appearance on earth is the threat posed by Ravana, an immensely powerful rakshasa, or demon. As a result of his superlative ascetic practices, Ravana had received boons from the gods Brahma and Shiva that made him invulnerable to all he deemed worthy of concern—excluding humankind, which seemed beneath consideration. Ravana proceeded to dominate the gods and threaten the dharma, or normative order, of the cosmos itself. At this pivotal moment of expectation,[8] Vishnu appears before the gods accompanied by his wife, Shri, and the gods beseech him to incarnate as a man to kill Ravana and restore the world to proper order. Vishnu consents, and dictates a series of incarnations in which gods will be born on earth as heroic figures who will prosecute a war against the rakshasas and defeat the demon king. Vishnu himself is born on the earth as Rama, son of Dasharatha, the great emperor of Ayodhya.

Thus begins the train of events that Kampan's audience would have known intimately: Rama and Lakshmana's journey with Vishwamitra from Ayodhya to Mithila, where he weds his beloved wife Sita; their long years of forest exile due to the machinations of Dasharatha's junior queen Kaikeyi; Ravana's abduction of Sita; Rama's alliance with the monkeys after he kills their ruler Valin; the brutal war in Ravana's kingdom of Lanka; Rama's triumph and his reunion with Sita; her public ordeal by fire to affirm her chastity during her imprisonment; their return to Ayodhya in Ravana's sky-chariot; and the institution of perfectly just rule under Rama's kingship.[9]

Much of the Ramayana is a tale of loss and cruel hardship, yet throughout, Kampan emphasizes that Rama is the supreme God, granting salvation to all who worship him.[10] This message is directed not only towards listeners, readers and devotees who approach the text with religious reverence, but towards the characters themselves: even beings killed by Rama's own hand, most notably the monkey lord Valin, proclaim his salvific grace. Yet Rama's divine omnipotence reveals itself only in flashes. This is the mortal riddle that gives his deeds extraordinary psychological depth: Rama is a man who experiences the world's limitations, its pains and instabilities, even as he is forever the divine overlord who transcends all such boundaries.[11] Regardless of their nature or condition—human, animal, god or demon—beings governed by partial knowledge attain a true awareness of Rama's nature when they are transformed by his presence on earth.

Kamparamayanam is profound. Each level in its scale of forms—the six books, their numerous chapters, and individual verses—has its own distinctive architecture and merits study on its own, for they are refracted by each other, offering new possibilities of meaning whenever the text is articulated. Even as it advances the larger narrative, a verse can describe an entire world. In sum, they reveal a lasting artistry that has entertained, guided, and inspired for nearly a millennium. Like any work of genius, *Kamparamayanam* is never interpreted once and for all. Whether approached from a position of reverence, enjoyment, criticism or opposition, the text has stood at the core of the Tamil tradition from premodernity to the present day.

Kampan and Valmiki

Composed in the late centuries BCE, the *Valmiki Ramayana* stands as the ultimate source for the countless versions of the Ramayana composed and performed the world over.[12] From early on, the epic assumed renown not only as a record of the deeds of the hero Rama, but his career as a god on earth. By the early centuries CE, literary consensus declared the text to be the first work of poetry, a status it asserts in its own introduction when describing the conditions of Valmiki's authorship. By the end of the millennium, in south India at least, the *Valmiki Ramayana* came to be treated with profound religious reverence. The epic was no longer only 'the first poem', but a work of scripture.[13]

Kampan invoked this primacy when he wrote his text. He was the first to compose a Ramayana in an Indian vernacular, using Valmiki's declaration of firstness to announce a concordant moment for the Tamil land and its culture.[14] *Kamparamayanam* assumes the universalist dimensions of its predecessor, but locates its founding mythology—the extirpation of evil and the restoration of dharma under the perfect rule of the god-king Rama—within the sociopolitical dimensions of Kampan's world, the late Chola empire. Kampan did not write to supplant *Valmiki Ramayana*, nor did he seek simply to calque it. In his prologue, he announces his modest stance:

> In the land that preserves the words of the noble ascetic
> who composed the great tale that brings us close
> to the archer who pierced seven shala trees
> with an arrow like a curse once launched,
> why would I begin my text when my words are too feeble to count?
> (I v. 5)[15]

He then supplies his own answer:

> The world will despise me, my character fouled,
> was this poem worth voicing at all?
> Only if I take the divine tale sung by this poet
> and make its majesty clear. (I v. 6)

Using the standard trope of humbling himself before his audience (avaiyadakkam)—which brings the poem's political context, a ruling court, to the fore—Kampan proclaims that he seeks to make 'its majesty clear' (matci terikkave). The choice of verb—used in Tamil both to indicate comprehension and physical presence—declares that he is not only rendering the Sanskrit Ramayana intelligible in Tamil, but also asserting that it takes place in the Tamil country.

While the *Valmiki Ramayana* is to some degree a work of synthesis, its first book being composed some centuries[16] after the core (and the seventh and last book even later), Kampan knew the first six books as a coherent whole. He structured his poem analogously, marking the same six divisions, and he followed the same basic tale.[17] *Kamparamayanam* converses with its model:

> Like a cat that approaches the roaring ocean of milk
> and starts trying to lick it dry,
> I tell this tale of Rama, perfect and triumphant
> just as absorbed in my own desire. (I v. 4)

Valmiki's text is an ideal beyond the imperfections of human authorship. Kampan relishes this vast and pristine source, a primordial milk ocean that fills him with yearning.[18] The simile turns on the shift from divine cosmogony, in which the milk ocean was churned to produce the ambrosia of immortality and Vishnu's consort Shri, to the realm of human pleasure and fulfilment. This is the ardent idiom of bhakti that suffuses the text. Kampan asks:

> I will make something clear to the best poets,
> experts in the set ways of threefold Tamil.
> Are the words of madmen, the childish, or devotees
> really to be heeded? (I v. 8)

The poet identifies with the childish (petaiyar), the madmen (pittar), and devotees (pattar, Skt. bhakta), embracing humanity in its faults and limitations, its follies and excesses. Worshippers, in Kampan's telling, are impassioned, heartfelt; instinctively transformed by Rama's presence at an intuitive level of feeling.

While Kampan's text offers an all-inclusive message of salvation, something entirely absent from the *Valmiki Ramayana*, his style is considerably less accessible than Valmiki's. The Sanskrit epic is composed largely in straightforward shloka quatrains, while Kampan's register is highly complex. He employs some eighty-seven varieties of meter—far more than any other Tamil poet.[19]

Kamparamayanam is a devotional work, and also an elite one. Its idiom, intertextual appeals, and modes of circulation demand a high level of reader competence. The great gods and myths familiar from Hinduism play essential roles throughout, but to speak of it only as a religious text constricts the role it has played in Tamil cultural history.[20] Composed in an age when Shaiva and Vaishnava texts were being anthologized into authoritative canons,

Kamparamayanam did not become part of devotional practice in temples or homes.[21] It has always been considered the work of a human author, has not garnered theological commentaries, and has been circulated in a pluralistic context that approached the work as a literary masterpiece.[22]

Kampan's meters, termed viruttam, are somewhat influenced by Sanskritic poetics, being distinguished by four metrically identical lines, but also by second-syllable rhyme (etukai) closely associated with Tamil verse, particularly in musical performance. Beginning in the 6th century, Tamil Vaishnava and Shaiva saints made extensive use of viruttam meters in their hymns, and by the 10th century, when the singing of these hymns had become integral to temple ritual, viruttam had become the prevailing register for narrative poetry.[23] Kampan's viruttam stanzas range from densely hypotactic to swiftly cadenced, intensifying the text's narrative dimensions with phonic care.[24]

Contrast, for instance, Kampan's description of Sita's birth with a quick series of verses expressing Ravana's fury when Hanuman scrambles through Lanka burning its groves and palaces. The first employs a stately cadence to emphasize the moment's divine significance, aligning Sita and her incomparable beauty with Vishnu's two wives:

> A yoke was placed on the mighty necks
> of a pair of bullocks with horns dark as iron,
> which pulled a golden plow inlaid with countless jewels
> fixed with a diamond plowshare, to prepare the field of sacrifice,
> and so we plowed endless furrows in the vastly powerful earth.
> On the blade of the tilling plowshare
> as though the earth goddess herself had revealed her true form,
> alive with the light of the dawning sun
> a princess was born, her qualities so splendid
> even the goddess who rose from the sea with the clear ambrosia
> was humbled, and fell back to worship at her side. (I vv. 757–58)

In the latter, the terse fluidity of the meter matches Ravana's urgency as he roars at his rakshasa court:

> 'Lanka has burned to the ground, and the fire
> finished it off with a burp all because of a stupid monkey?

The gods mock me now!' he said with a grim smile,
'Ravana, mighty in war.

'Whoever sees this feasting fire, seize him
and bring him to me!' ordered the conqueror of the gods.

'If you see the wretched monkey who did this,
catch him, before he slips away!' Ravana cried, seething with rage.
(V vv. 1226–28)

The Ramayana and Tamil Poetics

The characters in *Kamparamayanam* speak perfect Tamil. As the revelation of Rama's true nature emerges in Tamil verse, his deeds come to be attached to the land where the language is spoken.[25] Yet Kampan does far more to make the Ramayana tradition Tamil, both by appealing to Tamil's long poetic tradition and by imbuing a story everyone knew with ideals of literary sophistication crafted by his predecessors.[26] Beyond the requisite narrative elements arrayed in Valmiki's text, Kampan integrates a wealth of Puranic lore, southern bhakti devotionalism (however much steeped in the classic philosophical terms of the Samkhya), and local traditions unknown to Valmiki.[27]

From its first verses, the text declares its reliance on Tamil literary tradition: Clouds as white as Shiva's body drink seawater, and grow dark as Vishnu before they pour down rain that floods the Sarayu River to inundate the fertile fields of Ayodhya. For readers familiar with the earliest strata of Tamil classical poetry collectively known as cankam literature, Kampan's skill at blending the landscapes of Ayodhya with the Kaveri River running through his own homeland invokes an esteemed poetic tropology (see I vv. 29–32). The poet appeals to cankam landscapes by mixing them, describing how the river carries off goods from local areas and brings them somewhere new, changing them in the process.[28] It is, as he tells us, the flow of life, the sheltered oneness behind apparent diversity:

The water flowing from the mountains,
pouring down to mix with the sea

> is single at its source, like the sure truth offered by the Vedas,
> then divides, like the God described by the great religions
> whose scholarship branches into many different fields.
>
> ...the Sarayu spreads into many gardens dusted with flower pollen,
> like souls that enter different bodies as the texts describe.
>
> (I vv. 31–32)

Kampan later takes the motif of the rushing river and uses multiply interpretable phrases to compare it directly to the akam landscapes of the cankam corpus (tinai): the environments—heart-scapes, as it were—that connote particular experiences of love, relying on his audience's shared appreciation for classical tropes to refigure their significance:

> The heroes saw the Godavari River
> and it was like the poetry of masters
> An ornament for the earth goddess fine as poetic figures delightful to all,
> it flows over the five landscapes like the poetry that speaks of them.
> Nourishing the fields and carrying splendid treasures
> just as verse sustains wisdom and grants every human aim,
> the calm pools on its banks are like poetry's theme of inner life,
> its currents run clear and cool as sweet verses,
> and it sparkles with a light bright as the flames of poetic knowledge.
>
> (III v. 220)

Introducing the tinai landscapes to the storied locales of the Ramayana makes it live in the Tamil country, mapping a geography known through lore onto the world of readers' lives.

Kamparamayanam also invokes established themes of puram, the counterpart to the akam, or interior, world in cankam literature. Puram is the exterior, the land where akam values are imposed. Given the enormity of the Ramayana battle, which constitutes a third of Kampan's text, the variety of puram themes is immense: eyirkotal (storming the walls); eyirkattal (defending the walls); tanaimaram (nobility in battle, characteristic of a king who rushes to the battlefront regardless of consequence, or who has compassion for his foes because they have faced a powerful army); kattinittapal (relinquishing the throne); talinchi (a king who does not pursue and destroy an adversary in full retreat); and many more.[29]

Kampan is perhaps the finest Tamil poet to have rendered individual personalities and the world they inhabit.[30] Rama is divinely righteous yet fully human, and Kampan delves intently into what makes him so. We learn of his doubts, his anger, his frenzied madness when Sita is taken, his lack of compassion during her ordeal by fire. The rakshasas are monstrous, yet Kampan aligns his audience with their pleasures and sorrows, lending tragic depth to their fated destruction. He situates this psychological focus in highly detailed environments, using the technique of naturalistic description (tanmaiyani, Skt. svabhavokti), which by the 12th century had come to epitomize literary elegance. Yet the dramatic pace of the narrative, shifting between swift bursts of action and near suspensions of time, when continuous stanzas explore moods or offer expansive descriptions of natural beauty, does not falter; Kampan's text is regularly called *Kampanatakam* (Kampan's Drama) because of its absorbing plot.

Verses work multiply, developing the scene and furthering the plot as whole, yet also functioning singly to create their own self-contained worlds.[31] Consider a moment when young people stop to pick flowers and share them with their lovers:

> A man climbs a laurel tree to pluck flowers, and in his heart
> a woman with scented hair and a charming brow climbs with him.
> Men may become great, their wisdom grows,
> but will they ever conquer women with full, proud breasts?
> (I v. 1002)

A past moment becomes present occurrence, tied to an enduring maxim that closes with a question, directing thoughts to the future. Kampan delights in the play of motion and stillness, savouring the fluid dimensions of time that an eternal god born to live and die in the world provokes. For instance, when Rama and Lakshmana enter Mithila with their preceptor Vishwamitra:

> They saw bridled horses racing past, minds absorbed in speed
> coming into the turn like a potter's wheel as he spins it hard.
> They turn too fast for the eye to see them singly
> and become a constant whole
> like the insight of the sages, or the friendship of the noble. (I v. 566)

In a seminal essay on the use of clichés in *Kamparamayanam*, David Shulman identifies how the poet appeals to established tropes to achieve distinct effects.[32] Readers continually encounter the familiar: the 'sea-girt earth', 'woman with elegant jewellery', 'cloud-scraped towers' and the like. Such clichés have iconic power because they are so sustained and evocative, drawing a verse beyond the confines of narrative time.[33] Yet Kampan also transforms them in inspired moments that set a cliché to new purpose. When Sita cannot sleep, wounded by the lovesickness the sight of Rama has caused her, she cries out,

> White fire, you rose up in black fire
> the darkness known as encroaching night
> that kept growing stronger and stronger, coming to swallow the world!
> You confront us as an enemy, me and the pounding sea
> driven off in defeat by the hue of that lord
> whose magic will not leave me. (I v. 631)

The moon burning the skin of a lovesick woman is an oft-used trope, yet here, darkness, which normally offers cooling respite, is a fire that overwhelms the moon's power. Kampan celebrates colour, here the darkness of Vishnu's body. Yet here colour elicits pain, consuming Sita as swelling waves of fire, then water, then Rama's body itself, overwhelming one another in an otherworldly experience of night. As the clichés are reworked, the verse becomes difficult and strange, echoing Sita's tempestuous thoughts as she feels the first depths of passion.

Fate and Dharma

The emotional tenor of Kampan's poetry responds to his most pressing narrative obligation: how to portray Rama as a man who experiences the fullness of human life, yet whose deeds carry cosmic significance.[34] *Kamparamayanam* blends these divergent levels by interweaving a set of narrative frames that differ in knowledge of Rama's divinity. At the outermost level, that of Kampan and his audience, Rama is Vishnu the supreme being. The poet begins here, and reintroduces this frame throughout the text by using epithets that assert Rama's cosmic purpose. He is the 'fundamental principle' (mutal porul), the 'creator of the world' (ulakam inran), the 'first cause equal only to himself' (tan akiya takamaip porul), and many more. From within the narrative, the gods understand Rama's true nature, for it was they who begged Vishnu to assume human form (I vv. 197–200).

Does Rama know his own true nature? He effects intense change on those around him, but Kampan keeps Rama's self-understanding mysterious. Over the course of his life, he reveres his superiors—father, preceptor and the like—and he performs customary rituals of worship. He feels in knowable ways. The great sages, whose omniscient awareness transcends the flow of time, recognize Rama's divinity and proclaim it to him directly. After Rama has fulfilled his first heroic charge, protecting Vishwamitra's forest sacrifice from the depredations of the rakshasas, the sage declares:

> 'You created all the worlds, and later you protected them,
> swallowing everything living and still in your great stomach.
> The world will say I am blessed because you saved my sacrifice,
> but I think of it differently, I know you are far more.' (I v. 468)

Rama offers no response. When Parashurama proclaims him to be the supreme god, and hands him the divine bow Vishnu previously used to best Shiva in a contest between the two gods (I vv. 1376–79), Rama remains silent. This is the signal moment when a previous avatar of Vishnu confers the fullness of his power upon another, yet Rama remains taciturn. He is told he is God, he does not tell.

Rama effects extraordinary change in the world, establishing dharma through his justice and his martial prowess, but more than anything, he inspires love. This love situates his effects on the world at a level deeper than speech. It is an interior, intuitive feeling that leads others to strive to explain it when they are transformed by his presence. Sita, whose consuming love for the prince is first sparked by a single shared glance, tells Lakshmana, 'Those who have only known him for a day would give their own lives for him.' (III v. 819) So it is with Rama's brothers, with Hanuman, Guha, Sugriva, Jatayu, and so many others whom he meets during his travels. Do they know him as God? Kampan generally leaves this an unresolved question, asking if people could ever truly know that Rama was born to redeem them (I v. 294).

Indeed, over the course of the epic, Rama appears fascinated by the world, as if his effects prompt interpretation, rather than his interpretation of the world prompting him to cause effects. In one of the Ramayana's cherished scenes, when the dust from Rama's foot releases Ahalya from the long curse that caused her to stand as unfeeling stone, Ahalya 'stood there in her full beauty as if one with the ankleted feet of the lord who sees the truth'. (I v. 540) He is 'meyy unar pavan', the lord (Skt. bhavan) who sees—and here unar connotes an intuitive, felt knowledge, not a calculated act of cognition—mey, the truth, the real. Yet Rama's response to what has transpired is remarkable: 'How could something like this have happened in the world?' (I v. 542) He learns how to be God by living, and being God, as he grows and learns of his heritage and his destiny, performing deeds unthinkable for anyone else, means being a man who feels things fully. As Kampan proclaims, 'Truly, human nature has triumphed!' (manudam venrat' anre)

Where is the love that Rama creates found? The Tamil poets know this field well as akam, the province of uyir—flowing in-ness, life-breath, selfhood—transformed by love's powers.[35] This is the world of the cankam landscapes through which Kampan's poem begins its flow, vibrant, rhythmically alive, even as it flows, too, within the individual self. 'Uyir,' as David Shulman has gracefully described it, 'flows through bodies that seem to contain it but are really only precarious vessels for it. Moment by moment, the person breathes the entire cosmos in and out, and the cosmos itself, infused with uyir and moving with its rhythm, is also breathing in and out.'[36] Kampan's Rama is the fundamental principle (mutal porul) behind this flow: 'They say he is present within and without, like body (un), life-breath (uyir), and feelings (unarvu)' (II v. 1), but he does not stand beyond it: he feels it, he revels in it, and for most of the Ramayana, he suffers its pains.

Rama's beauty is perfect; Sita is so beautiful that she causes mountains, walls, granite and grass to flow with love. When they first see each another as Sita stands on a palace terrace (a celebrated innovation of Kampan's that depends wholly on the larger rhythms of shared uyir) their inner selves take hold of one another, destined for a oneness they, as Vishnu and Shri, have always already had:

Then their eyes met, seized each other, consumed each other,
their hearts did not stay in them, but went out to become one
as the lord looked at her and she looked at him.

Her eyes as they watched him were two sharpened spears
that sank into the arms of that strong, well-built man,
and the red eyes of the hero who wore ringing anklets
bored into the breasts of the girl gorgeous as Shri.

Bound together by their eyes as they drank each other in,
their inner selves pulled and drew each other close.
The lord with a sturdy bow, and the girl with eyes like swords
felt their hearts travel out to be one on their shared journey.

The girl with no waist and the man beyond reproach
became a single soul, two bodies uniting,
two beings set apart, pulled from their union in bed on the sea,
once more joined with each other: what need is there for words?
(I vv. 590–93)

Every moment of separation they endure from that moment on is tortuous. When Rama loses Sita to Ravana's wiles and first knows the pain he will suffer, he is driven to madness beyond endurance, for he has been broken from within. He stands 'like the sweet life-breath split from its vessel, the body, and keeps searching for sign of it, but does not find it.' (III v. 962)[37]

Rama's anguish over his loss of Sita must be contrasted with his larger view of the fate provoked by dharma. Terrible hardship can occur, and such trials, when they lie beyond the failings of personal responsibility, must be dealt with calmly. When Lakshmana threatens mass slaughter of anyone who might prevent Rama from becoming king after their banishment to the forest, Rama asks him to consider the nature of the world, contrasting the fate that dharma brings with individual blame. Fate is to be endured, blame (pizhai) must be rectified:

A river is not to blame if its sweet waters run dry,
and so it is that the king bears no blame, nor the woman who raised us.
Wisdom bears no blame, and blame does not lie with Bharata,
fate itself is the one to blame, so how can you be so angry, brother?
(II v. 426)

Evil is itself encompassed by dharma, and Kampan embraces hardship and tribulation: Rama's presence on earth occurs within such conditions, it does not reject them.[38] Contrast his statement to Lakshmana to his frenzied madness after Sita has been taken, when he declares that he alone is to blame. 'This is the deed that has ruined me!' he thinks, and cannot stop thinking until his heart is crushed by the weight of it (III v. 960). Valin's death, too, is in Kampan's telling the result of his own blameworthy acts. Rama rebukes him for treating his brother Sugriva with contempt and threats, and for violating Sugriva's wife's chastity. But Kampan repeatedly asks, can be so certain that fate dictates the conditions of life? Does blame lie in transgressions against dharma, or fall within dharma itself? The poet complicates things from the beginning, raising questions about fate, dharma, and blame that knot them into tangles. When Vishwamitra urges Rama to slay the rakshasi Tataka, the young prince is troubled. She is a woman; is it not a crime against dharma to kill her? Vishwamitra's response that her monstrosity makes her a non-woman seems specious, and it is only Rama's belief that following his preceptor's order constitutes dharma that causes him to proceed. As Valin nears death, he makes the pitiable point that he could have offered Rama great help if fate had only been kind to him (V 7 vv. 140–41). Fate, dharma, blame: the compelling response to the insoluble problems they raise, Kampan asserts, is to love God devotedly. However flawed, devotees are loved in return.

Kampan's rakshasas merit their own substantial treatment, and while we can only sketch things in brief here, the epic's two most prominent demons, Shurpanakha and Ravana, reveal the depths of madness, fury and the brokenness that separation can provoke when a loving self commits to—and is imprisoned by—an unattainable union. When Shurpanakha first sees Rama and attempts to seduce him, he rejects her out of hand, toying with her as her desire grows and with it her deceit. The poet adds a heartrending scene to Valmiki's sparing rendition of the tale, in which Shurpanakha lies awake through the night, enduring the anguish of separation that Rama and Sita themselves had felt when they first saw each other. Kampan asks his audience to identify with her pain.[39] Love is central to the rakshasas' nature: the love shared between Ravana and his siblings; Mandodari's love for her husband Ravana; Indrajit's love for his father; Ravana's tragic love for his ill-starred son. Rama and Sita call the rakshasas evil, and their carnivorous ferocity should not be minimized, but to call them evil diminishes the complexity of the term unless such evil operates within the redemptive dharma that governs the Ramayana war, not beyond it. Rakshasas exhibit nobility, deep devotion to family and the ideals of martial loyalty evocative of the Ramayana's protagonists. Kumbhakarna, when faced with an impossible fusion of dharma and fate, goes willingly to his death out of loyalty to his brother Ravana, while Vibhishana, who offers devoted love to Rama, abandons his family and turns spy against them. Dharma proves complex for individual lives, and it is the rakshasas' sheer identity as rakshasas, serving Ravana as he masters the worlds, that assures their fate.

Shurpanakha's encounter with Rama and Lakshmana is Kampan's prelude to the exploration of these questions. She is helpless in her desire, yet her actions are predicated on lies. Rama is defined by his truthfulness and Sita her faithful constancy, both revealed in physical beauty. Shurpanakha's beauty, by contrast, is artifice, crafted to deceive. She has none of the shame expected of this patriarchal world, and compounds her lies by declaring Sita to be the real rakshasa. When she moves to kill Sita while the brothers are away (III 5 v. 92), her true anthropophagic nature drives the discontinuity between her invented form and her genuine desires beyond resolution. Lakshmana's violence against her is brutal, creating still another form for her: the horrific, so disfigured that Rama does not recognize her when he later finds her wailing in the forest.[40] Her mutilation triggers the series of events that cause the rakshasas' downfall, resonating in the savagery of war and Ravana's own mutilation as he loses his ten heads, conscious of his emergent ruin at every step.

Ravana is a profound figure. An immensely powerful king whose court is as commanding and elegant as any, his character is drawn from Valmiki's Ramayana and strong south Indian religious currents that proclaim him a great devotee of Shiva. Indeed, when Shurpanakha first calls to him after having been mutilated by Lakshmana, she stresses the power he has gained through this devotion, praising how he lifted and shook Shiva's mountain home Kailasa, and how in return for his extreme austerities, the god gifted him the sword Chandrahasa. Kampan does not portray Ravana as monstrous, as his devotion to Shiva, his commitment to masterful rule, and his intense love for his family make clear. Ravana is a brahman, superb musician, speaker of polished Tamil, a reciter of the Vedas. He exalts in power, and this proves his undoing. When he shakes Mount Kailasa to demonstrate his peerless might, his realization of the immensity of Shiva's power when the god crushes him with his toe leads to total devotion to the god. The boons he subsequently receives, however, convince him that no living thing can hinder him.

Ravana is tortured by his desire for Sita, and his uyir—his wholeness—fragments as his heart travels out to this woman he has never seen but who now dominates his consciousness. Like Shurpanakha, his approach is predicated on deceit. He arrives before Sita in the guise of an emaciated ascetic (III 9 vv. 20–25), leading her to believe that his words must carry the power of truth. In pride heated by an intense mix of envy and resentment towards Rama, he praises himself beyond all measure in the third person, claiming Ravana to be the master of the world (III 9 vv. 41–50).[41] When Sita mocks the rakshasas, noting that Rama, a mere man, has killed Viradha and Khara, he bursts into his true form, paralyzing her with fear (III 9 vv. 64–65). The duplicitous veneer has fallen away and appearance reflects character. Overwhelmed with lust, the mighty rakshasa king is ready to carry her off.

Sita is imprisoned within an ashoka grove in Lanka, but Ravana becomes the true prisoner, captive to his own illusions of limitless power and his desire for Sita. When he first responds to Shurpanakha's anguished cries, he proclaims:

> Those who committed this crime inflicted it on me
> they acted with such zeal, but they are only men
> and still they breathe with life (uyir)!
> But here is my sword, these are my shoulders,

> I have a long life thanks to Shiva who drank the flooding sea's poison,
> and I, of course, am still here! (III 7 v. 60)

This is a masterstroke of irony. Ravana, contemptuous of the lives of these mortal men, readies to destroy them, but Rama's uyir is the life of the world itself, within which Ravana's own existence plays out. He accuses Rama and Lakshmana of crime (pizhai), yet his abduction of Sita is the true crime. 'I, of course, am still here!' (naann ulenn anro) he cries, and boasts of his sword and long life, yet already his life is beginning to wane, breaking under the power of his desire for Sita, whose uyir blends as one with Rama's own. For Ravana, the rest of the Ramayana is a tale of loss. He will lose his army and much of his family, his royal fame, his son Indrajit, his kingdom, and each of his ten heads till he dies. His destruction is fated because of his pride and avarice, but that makes it no less brutal: Kampan's description of Ravana suffering as he wanders the battlefield to find the body of his son is one of the text's most poignantly rendered episodes (VI 28).

When Rama first defeats the rakshasa king and refrains from killing him because he lacks weapons, and perhaps, as Rama says, because the rakshasa's failure has caused the evil within him to die, Ravana cannot stop. The forces that have led to the disintegration of his consciousness and the ruin of his kingdom have a momentum of their own. He is by this point miserable, a superhuman being driven to a ruin inevitable from the moment Vishnu and the other gods took mortal form on earth:

> He had always been triumphant; if he fought it was to conquer,
> yet now he had lost his jewelled crown at the speed of sound
> and he seemed like the daytime or nighttime
> if the sun or bright moon had gone missing.
>
> Even though he was great and had vanquished the worlds
> the rakshasa who lost his crown heavy with flawless gems
> seemed like a man robbed of all his astonishing fame gained in war
> by a verse of abuse sung by a masterful poet.
>
> He looked down at the ground,
> the glow gone from his face, empty hands at his sides,
> his body like a banyan tree with its hanging roots.

'This is how it ends,' yelled the world,
'for those who transgress dharma!'
His body turned dark, and he scratched the earth with his toe.
(VI 14 vv.46–48)

In the end, he is little more than Sita's jailer, who meets Rama not as an equal but as a failure.

Rama and Sita, however, are not made whole, for the separation of their inner lives—the suffering that conditions most of the epic—resumes when Rama threatens to banish his love because she may not have been chaste during her long captivity (VI 37). Love, in the Tamil poetic consciousness, is volatile, and Rama's abandonment of Sita reveals the inherent possibility of separation even when love in union seems lasting. Outraged, Sita proclaims her chastity, which proves so pure that in the fire ordeal that follows she burns the fire itself. But the latent rejection remains, affecting the couple's life thereafter. 'The final meeting of Rama and Sita,' as Shulman argues, 'follows the more general paradigm of the lovers' thorny career in Tamil poetry and its extensions into the sphere of *bhakti* devotionalism. Lovers, like devotees, are not meant to be at peace.'[42]

Kampan's Date

Kamparamayanam was a text consciously written to last, and fittingly, Kampan did not bind his work to a particular time. Its date, however, has been subject to some dispute, and deserves analysis.[43] Scholarly discussion regularly turns to prefatory verses penumbral to the text, or fleeting allusions to ruling kings of the Chola empire (9th–13th c. CE), yielding dates of either 885 or 1185.[44] Turning to the text proper, a well-known verse (VI v. 2695) describes Hanuman beholding the land of Uttarakuru, 'which is like the lands by the golden Kaveri River ruled by Tyakamavinotan, the lord crowned with a garland of blossoming flowers'. As Vaiyapuri Pillai has noted, Tyakamavinotan (Skt. Tyagamahavinoda) is a title of Kulottunga III, whose reign—if Kampan is referring to a contemporary king—accords well with the 1185 attribution.[45] Yet the text also mentions a king Amalan ('The Stainless'), whom the 12th-century poet Ottakkuttar identifies as Kulottunga II (*fl.* 1133–50),[46] and it regularly employs the term Uttaman (the Supreme), leading some to argue that the work should be dated to the reign of Uttama Chola (*fl.* 970–85). Such variations, clearly, offer little help. The prefatory stanzas are not part of the text proper, and the allusions to royal titles are too fleeting and nebulous to be reliable.

A more productive approach is to evaluate *Kamparamayanam*'s style, poetic figuration, and thematic structure to determine intertextual parallels and the author's cultural milieu. Taken together, these features suggest that the text was composed in the Kaveri heartland in the late 12th century.

Political Context: The Late Chola Empire

Although reading *Kamparamayanam* through the lens of Kampan's political world by no means exhausts the range and complexity of his masterwork, he invokes political means for cultural ends.[47] If the poem is not read with the Tamil political landscape in mind, we cannot appreciate all that Kampan achieved. By its very nature, a Ramayana declares a beginning, a new cultural order.[48] Kampan would not displace Valmiki's epic, which as we have seen was by Kampan's time understood as a religious work subject to exhaustive theological exegesis, but would stand with it, sharing its guiding concerns with polity, kingship, martial valour, and human suffering.[49] Kampan's creation of an idealized Tamil geography governed by perfect rule is a political assertion. Through its articulation, it encourages its audience to recognize in the text's verses the conditions of their own lives and place in Tamil history.

Kamparamayanam is a courtly work. He regularly praises his patron, Cataiyappan of Venneynallur, presumably a wealthy local noble (no information on his identity or town is today available).[50] He participated, therefore, in the scale of political forms that composed Chola rule.[51] With its vivid descriptions of Dasharatha's and Ravana's courts, and its concern with the nature of kingship imbued with divine power, *Kamparamayanam* is inherently linked to royal concerns.[52] When Kampan composed his poem in the late 12th century, he wrote in a period of general political stability that followed some three centuries of political expansion that had seen the Cholas win victories throughout south India, up the east coast to the Ganges, and the Sumatran kingdom of Srivijaya. While no longer at their territorial apogee—Chola control over Sri Lanka, for example, had by this point been lost—it was a time of exceptional cultural continuity. The Cholas sustained social conservatism, and Kampan's poem resonates deeply with that goal. Perfect rule is contrasted with a demonic Other, and adherence to political will ensures dharma will triumph.

For some five hundred years, Tamil had been moving from a vernacular used in speech and documentary inscriptions to a literary register, subject to myriad governing treatises that regimented its expression and documented its history.[53] With Kampan, the language, for many, reached its apogee, but the textuality that conditioned his work began earlier in the Tamil country. Adaptations of the Sanskrit Mahabharata were composed in Tamil and the 9th and 10th centuries.[54] As would be true for Kampan's Ramayana, the vernacularization of the Mahabharata, which explores the nature of Indian kingship, its continuance, and the means of its territorial extension, appears to have been foundational to the realization of a regional polity with reflexively cosmopolitan dimensions.[55] There may have been earlier Tamil Ramayanas as well: a commentary on *Yapparunkalam* (11th–12th c.) mentions a Ramayana that may very tentatively be ascribed to the 7th century, and we also find reference to a Tamil Jain Ramayana in the commentary on the *Viracholiyam* (late 11th c.) and the *Shripuranam*.[56] The fact that neither of these Ramayanas is in any way extant, however, runs counter to the pioneering importance that originative vernacular renditions of the epics have had throughout South Asia, and casts doubt on the possibility that they were ever finished, or preserved in a substantive way.

Kampan evoked the ordering cultural values of the Cholas, the most powerful kingdom south India had known.[57] The period of the later Cholas has long been described as a Tamil 'golden age', primarily because of the political and cultural integration that led to extraordinary artistic efflorescence.[58] They are the most intently studied south Indian dynasty for a reason: the age witnessed an effusion of literature, architecture, religious and philosophical theorization, and confident political self-assurance still upheld as a period of unique cultural merit. This is not to say that the state exercised a monopoly on coercive power, or on judicial or fiscal administration. Political affairs remained largely at the local level, and this decentralization of state power was on the increase by Kampan's time.[59] But the Chola imperium created the stable conditions for commissions like *Kamparamayanam*. The Tamil language had become translocal, spread on maritime routes that extended out to Southeast Asia, coastal areas on the Red Sea, and China. This was a 'universalist ethos', which to judge by the number of pioneering works of literature composed under Chola rule, was sustained at all levels of lordship, from the king to ambitious local patrons.[60] Kampan's text embodies this confidence and honours its achievements, consolidating the emergent ascendancy of a Tamil literary field that mapped onto lived reality. His text told his audience who they were.

Literary Context

This universalist vision of Tamil was inflected by categories that emphasized Sanskrit poesis.[61] As Sanskrit and Tamil shaped each other in ways that defy easy separation of the two, the resultant 'multi-statal grammatical or constituent complexity' of these languages, as Rich Freeman has termed it, provoked the creation of meta-treatises on poesis and grammar that aimed to systematize and promulgate this shared sense of a unique era when the riches of Tamil literary history, properly understood, offered imaginative possibilities for the future.[62] In the field of literature, this wave of creativity inspired authors to find new ways to write, but it also stemmed from a growing ambition to look back and order the past. This was a culture absorbed in conserving and shaping its history, advancing itself as an epistemic consummation. The Cholas brought Tamil under the aegis of philology. The 10th through 12th centuries witnessed the composition of grammars and theoretical texts on poetry, as well as their attendant commentaries, and in the 11th century the age of the great commentators begins, in which culturally central texts were interpreted according to emergent theorizations.[63]

In the field of religion, similar processes of historical reflection and re-articulation were at work. Tamil hymns of religious saints from centuries past were anthologized and standardized. For both Vaishnavas and Shaivas, these canons were instituted through Chola political will, and came to be regarded as equivalent to—if not superseding—the Sanskrit Vedas. The Vaishnava Tamil canon, *Nalayira Divyaprabhandam*, comprises the hymns of the saints known as the Alvar ('The Immersed', 6th–10th c.).[64] Perhaps a half-century later, a tale of textual loss and recovery occurs among Shaivas. Nampiyandar Nampi, a priest of the Chidambaram temple, is said to have miraculously regained Tamil hymns of the three greatest Shaiva saints (Nayanmar), Appar, Campantar, and Cuntarar (7th–9th c.?) from one of the temple's locked chambers, and anthologized them as the text *Tevaram* at the behest of Rajaraja Chola I (985–1014).[65] As is the case for Tamil Shaiva texts in general, they garner no premodern commentaries. Tales of ancient hymns lost to time and then miraculously recovered, collated and promoted in temple practice advance Tamil as a principal mode of elite cultural expression. *Nalayira Divyaprabandham* and *Tevaram* are deeply concerned with the geography of temples and pilgrimage links in the Kaveri River heartland. By Kampan's time, this had crystallized into a religiosity articulated in temple practice, denoting a sacred geography that the poet was able to invoke as he crafted his own vision of a land pervaded by the living presence of the divine.[66]

The Chola period is also famed for a new development in temple artistry: portrayals of Ramayana scenes. Two points must be emphasized here. None of these temples was dedicated to Rama, and in the Tamil country, they are all Shaiva, corresponding to the Cholas' own commitment to Shiva worship.[67] Six temples offer prominent Ramayana representations (though this does not indicate an emergent Rama cult in the Tamil country): Nageshvara temple in Kumbakonam (more than sixty scenes in relief); Brahmapurishvara temple in Pullamankai (over sixty); Cataiyar temple in Tirucennampunti (over sixty); Naltunai Ishvara temple in Punchai (forty-two); Samavedishvara temple in Tirumankalam (some twenty); and Kamakshi temple in Dharmapuri.[68] The period is also well known for bronzes of Kodanda Rama ('Rama wielding the bow'), Sita, Lakshmana and Hanuman. These bronzes might seem to indicate the emergence of Rama worship, but their popularity should not be overstated. They are limited to the reign of Aditya Chola (*fl.* 870–907), who himself bore the title Kodanda Rama. If the Ramayana bronzes indicate a link between Tamil religiosity and political ends, the tale halts with Aditya.[69] In sum, Kampan's cultural environment included a substantial array of Ramayana narratives wrought in the plastic arts under a Shaiva mantle.

The Ramayana narrative was also moving in textual and oral currents through the Tamil country, as is evident from the earliest literary strata. Cankam literature makes fleeting note of Rama: *Purananuru* 378 refers to Ravana's abduction of Sita and forest monkeys comically wearing the jewellery she casts down as a trail for Rama; *Akananuru* 70 refers to Rama's war council in Dhanuskodi prior to his invasion of Lanka; and *Purananuru* 358 is attributed to Vanmikiyar (Valmiki).[70] Ramayana episodes are found in cycles of the post-cankam work *Paripadal* (19–50), while the grand poem *Cilappatikaram* (6th–7th c.?) describes the Chola seaport capital Kaveripumpattinam once Kovalan and Kannaki had left it as looking like Ayodhya after Rama departed, and later notes how the Jain nun Kavunti consoles the hero Kovalan by describing how Rama suffered (13.64–66; 14.46–48).[71] Religious sources, however, shaped Kampan's vision of the Ramayana far more. As Friedhelm Hardy has demonstrated, this devotionalism takes separation from the beloved as a principal mode of interacting with God in the world.[72] *Kamparamayanam* is largely a tale of loss and separation, and Kampan draws deeply from the hymns of the Alvar (and to a lesser extent, Nayanmar) to develop the narrative elements in his Ramayana that depict Rama as the supreme being.

The Alvar knew the Ramayana well, including elements not present in Valmiki's text that must have been moving in oral currents in the south.[73] The epic, as Archana Venkatesan has argued, provided 'numerous examples of a devotee's paradigmatic surrender, of god's boundless grace and of the fundamentally reciprocal relationship between god and his devotees'.[74] The Alvar express their devotion to Vishnu both through reference to narrative elements of the epic and through the adoption of first-person voicings of individual characters. Such allusions introduce two features of the Ramayana that Kampan will employ: they associate characters in the epic with a paradigmatic relationship between the devotee and God, and they place the Ramayana's geography in the Tamil country by superimposing stories from the epic onto Vaishnava temple sites. In Andal's *Tiruppavai* (9th c.), for example, the saint sings of how Rama's anger is roused properly on behalf of the devotee, who is associated with Sita after she has been abducted by Ravana.[75] Scores of examples could be given of the Alvar's references to the Ramayana, and Kampan regularly draws from these depictions, sometimes directly reproducing them, more often through indirect reference and suggestion.[76]

Two Alvar in particular are vital to Kampan's text: Kulacekara Alvar (9th c.) and the greatest of them all, Nammalvar (*ca*. 8th–9th c.). The hagiographical tradition states that Kulacekara delighted in hearing the epic, and became so distressed by the thought of Rama heading off to face the rakshasa army that he summoned his own troops to go to Rama's aid.[77] His *Periyal Tirumozhi* is a folksong lullaby that narrates Rama's life sung in the voice of his mother Kausalya (8), assumes the voice of Dasharatha to express the anguish of separation from Rama after he has been sent off to the forest (9), and then asks, 'When will the day come when we can see Rama, our eyes shining with joy,' thus beginning a narrative summary of the Ramayana entire (10).[78]

Nammalvar is the most revered of the Alvar, not only because of his four works in the *Divyaprabandham*, which are equated with the four Vedas, but because he is held to be the first Shrivaishnava spiritual master (acharya), a yogi whose verses are suffused with descriptions of his mystical experiences.[79] Nammalvar draws deeply from the conventions of akam poetry, developing an aesthetic in which the experience of divine love is figured as a reshaped expression of cankam conventions. The love between hero and heroine is transformed into the experience of the divine beloved: emotionally charged, intimate, and overwhelming.[80] The beloved is, like the hero of cankam verses, often absent. Among his four texts in the *Divyaprabandham*, his hundred-verse poem *Tiruviruttam* stands supreme.[81] Kampan's grand poem is suffused with *Tiruviruttam*'s theology and poetic register. Most obviously, this occurs at the level of meter, for *Tiruviruttam*, as its name reflects, consists of interlinked verses composed in the viruttam meter, instilling the performative, musical qualities with which this meter is associated. Like *Tiruviruttam*, *Kamparamayanam* is a work to be performed and enjoyed, and which like its bhakti predecessors not only describes god acting in the world, but is held to effect his favour:

> For those who narrate the power of Rama's arms
> when he wields his bow, wreathed in a victory garland,
> and how Shri looks on with love in her eyes
> as the rakshasas crumble and he paves the way to release,
> all that they seek will come to hand in wisdom and in fame. (I v. 12)

For Nammalvar too, Rama is God supreme, the refuge through which all things living and still will be saved.[82] He does not envision Vishnu only as Rama—indeed Krishna, not Rama, is instanced more frequently as the divine presence on earth—but his verses in praise of Rama declare that he liberates his devotees as the master of a perfect dharmic order:

> Will the wise study anything but Lord Rama?
> In grand Ayodhya, he esteems the living and still
> right down to the ants, right down to the grass
> in the world that four-faced Brahma has made.
>
> He was born on earth and endured misery for all humankind,
> hunting down rakshasas who punished the earth so he could destroy them,
> protecting the land and granting salvation! Learn of his deeds,
> and who on earth would belong to anyone but Narayana?
>
> (*Tiruvaymozhi* 3605–06)

Kampan's Rama invokes Nammalvar's vision of the avatar enacted on an epic scale and glorified in the fulness of his humanity.

Kamparamayanam contains a wealth of mythological lore not found in Valmiki's telling, which largely derives from the most influential bhakti work of all, the *Bhagavata Purana,* composed in the Tamil country at roughly the same time when the Alvars' hymns were being anthologized into the *Divyaprabandham* (*ca.* 10th c.).[83] Kampan further appeals to the Shaiva anthology *Tevaram,* which makes frequent reference to Ravana's glory. The rakshasa is described as the superlative devotee, willing to endure agonizing pain because of his devotion to Shiva. The hymns refer to Ravana shaking Kailasa, only to be crushed by Shiva's toe. Ravana responds by crafting a lute using the sinews of his arm as the strings, then chanting the *Sama Veda,* which pleases Shiva so much that he grants him the boon of prolonged life and the divine sword Chandrahasa.[84] *Tevaram* exalts his power in almost every decad.[85] Kampan's Ravana draws on his *Tevaram* character: his supercilious scorn that leads him to try and shake Kailasa; his pain when Shiva crushes him; his devotion made pure by the loss of pride; Shiva's delight in the rakshasa's music and ascetic practice; and the gifts of prolonged life and the divine sword.[86]

While Kampan drew upon the recently anthologized hymns of the Vaishnava and Shaiva saints and puranic lore, other literary masterpieces of the Chola period had greater influence on his Ramayana. As scholars have long noted, the outstanding treasure of Tamil Jain literature, *Civakacintamani* of Tiruttakkatevar (late 9th–early 10th c.), was Kampan's principal model.[87] While *Civakacintamani*'s plot derives from earlier Jain texts in Sanskrit and Prakrit, the work itself is steeped in contemporary Tamil culture, particularly the thriving urban and mercantile setting of the emergent Chola imperium, including its role in maritime trade.[88] Kampan knew this text intimately. He emulates *Civakacintamani*'s grand scale and adheres to its chaptered structure. In a point of convergence with his recourse to Nammalvar's *Tiruviruttam,* he follows *Civakacintamani*'s innovative use of viruttam meter in a grand poetic work. Tiruttakkatevar's use of this meter brought its performative, artist-centred quality out of the context of bhakti hymns linked to temple practice and into the realm of courtly literature. The text's varied scenes, including everything from philosophy, theology, erotics to mythological lore, offered Kampan a model for his own vast narrative range.[89] He also reproduces specific topical chapters, and indeed individual verses, sometimes word for word.[90]

While *Civakacintamani* provided a template and its eroticism helped shape Kampan's aesthetic, more than a third of *Kamparamayanam* contains minutely detailed descriptions of war. Here too Kampan had archetypes, most famously the earliest work of Chola court poetry, the *Kalingattup Parani* of Cayankontar (early 12th c.), which describes the Chola military assault on Kalinga (contemporary Odisha) in 1112.[91] This poem delights in a typically Tamil blend of the grotesque and the comic, as ghouls, vultures and jackals approach to feast on the gore of battle. Kampan employs similar conceits, such as ghouls who feast on brains and spilled intestines; vultures dipping their wings in blood; jackals roaming the field; and rivers of blood dragging bodies into the sea. Throughout, the anguish the Ramayana war causes to both sides is complemented by the joy it causes to the creatures who treat it as revelry. In the 12th century, the great Chola court poet Ottakkuttar transposed the *parani* genre's themes to the ancient myth of Shiva destroying Daksa's sacrifice in his *Takkayakap Parani*, in which Daksha's proud egoism is laid low. The annihilation of egoism and triumph of the perfect soul reads beautifully against Kampan's own *parani*-like descriptions of battle, as Ravana's pride, swollen by the life-giving boons he has received, is crushed in *Yuddhakanda*'s fourteen days of battle.

Ottakkuttar also provided models for Kampan with his *ulas*, or procession poems, which focus upon women who are overcome with erotic desire as they watch a hero pass by.[92] As the *ulas*' sole audience for the procession, the women become emblematic of the world as a whole, reacting to the hero's presence with instinctive longing. Kampan includes a chapter dedicated to *ula* (I 19), describing Rama's grand procession for his wedding day.

This section is uniquely Tamil, incorporating the processional trope that Kampan's audience would have known as a standard means of signifying the majesty of the occasion. It demonstrates that Kampan knew Ottakkuttar's *ulas*, and employed the genre's glorification of a hero to dramatize elegantly the crucial moment when Rama joins his perfect bride. In addition to *Kamparamayanam*'s reliance on *Civakacintamani* and *Kalingattup Parani*, this section also provides crucial evidence for Kampan's 12th-century date.

Kampan follows Cayankontar and Ottakkuttar still further by incorporating a royal genealogy into his Ramayana, told when Vishwamitra first describes Rama's line to King Janaka.[93] In another lamination of his Ramayana on the Chola political world, the genealogies reveal intertextual consonance as Vishwamitra calls attention to figures central to the Cholas' own solar lineage.[94] The correlation is strengthened by the fact that the Chola kings, while Shaiva, are described in these genealogies as mortal emanations of Vishnu, the earthly agents of Shiva's transcendent will. Given their manifold parallels, *Kamparamayanam* must necessarily have been composed after Ottakkuttar's *ulas*.[95]

A Shaiva *Kamparamayanam*?

Kamparamayanam emerges at a time of extraordinary artistic and intellectual creativity, which sought to order a Tamil past by governing the practice of writing literature in accordance with new grammars and theories of poetic practice; the anthologization of religious texts and their institution in temple practice; and a prolific increase in the construction and renovation of temples, in which Ramayana narratives took increasing prominence. Why would an epochal text that asserts the supremacy of Vishnu be so closely associated with a time of state-sponsored Shaivism, in which Chola rulers committed vast resources to public demonstrations of piety?[96] Tamil literary history is not a function of religion, as the influential texts authored by Buddhists and Jains during the Chola period indicate.[97] Yet there is a sustained current of thought that Kampan had Shaiva leanings. Such assertions should recognize the fideistic commitments they can entail.[98] But there are cogent reasons for taking this position. As noted, *Kamparamayanam* never became an important text in Shrivaishnava theology, and it garnered none of the commentaries usual for such discourse. The fact that it has no commentary aligns it, rather, with Shaiva texts, which did not prompt exegesis in premodernity.

Shiva is not diminished by Kampan's devotion to Rama. Rather, he acts in signal moments. When the gods seek a means to destroy Ravana, they first approach Shiva, who demurs, for it was he along with Brahma who conferred tremendous power and seemingly everlasting life on the rakshasa king. But when Vishnu declares he will incarnate as Rama, Shiva agrees to incarnate as Hanuman, sharing the monkey's body with the wind god Vayu.[99] In the dramatic moment when Rama appears unwilling to take Sita back, Shiva appears before Rama and exhorts him to accept his queen, telling him that he has forgotten his divine identity and that of his wife: 'Apparently you don't understand yourself at all! You are the living primordial god, and Sita, your queen, is the mother of the three worlds, clinging to your chest.' Though he has been told he is god many times, Shiva's counsel affects Rama deeply, prompting him to accept that he must reject the contempt he has shown his wife.

Kamparamayanam's textual history, moreover, strongly suggests that Shaiva thought influenced its transmission. In Southeast Asian renditions influenced by Kampan, Shiva regularly stands supreme, directing Vishnu throughout his life as the avatar Rama.[100] In the puppetry tradition of Kerala, in which Kampan's verses are dramatized with extensive commentary by the puppeteers, Rama is Shiva's devotee. The plays are performed during festivals for the goddess Bhagavati, and in the origin mythology of the plays, Kampan is himself an incarnation of Shiva.[101] As Meenakshisundaram recounts a Malayalam anecdote, 'Kali, guarding the Lanka of Ravana, was requested by Shiva to depart. She was therefore not present to witness the Ramayana war. To make up for this, Shiva, born as Kampan, composed the *Kamparamayanam* consisting of the thirty-two dramas enacted even today as a part of the ritual during the annual festivals in the temples of Shiva in the northern part of Kerala.'[102]

Kampan's Ramayana flows in the Shaiva worldview of the Cholas, who claim Rama as their ancestor. In south India, Rama-bhakti flowed within larger Shaiva and Shrivaishnava currents; it did not take on an independent life of its own.

Geographical Context

Valmiki Ramayana knows the magical world of the forest and Ravana's Lanka as distant realms populated by superhuman beings, far removed from the familiar northern strongholds of Ayodhya and Mithila. Once Rama crosses the Ganges and heads south, he enters a land that Valmiki's audience did not know. The epic's Lanka is likely not Sri Lanka. As Goldman notes, 'the most that can be said with any certainty is that the poet knew of an island kingdom, whether real or mythical, said to lie some distance off the coast of the Indian mainland.'[103] Not so for Kampan and his audience. For Tamils in the Chola period, Rama's sojourn in the south maps onto actual places they knew, and the tale of Ravana in Lanka was likely taken to resonate with Sri Lanka's ancient history.

This territorial lamination begins early in Tamil literature. Sustained geographical identification based on Ramayana mythology, however, begins with inscriptional discourse glorifying military conquests in Sri Lanka. The Kasakudi Plates of the Pallava king Nandivarman (8th c.), for example, describe his ancestor Narasimhavarman (7th c.) as 'surpassing the glory of the valour of Rama by (his) conquest of Lanka,' and Nandivarman himself as the equal of Rama in archery.[104] The Tiruvalangadu Plates of Rajendra Chola (*ca.* 1018) proclaim that whereas Rama needed a monkey army to build his bridge and help him conquer Ravana, 'my general crossed the ocean in ships and easily destroyed the lord of Lanka—and so put Ravana to shame'.[105] In a memorable interpretation of one of the Ramayana's well-known scenes, in which Maricha takes the form of a golden deer to lure Rama away from Sita, the Kanyakumari inscription of Virarajendradeva Chola (*ca*. 1030) describes an eponymous 'King Chola' who is drawn into the south by a rakshasa in the form of a magical deer until he reaches the Kaveri River. He sees no brahmans there, so he calls them to migrate down from the north, establishing the Chola realm.[106]

Though knowledge of the Cholas' succession of military campaigns into Sri Lanka may have affected Kampan's understanding of a Ramayana geography, his poem is not a *poeme à clef* asserting Tamil supremacy over a demonized Sinhala population.[107] The political interplay between Tamil and Sinhala forces in the centuries prior to Kampan's life is fluid and complex, and once Rama enters the forest, Kampan is careful to preserve Valmiki's sense of remote, enchanting wildness. In Ayodhya and Mithila, by contrast, the poet uses great skill to ground the text in a Tamil landscape evocative of the Kaveri heartland, asserting fantastic deeds of the past as local history. When Rama arrives at the wedding canopy in Mithila and the royal families assemble to witness the event, Kampan takes great care to list the kings present, mapping out an expanding circle of lordship that starts with the southern dynasties and rotates outward, in which the poet's contemporary landscape is instantly recognizable:

> There were Gangas, the Kongus, Kalingas and Telugus,
> the rulers of the Sinhalas, the Cheras, the Pandyas,
> the kings of Anga, Kulinga and Avanti,
> the Vanga kings, the Malwa kings, the Cholas, the Marathas,
>
> The mighty kings of Magadha, the Maccha kings, foreign kings,
> and still more, the heroic Lata kings, the kings of Vidarbha,
> the Chinese kings, the Seguna kings, the Sindhi kings, the Panchala kings,
> the Sonaka lords, the Muslim kings, the Kuru kings,
>
> Joined by armed Yadavas, the kings of Chedi
> and the seven valiant Konkani kings,
> the finest of men all crowded close,
> kings with shining crowns beaming light into the sky. (I v. 1186–88)

Kampan also incorporates details that carefully situate narrative action, invoking iconic Tamil landmarks. When the monkey lord

Sugriva sends Hanuman to the south in a search party for Sita, he instructs the party to search the Vindhya Mountains (the idealized northern border of the Tamil land), the great temple site of Tirupati, then on through the Tondainadu (northeast Tamil Nadu), the Chola heartland surrounding the Kaveri River, the Pandya country, and off to the southern ocean (IV 2).[108] The linchpin between the epic narrative and the Tamil country is the Ranganatha icon at the great Shrivaishnava centre of Srirangam. Early Alvar poetry identifies Ranganatha with the family icon, passed down from the sun's grandson Ikshvaku to the heirs of the solar line in Ayodhya, which Rama gave to Vibhishana in thanks for his loyal service in the war against his older brother Ravana.[109] While returning home to Lanka from Ayodhya, Vibhishana stops by the Kaveri River to bathe, and places Ranganatha on the island of Srirangam. When he attempts to carry the island further, he cannot lift it: Ranganatha will remain in Srirangam, though he favours Vibhishana by keeping his gaze directed southward, his back to the north (an atypical axis for a temple deity).[110] Kampan knows this tale well, and emphasizes the Raghavas' possession of Ranganatha in his poem. Taken together, Kampan's appeals to the Tamil literary tradition and the political culture of the Chola imperium, as well as his skilful lamination of the epic onto a distinctly Tamil geography, regionalize a translocal narrative, placing the Ramayana's universalist ethos squarely in the Tamil land.

Legends of Kampan

Because we know essentially nothing of Kampan, his vaunted place in the Tamil literary tradition moves in hagiographic currents.[111] Traditional accounts about the poet converge on the brief personal details that Kampan was from Tiruvazhundur, and may have been of the uvaccan caste, a drummer in a Kali Temple (note again the Shaiva associations).[112] A strong folk tradition holds that he died in Nattaracan Kottai (Sivaganga), where local villagers still mix milk with a trace of soil from his tomb grounds and feed it to newborn babies to instil Kampan's poetic gift. Though subsequent tales draw him closely to the Chola court, Kampan's text makes no such claims. His devotion is to the supreme being who incarnated as Rama. This prompts his primary use of the first person in his verses, stressing that the grand poem he is creating is bound to his own religious experience. Rama, he writes, 'has taken me as his slave'; he is 'the storm-coloured god who rules me'; so too he is a slave of Vishnu and his eagle mount Garuda.[113] Rama is, for both Kampan and his audience, em piran, 'our lord'.[114]

Kampan's devotion carries him, and thereby his text, beyond stubborn prescriptive judgements about what literature in medieval India was supposed to be. His is a text made with love, the consuming emotion that drives the Ramayana narrative in its triumphs and in its desolations, which it explores with such psychological acuity. This declaration of passion, childlike constancy, and love, and the devotion that provokes and guides them, strongly affects the traditional accounts of Kampan's life. He is spontaneous, natural, a man intimate with the Goddess and familiar with her wildness, who drinks deeply of the world and its varied experiences, indeed he is said in a variety of tales to have improvised his entire work.[115] This is the Kampan said to have composed numerous single stanzas responding cleverly to circumstance or his preternatural powers of insight.[116]

The Srirangam temple contains a 13th-century Hoysala hall associated with the poet, yet prominent accounts emphasize Kampan's close relation to the Chola king, which given the poet's unrehearsed, instinctual ability to create verse, is rife with tension. He is presented as being close to Kulottunga Chola, enjoying the king's company and largesse even as he vexes him with his wilfulness and arrogant independence. Kampan deigns to let Kulottunga enjoy his verse; it is the poet, not the king, who is the true benefactor.[117] Indeed a common story has Kampan murdered by the Chola king's own hand, the victim of the king's seething jealousy.[118] He is unschooled, a man of passions who takes up with courtesans, enjoys his leisure and sleep, and lives with a dancer from the Shaiva mutt at Tiruvottiyur.[119] In some tellings, the poet is a devotee of goddess Kali, who appears before him to confer his poetic genius, and holds a torch so he can compose his verses in the still of night.

Wonderful tales focus on Kampan's conflict with Ottakkuttar, whose pedantic insistence on formal refinement is no match for Kampan, the gifted free spirit.[120] After Cataiyappan commissions him to render the Ramayana in Tamil, Kampan makes no headway, leading the lord to complain to Kulottunga Chola. The king devises a contest to ensure the work will be completed as quickly as possible: both Kampan and Ottakkuttar will author a Ramayana. Ottakkuttar quickly drafts the first five books and is at work on the sixth by the time the king demands to hear what the poets have accomplished. Kampan has done nothing, but claims to have finished even more than Ottakkuttar.[121] The king orders Kampan to recite the chapter, and the poet sings out seventy verses in impromptu brilliance. Ottakkuttar latches onto a point of grammatical discord that he hopes will ruin the performance, for Kampan has used a colloquial word for 'droplet' (tumi rather than the appropriately formal tuli):

> The grand mountain that Kumuda hurled in the sea
> seemed like a dancer plunging into rhythm,
> the spray of water [tumi] of the sea's reeling waves
> entered heaven, and the gods leapt up greedy
> for the ambrosia sure to emerge once more. (VI v. 657)

Kampan prays to Saraswati, goddess of poetry, for help, and she appears before him in a vision, telling him to bring Ottakkuttar and the king down to the street the following morning. There she conjures a pastoral scene, taking the role of a milkmaid who cautions little children around a churning pot, 'Careful, children, drops [tumi] of buttermilk will splash up!'[122]

When Ottakkuttar later returns to the street and finds it empty, he realizes that Saraswati herself saved Kampan, and his own poetry will fail in comparison. He manages to complete his Ramayana, but in an outburst of despair starts to tear it apart. Kampan stops him only in time to save the last book, the *Uttarakanda* the Tamil tradition attributes to him today.[123] As *Vinodarasamanjari* tells the story, Kampan allows Ottakkuttar's *Uttarakanda* to be appended to his own Ramayana because he has no interest in composing it himself given its tedious subject matter, and the contrast between Ottakkuttar's poetry and his own will cause everyone to acknowledge him as the superior poet.

Transmission of the Text

Legend holds that Kampan first attempted to premiere his text at Srirangam before assembled Shrivaishnava brahmans. They demur, however, for the poem is not in Sanskrit, and appears to praise its patron Cataiyappan, which they declare unacceptable for the divine tale of Rama. The brahmans demand that Kampan provide them with an endorsement of the text from the fabled 3,000 Dikshitar brahmans of the great Shaiva temple at Chidambaram, presumably the proper arbiters of a grand Tamil poem. In a series of complex manoeuvres involving rebirth from death, Kampan gains the sages' approval, then returns to Srirangam, where the Shrivaishnavas demand an ever-increasing number of approbations from representatives of different social strata. At last, the Shrivaishnavas personified by Nathamuni, compiler of *Nalayira Divyaprabandham*, accept the poem's divine significance and stylistic perfection. Ranganatha himself, speaking through a possessed priest, agrees to accept the work as his own. At last, Kampan sits in Srirangam's grand hall, ready to premiere his text before assembled brahmans, kings, and Sanskrit and Tamil pundits. He delivers the work brilliantly, as Nathamuni himself defends against criticisms and objections raised along the way. When he reaches the tale of the asura Hiranyakashipu, the audience protests this innovation in the Ramayana narrative (the tale is absent in Valmiki), but their doubts are quelled by an image of the god Narasimha himself, the slayer of that demon, who shakes his crown and lets out a triumphant roar.[124]

For most of its history, *Kamparamayanam*'s transmission was not dependent upon the printed word. It was instead shared in a dense confluence of manuscript circulation, performance (routinely by professional reciters), and educational recitation, with all three of these interactive constituents contributing to textual stability. For this reason, the poem was resistant to textual drift: in some thirty to forty extant palm-leaf manuscripts, variations are almost always trivial.[125] It is clear that historically the poem quickly gained success, for a Kannada inscription *circa* 1377–78 alludes to two itinerant Kampan performers from a family of professional reciters.[126] The text proved enormously significant in Tamil literary culture, influencing works from Pukazhendhi's 13th-century *Nalavenpa* to the poetry of Ativirarama Pandya (16th c.) and Kachiyappa Sivacharya's compendium of south Indian Shaiva lore, *Kandapuranam* (17th c.).

Kamparamayanam moved beyond Hindu religious boundaries as well: in the 17th century, the Muslim poet Umaruppulavar used Kampan's poem as a model for his own epic work *Cirappuranam* ('The Prophet's Holy Life').[127] An early instance of the emergent idiom of Muslim Tamil, *Cirappuranam* envisions the Hijaz as classic Tamil cankam landscapes in which the prophet 'descends' (avatara).[128]

Sectarian identity does condition this history, most notably in the case of the brilliant intellectual Civajnana Munivar (d. 1785), an ascetic at the Tiruvavaduthurai Mutt who wrote authoritative commentaries on the canonical grammar *Nannul* and the foundational text of Tamil Shaiva Siddhanta, *Civajnanapotam*. Civajnana, a staunch Shaiva who prohibited the study of Jain texts in the Mutt, was a master of Kampan's Ramayana. As the story is told, when confronted by 'haughty' Shrivaishnavas who proclaimed the genius of Kampan and claimed him as their own, Civajnana responded by listing twenty-two errors in the first verse of the text. Humiliated, the Vaishnavas prostrated themselves before him, crying that they had not truly understood the text. Civajnana responds by crushing each of his own arguments. The Vaishnavas are stunned, and when the Shaivas of Kanchipuram request that the performance be committed to text, Civajnana writes *Kamparamayanam Mutal Ceyyul Cankottara Virutti* ('A Critical Exposition of Potential Flaws in the First Verse of Kamparamayanam, and Their Resolution').

In the 19th and 20th centuries, *Kamparamayanam* stood at the forefront of educational practice both traditional and in government schools, as the text moved into print even as it continued to be transmitted as a received text through mansucript circulation and performance. In the early 1920s, U. Ve. Caminataiyar published his autobiography in serialized form. In it and in his biography of his teacher Minatchicuntaram Pillai, the greatest Tamil poet and scholar of the 19th century, Caminataiyar offers a view of elite literary culture, from traditional study at the Tiruvavaduthurai Mutt to his work at Kumbakonam Government College and extraordinary career publishing classical Tamil texts. Kampan runs like an authoritative thread throughout these texts, introduced time and again as Caminataiyar refers to his own teachers and learned scholars of the era.[129]

He speaks of men of his great-grandfather's generation being renowned for their discourses on Kampan, and describes his own young life assisting his father in evening Ramayana performances, which delighted large crowds and brought in a substantial income.[130] Minatchicuntaram Pillai, a devout Shaiva who never failed to recite daily hymns, was a master of the text, and thrice copied it on palm leaves in his own hand.[131] In one of the autobiography's famed passages, when Caminataiyar attempts to impress a local munsif with his knowledge of Tamil literature, he cites text after text to no avail, then realizes, 'I've forgotten the most important book of all! If I had mentioned it first, he would have judged me correctly!' He declares that he has studied *Kamparamayanam* with Minatchicuntaram Pillai, and read it in its entirety two or three times.[132]

Kampan in Modernity

In the early 20th century, printed editions and inexpensive paraphrases available in the markets made the text available to a far wider readership, and interest in Kampan soared.[133] The text assumed a central place, moreover, in larger claims to south Indian emancipatory politics and cultural dignity being asserted by the emergent independence and Dravidian movements. The Kampan movement began in full in 1921 with the publication of V.V.S. Aiyar's *Kamba Ramayanam—A Study*, a book of character studies and extended translations that sought to bring Kampan to an English-speaking audience.[134] V.V.S. Aiyar viewed the epic not only as a literary masterpiece, but as vital to Hindu self-regard. If men prevailed in public renditions of the text, women, as A.R. Venkatachalapathy notes, held their own reading circles, which 'bred a sense of gender solidarity among women who often identified their problems in an oppressive patriarchal world with the plight of ballad characters like Sita'.[135]

Kamparamayanam was also invoked to counter some contemporary arguments that Valmiki's epic narrated the Aryan conquest of a south India populated by monkeys and evil rakshasas. In 1928, the Dravidianist scholar M.S. Purnalingam Pillai published *Ravana the Great*, a Shaiva reading of Kampan that declares the rakshasa king to be the hero of the tale, Hanuman a Dravidian hero, and Sita a Dravidian worshipper of Shiva.[136] 'A careful reading of it,' he writes in his primer on Tamil literature, 'will discover that, though the epic celebrates the life and exploits of an Aryan King... it is full of side hints as to the superior civilisation of the Dravidians to that of the Aryans.'[137] Valmiki's text was also subject to such readings. Rama became denigrated as an effete warrior manqué, and Ravana championed as a manly hero and superlative devotee who sacrificed himself to promote Shiva-bhakti.[138] The Dravidianist party Dravida Kazhagam promoted such readings in drama, most prominently C.N. Annadurai's *Niti Tevan Mayakkam* ('Seduction of the Just King,' 1947), in which Ravana (played by Annadurai himself) summons Kampan to his court and charges him with the offense of libelling him as a demon.[139] The founder of the Dravida Kazhagam, E.V. Ramasamy (Periyar), linked a proper reading of the Ramayana to his desire for an independent Tamil state, and critiqued the epic in the strongest terms as an apologetic for brahmanical Hinduism.[140] His strident actions, however, which included beating pictures of Rama with his sandals and setting them on fire, targeted his attack on Valmiki and avoided criticizing Kampan directly.[141] Kampan's role in the assertion of south Indian identity appeared to insulate it from attack.

Kamparamayanam is still a celebrated text today, though its rich medieval idiom is no longer as central to the curriculum as it once was. Kampan societies are found in Tamil Nadu's major cities, and the poem is read, taught in schools, performed in Kampan festivals and kalakshepas (narration with accompanying musical performance), and rendered dramatically in puppet plays at some one hundred Bhagavati temples in Kerala.[142] Experts have the title '*Kamparamayanam*' prefixed to their names to demonstrate their mastery of the text.[143]

From its inception to the current day, Kampan stands at the forefront of Tamil literature: his vast and compelling work does honour to the language and, like its hero Rama, reveals the power of the human endeavour. A premodern work that has powerfully shaped the contours of Tamil modernity, *Kamparamayanam* is a rich vein running through the biographies of Tamil Nadu's foremost scholars, partisans, religious teachers, politicians, and more, reaching beyond sectarian identity to stand as a measure of Tamil's linguistic elegance and expressive possibilities.

Balakandam

Rama's Youth

Kampan's *Balakandam* tells of a man-god born into the world. As he matures, he learns how he transforms the earth, but also how it affects him. It is, above all, a book of questions, and Rama is the one asking them. Such is the riddle of the man-god, for Kampan is clear from the outset that Rama is the absolute lord, an avatar of Vishnu. The poet's devotion to this god is consuming, embracing the joys, tragedies, madnesses, and vagaries of life. Here Rama learns of the land he will come to rule in perfect justice. Under the tutelage of his preceptor Vishwamitra, he is first exposed to the magical wilds of the forest, the viciousness of the rakshasas, and the sages and gods who reveal his true nature to him in scenes that presage the narrative arc of the Ramayana as a whole. He will marry, winning the hand of Sita and knowing perfect love. The book concludes with Rama's first true test of manhood: a conflict with Parashu Rama, the previous avatar of Vishnu known for his savage power in combat and uncompromising commitment to his vision of dharma. Parashu Rama is defeated and, handing his own bow over to Rama, proclaims him the true incarnation of Vishnu:

> Since it is clear you are the lord who wields the discus,
> garbed in yellow, your feet adorned with finely wrought anklets,
> what sorrows will the earth now bear?
> I gave you a bow that was already yours,
> no match for your own strength. (v. 1377)

The vast majority of *Balakandam* is Kampan's own creative work, based not upon Valmiki's own brief text but drawing from puranic lore and Tamil literary masterpieces for inspiration. It begins with a famed passage on the Sarayu River as it flows into Dasharatha's kingdom of Ayodhya, 'like the breast of a mother to every life that lives on this sea-girt earth' (24); 'like souls that enter different bodies as the texts describe' (32). Like the river, the world is premised on change, and larger forces at work affirm this. The rakshasas, demonic beings that roam the earth, are tormenting the three worlds under the reign of Ravana, who has been granted what he believes to be eternal life, and the gods desperately need to destroy them. They approach Vishnu and beseech him to slay Ravana, for 'only Vishnu, the sea of compassion, dreaming on the sea, could end the gods' suffering by confronting him in war' (190). Vishnu accedes, and the other gods agree to incarnate as Rama's three brothers and the preternaturally strong monkey army, with Vayu and Shiva together incarnating as the monkey Hanuman, later to become Rama's chief ally.

On earth, Dasharatha's preceptor Vasishtha is aware of all that has transpired in the heavens, and also knows that Dasharatha, after ruling for 60,000 years, faces the classic Indian crisis of the transfer of power: the need for sons. Through a complex release of ascetic force, Rama and his brothers are born, and come to share extraordinary closeness. This notion of consummate love, of two living hearts flowing out to join another, becomes central to the themes of bhakti devotion developed in the *Kamparamayanam*. It is immediately tested when the royal sage Vishwamitra comes to demand that Rama and Lakshmana accompany him to the forest to fight off the rakshasas who have been ravaging the sages' sacrifices, provoking the first opposition between the just rule of the city and the unpredictable, dangerous world of the forest.

As they travel, Rama and Lakshmana's introduction to the world at large is developed by questions the boys ask Vishwamitra as they pass notable locales. The sage addresses their queries by crafting a sacred geography, invoking a wealth of lore from the ancient legends. These larger, epic concerns develop stories within stories, as Kampan's audience learns with young Rama the contours of his world and its mythic past. These sites, of course, become even more sacred precisely because Rama and his brother have visited them.

Rama faces his first taste of combat when he slays the rakshasi Tataka, and his initial instinct—most interestingly for a god come to earth to change the world—is a reluctance to engage. He does not want to kill Tataka since she is a woman, and so ensues an urgent disquisition in which Vishwamitra demands he ponder the deeper nature of dharma, and how difficult it is to know its proper role within the larger workings of fate. After Rama kills her with ease, Vishwamitra confers on him mantra-controlled weapons of enormous power:

They were overjoyed to unite in him,
as though the fruit of all good karma
had come seeking to join him in the next rebirth.

The divine weapons exclaimed,
'We have joined you, hero, and we shall never leave!
Like your brother, we shall always be at your just command.' (vv. 413–14)

There are intriguing moments of narrative conflation as the trio continues its journey, such as at a grove where Vamana—Vishnu in his dwarf incarnation—once claimed the universe from the asura Mahabali. When questioned, Vishwamitra tells the boys,

'Listen still further! Mal* with red lotus eyes,
whom no one, not even the Vedas or gods, can know
stayed here and did penance for the good of the world.

'He is called by his own holy name when prayers are recited
to cut through karmic bonds on earth and in heaven.
They describe him by asking who can ever fully know
the ways he warps reality through the power of his illusion?
He is the pristine form, we cannot know his aims,
and he performed great ascetic deeds here for a hundred aeons.' (vv. 427–28)

He is describing the universal lord to himself, a boy still learning what he is. Vishwamitra can be more direct. After Rama and Lakshmana with superhuman skill kill the rakshasas who are ravaging his sacrifice, the sage proclaims:

'You created all the worlds, and later you protected them,
swallowing everything living and still in your great stomach.
The world will say I am blessed because you saved my sacrifice,
but I think of it differently, I know you are far more.' (v. 468)

Yet again, Vishwamitra's revelation is not explicitly registered; either this is a truth Rama keeps silent about within himself, one

*A prevalent Tamil name of Vishnu.

he is still learning to make sense of, or Kampan chooses to keep the knowledge of Rama's true being beyond the realm of his explicit recollection.

Yet there are signs that Rama only gradually grasps the truth of his nature. In a famed episode, when the dust from Rama's foot drifts over a black stone and transforms it into the beautiful Ahalya—the sage's wife who had been literally petrified as punishment for her adultery—he is not quite sure what has happened. He is told that through his presence on earth the consequences of karma are coming to pass, through his ability both to kill, in his slaying of Tataka, and to restore, by reviving Ahalya. For both beings—though in very different ways—he has brought about release:

> 'The deeds that make the present were made in the past,
> and now, for all the worlds, what is there to suffering?
> Nothing but gaining salvation!' (v. 551)

In Mithila, where Rama and Sita first see each other, they instantly fall in complete and total love: hearts flowing out to join as one. The lovesickness they endure that night presages the enormous suffering they will endure during the long period of Sita's captivity. Here too, he is learning what it is to be human.

After Rama breaks Shiva's war bow, demonstrating superhuman strength without further explanation, Kampan introduces a long set of chapters describing the joyful procession of Dasharatha's retinue to Rama and Sita's wedding. Chapters such as 'Seeing the Mountain', 'Picking Flowers', 'Playing in the Water', 'Drinking and Making Merry' depend heavily upon earlier Tamil literature (in particular *Civakacintamani*) and the narrative conventions of Sanskrit court epics. They contain some of the most beautiful verses in the text, many of which can be—and were—read on their own as self-contained works. Time nearly halts, allowing readers to ponder a verse on its own terms, appreciating its poetic beauty and deep psychological purchase.

By the time Rama processes in state to his wedding, he is moving into manhood. He captivates the women who have heard of his mighty deeds and rush to see his incomparable beauty. He is becoming dominant in the world. Vishwamitra disappears from the tale, for the time of the preceptor's teaching is over, and Rama has entered married life. It is a new world of sexual experience, the consummation of a love with Sita that will soon be challenged, and forbidden to Ravana no matter his desire or powers.

As the couple returns home after the wedding, and Rama defeats Parashu Rama and takes his bow for himself, he lets his arrow fly to collect the entirety of Parashu Rama's power and claim it as his own. Parashu Rama, a kshatriya-like brahman who cleansed the earth of kings, confers his powers on a kshatriya who affects brahman qualities during his forest sojourn, and who will cleanse the earth of a different class of ruling beings. As Dasharatha proclaims:

> 'Could anyone in all three worlds do the manly deeds
> that Rama has done in childhood, free from any guile?
> Since this is true,' Dasharatha exclaimed,
> 'this young man is the creator
> here to ripen the fruits of karma
> for every virtuous being, in this life and the next!' (v. 1383)

In the poem's coming books, Rama will need this power, for things soon go awry. But *Balakandam* ends on a joyous note: Rama a dominant young man with a powerful and devoted ruling family, blissful union with a loving wife, invincible weapons, and a knowledge of his past and his destiny.

Note on Text and Translation

This translation is based on the edition of the renowned Tamil scholar U. Ve. Caminataiyar, and his commentary, which—reflecting his training—expresses not only his own views but also the traditional readings of his teachers. No true critical edition of the text exists, but given the lack of serious variation in the manuscript tradition that published editions of *Kamparamayanam* record, this does not preclude us from making the text as it stands available to an English-speaking audience. Caminataiyar's own editorial principles are not explicitly described. While he records manuscript variants without defining his principles of selection, he clearly aimed to secure the best reading through collation of the manuscripts available in the Tiruvavaduthurai Mutt and his own vast learning.[1] And indeed, readers today continue to profit from Caminataiyar's graceful and lucid exposition.

Kampan makes occasional use of paronomasia (Skt. shlesa, Tamil ciletai) in his verses.[2] Paronomastic verses have a primary and secondary reading, linked together through implicit simile. In this translation, I have sought to incorporate the two readings by turning the figure into an explicit comparison, thereby rendering the secondary meaning clear, as far as possible, within the clearly presented syntax of a single verse.

If the translation offered here inspires others to learn Tamil and enjoy its extraordinary wealth of literature and profundity of thought, it will have achieved its purpose. In the meanwhile, I hope that it will offer new opportunities to recognize the beauty and significance of Kampan's grand poem, and to acknowledge that, if Western theorizations of literature can inform new understandings of a world classic, they also have much to learn from it.

Prologue

1.
Creating, sustaining, destroying
the world and all within it,
he never rests in his endless game.
He is the master, and our refuge lies
solely in one like him.

2.
The wise know little of his true state and I cannot perceive it,
he is purely the first of the three ordered natures.
He is supreme, and how fine it is
to bathe in the sea of his virtues.[1]

3.
Reciters of the Vedas, infinite and timeless
chant Hari's name at the beginning and the end.
They have passed from attachment, except for attachment
to the feet of the constant lord, where the true path lies.

4.
Like a cat that approaches the roaring ocean of milk
and tries to lick it dry,
I tell this tale of Rama, perfect and triumphant,
absorbed in my desire.

5.
In the land that preserves the words of the noble ascetic
who composed the great tale that brings us close
to the archer who pierced seven shala trees
with an arrow like a curse once launched,
why would I begin my text when my words are too feeble to count?[2]

6.
The world will despise me, my character fouled.
Was this poem worth voicing at all?
Only if I take the divine tale sung by this poet
and make its majesty clear.

7.
To ears used to hearing collected verse
and a wide range of themes sung in meter,
when I sing, my verses will seem like a drumbeat
to the fine ears of an acunam
who loves the honeyed tones of the lute.[3]

8.
I will make something clear to the best poets,
experts in the set ways of threefold Tamil.
Are the words of madmen, the childish, or devotees
really to be heeded?[4]

9.
When children play in their rooms or climb on the stage to dance,
does it vex the carpenter if they draw a line on the floor?
How could my bad verses, which bear no trace of learning,
anger those who savour books written according to rules?[5]

10.
Three poets have composed this tale
in the language of the gods.
I heed the style of the finest among them
to relate it myself in Tamil verse.[6]

11.
Presented in Cataiyan's town of Venneynallur,
this grand, pristine and noble tale, filled with poetic charm,
is the Descent of Rama, who lived as an embodiment
of the highest lord, steadfast in deeds.[7]

12.
For those who narrate the power of Rama's arms
when he wields his bow, wreathed in a victory garland,
and how Shri looks on with love in her eyes
as the rakshasas crumble and he paves the way to release,
all that they seek will come to hand in wisdom and in fame.

The River

13.
Now I speak of that jewel of a river that graces the Kosala land,
where arrows, the five senses, which lead to restless mistakes,
and arrows, the eyes of women who wear jingling breast bands
never go wide of their mark.[1]

14.
Clouds the colour of Shiva's ash-covered body
spread beauty as they roam,
they dive down to drink seawater, then rise again, now dark
like the lord who married Shri, who cannot be shared,
and covers her breasts with fragrant oudh cream.

15.
The clouds grow thick and roll out so far
Shiva's father-in-law, Himalaya, must be roasting up there
beneath the sun, craving water to ease the heat,
for the ocean down here seems to have climbed
to the top of that immense mountain.

16.
The mountain is splendid, dappled with colour,
it looks like solid gold,
so the clouds pour down sheets of rain,
silver bars plunging deep to dig the mountain slopes.
Each cloud is a generous patron who knows
giving up all he owns is a joy.

17.
The rising waters flood out like gifts for brahmans
who preserve the four Vedas and are foremost in wisdom,
like the fame of an honoured king who upheld dharma
and followed the laws of the first king Manu.[2]

18.
It sweeps over the mountain's peak, sides and base
the way she strokes heads, chests and feet,
it never stays in one place long, lingering but a moment
like she never truly gives her heart, faithful for a second,
it gathers all that the mountain holds in its torrents
the way she takes a mountain of wealth then rushes off:
the flooding river is like a courtesan.

19.
Gems, gold, and peacock trains,
fine white elephant tusks and oudh,
sandalwood that cools like nothing else:
picking up goods and hurrying on,
the flood seems like travelling merchants.

20.
Carrying bright trails of flowers dusted with pollen
and blending their nectars into the water,
spread with rosy gold dust and mixed with pouring rut,
the flood looks just like a rainbow.

21.
Picking up mountains and ripping out trees,
snatching all in its path right down to the leaves,
the flood is like the monkeys who once resolved to build
a bridge over the wave-tossed ocean.[3]

22.
Flies and bees gather as if swarming heavy drinkers,
power increases and clarity dims
as if passions were surging to overwhelm reason,
the flood rushes down, smashing the teak trees,
the way men might keep drinking, releasing loud belches:
the sweet waters are drunks who delight in poured liquor.

23.
With a roar as it sweeps off elephants and forest beasts
like an army shouting for battle
as it seizes horses and broad-faced tuskers,
and since it digs into the banks, as if advancing and holding fast,
while beautiful green boughs wash by like beautiful banners,
the flood seems to face the sea as if arrayed for battle.

24.
Bound to the grand order of protection
the countless kings of the solar line have upheld,
the Sarayu is like the breast of a mother
to every life that thrives on this sea-girt earth.[4]

25.
Scented powders ground by mountain women,
saffron flowers, costus shrubs, cardamom, refreshing sandalwood,
vermilion, lemongrass, gamboge, cassia flowers,
mountain ebony flowers, kino blossoms, myrobalan flowers, herbs,
sweet honey and oudh from the neigbouring mountains:
the riches of the mountain spread their fragrance towards the water.

26.
The flooding river makes people from hunters' villages run
and the women beat their stomachs in terror as they flee.
As the surging torrents snatch up bows and sharp arrows,
the river seems like armies of triumphant kings on the march.[5]

27.
Because it steals hanging pots of rich milk,
butter, curds, and golden ghee to eat,
breaks wild lime and arjuna trees and shoves them aside,
snatches away the bangles and clothes
of herding women with innocent eyes,
the river is like worthy Krishna
dancing on a serpent covered with spots and stripes.[6]

28.
It crashes against sluice gates like a tusker smashing down doors
while plowmen throw up their hands like soldiers, roaring with joy,
then it runs down to fill the channels with water,
scattering piles of gems as if ripped from caparisons,
it crushes new green shoots with its powerful waves
the way the beast smashes its hitching post with its powerful trunk,
provoking the bees that eat nectar and pollen:
the river pours into the fields like an elephant raining down rut.[7]

29.
Turning forest pastures into mountain slopes,
and the seashore below into treasured flooding fields,
because it mixes different things in very different places,
the river flows like good and bad karma,
taking the different paths of lives being led.[8]

30.
The rushing river lengthens and spreads,
flowing into canals as it digs into the earth,
and plowmen pound drums to announce the floods are coming.
Racing past the sluice gates, the waves hurl pearls, gold and rosy spray:
the river is like the human race, branching from its source.

31.
The water flowing from the mountains,
pouring down to mix with the sea
is single at its source, like the sure truth offered by the Vedas,
then divides, like the God described by the great religions
whose scholarship branches into many different fields.[9]

32.
In champak-tree forests, in many lakes where flowers bloom,
in areca groves bordered by hiptage,
in tanks with new sand, and in the many fields,
the Sarayu spreads into many gardens dusted with flower pollen,
like souls that enter different bodies as the texts describe.[10]

The Land

33.
The sage Valmiki, inspired to compose verses,
wrote poetry so sweet the gods sought to hear it.
Now I will describe the land he praised,
sipping the liquor called love,
as if I were a mute man speaking his first words.[1]

34.
Conches lie in the canals where water leaps and splashes,
pearls lie along the fields' channels, gold flecks on the flooded dams,
red lilies lie in watering holes where buffalo wallow,
geese in all the paddy fields, coral on all the bunds,
sweet honey at the fields' borders,
and swarms of joyful bees fly through every charming garden.

35.
The noise of the river racing past the flooded fields,
the call of plowmen at the sugarcane press,
the splash of cane juice flowing,
the blare of conches on the seashore,
the pounding of bulls as they shove each other,
and the low of buffalo lolling in the waterholes
all clash against each other.

36.
Peacocks dance in the gardens, lotuses hold their blossom lamps,
clouds thunder like drums, blue lilies bloom like unblinking eyes,
clear waves look like ornate curtains,
and bees sing like the lute's honeyed strains,
as the pastoral world of flooded fields rules its own domain.

37.
The bees that dwell in the lotus are the gorgeous goddess Lakshmi,
and women's eyes are Kama's arrows
striking men who wear cool garlands.
Born of the rains, the sea is full of coral and shining pearls,
and the truth that rests on everyone's tongues
is the essence of the holy texts.

38.
Conches lie in the ponds, buffalo slumber in the shade,
bees rest merrily on flower garlands, Lakshmi dwells in her lotus,
turtles live in the mire, pearl oysters live in the coves,
geese dwell on heaps of paddy sheaves
and peacocks live in the gardens.

39.
Gold turned up in plowed rich soil, pearls born of conches,
heaps of different gems pressed against the fields' embankments,
the green hue of paddy, crops of sheathed sugarcane,
fish, bees, and flowers are a wonder to the eye,
like the eyes that sparkle on the kataiciyar women's faces.*

40.
Bards who play stirring music on their lutes sip toddy
as the drums strung with catgut ring out,
and far and wide their music awakens women
graceful as peacocks with haunting dark eyes
in gleaming mansions' upper storeys, on their golden beds.

41.
Juice from sugarcane crushed in a press,
juice from fruits in the gardens,
toddy from sliced palm spathes, honey from hives,
and nectar that splashes from garlands all constantly pour
into the sea where ships roam,
and fish rejoice as they drink it down.

---

*Kataiciyar: landless labourers who work in the fields.

42.
Strong plowmen do no weeding and toddy runs from their mouths,
they stand there overwhelmed with greed,
for they see no other weeds apart from flowers
like the wide eyes, hands, feet, faces, and mouths
of the kataiciyar women who speak melodious words.
When the lowly feel desire for women,
how can they be at fault?[2]

43.
When women bathe in new floods sent by dark ocean waves
and the scent of flowers, musk and sandal drifts from their hair,
can we say how many women there are
with waists like lightning bolts and mouths speaking childish words
who fill men with lust, casting glances with eyes like swords?

44.
As the flooding water where handsome men bathe
drains into the silt and soil
of the gardens, the paddy fields, and nearby places,
the bees swarm, drawn to the scent of dissolved sandalwood cream
and the velvety sandalwood mixed with fragrant saffron.[3]

45.
Red-legged geese wander the fields
like women with eyes that shine like fish,
and their chicks, nurtured on beds of lotus blossoms,
drink the milk that flows from water buffalo with muddy legs,
bleating as they think of their calves,
then they sleep to the song of green frogs
that calms them like a lullaby.[4]

46.
Cuckoos mating in gardens and peacocks dancing on branches
are finer than women dancing on stage, their eyes like sharp spears.
Bees sing out in the pastoral mode, so royal geese with thick feathers
open their eyes and rise from their comfortable lotus beds.[5]

47.
People who marry women who are right for them,
people who delight in the gift of a kite's musical call
like a shadow matches flight when the bird takes to the wing,
people listening intently to questions posed in great texts,
people who feast when they see guests' cheery faces,

48.
People who send fighting cocks into battle, the birds filled with rage,
feeling a new fury as they attack with spurs tied to their legs,
resolute in their cruel war, cockscombs redder than their eyes,
fearless, ready for a fickle death if their heroic lives are sullied,

49.
Bull calves born of water buffalo cows
pound into each other, eyes red with rage,
crashing like thunder as they face each other again and again,
and men roar to the clouds, bees fleeing their topknots
as they watch darkness split apart, and then attack in fury,[6]

50.
White shoots sprout from lotuses with thorny stems,
gems scatter, wondrous conches blare,
gold and pearls are swept aside, murrel fish hide in the borewells,
fish leap and thrash in the furrows, turtles hide in their shells,
as men drive their buffalo forward when they plow the fields,[7]

51.
Plowmen take the reaped sheaves of grain
and place them in heaps that reach the sky,
then trample them with buffalo alert to their drivers' commands.
They gather threshed grain into piles, offer gleanings to the poor,
then load it in carts that hide it from view
to take it home so guests might have feasts,
and drive them forward, each one so heavy
it bends the earth beneath it.

52.
Plowmen harvest fields filled with different grains,
fragrant gardens, trees heavy with ripe fruit, cultivated drylands,
creepers grown from cuttings, and tubers dug from the earth,
like bees collecting nectar from the blooming flowers.

53.
Brahmans and high castes all dwell happily in their homes,
sitting down together with relatives and guests
and eating their food with zeal:
the three best fruits,* all sorts of dals, rice soaked with ghee,
and rice mixed with sugar and thick golden curds.

54.
Great Dasharatha was kind to each life in his realm,
a king learned in the law, growing angry when merited,
taking only the tribute required, spurning crude desires.
He protected his land so the earth could take a deep breath,
and boats had their cargo unloaded, easing the pain in their keels.

55.
The male bees in the fertile fields
think they have found enamoured mates
when they see the beautiful, dark eyes streaked with kohl
on the lotus faces of fine women, and they hover there
spurred on by the love and passion that drives them.

56.
In rich fields, women with eyes deadlier than Kama's arrows
have firm breasts that bend men to their will.
Plump scabbard fish swim, confident and peaceful,
drinking toddy that trickles from spathes of the coconut palm.

---

*Jackfruit, mango and banana.

57.
Black water buffalo that move like rainclouds roaming the earth
dip into cool waterholes where they relax.
They pour nourishing milk from their udders
when they think of their calves resting back in the village.

58.
The flood of water that washes rice in large pots,
which bubble loudly as they cook in well-stocked kitchens,
flows into gardens where areca palms tower over the seed beds
and nourishes paddy seedlings transplanted to nearby fields.

59.
White roosters with red cockscombs scratch through the trash
kicking up splendid gems that lie scattered, sparkling.
Flocks of chickens mistake them for glow-worms
and peck at them to take them back to their nests.

60.
White conch bracelets conceal the sound of the churning staff
pounding down again and again as it churns the creamy curds,
mouths call out, and waists tremble as they wear away
when cowherd women churn, until they hurt their hands.[8]

61.
Little fisherfolk girls whose dark eyes do not yet hurt men
scoop up sand in toy winnowing fans
to build little castles in front of their huts.
As they sift through the sand, they collect scattered pearls
that lie among pieces of crushed areca nuts.[9]

62.
Rainclouds flash with lightning as they drift over the mountains,
they dread the crash of fearless rams born of gentle ewes
attacking each other with striped horns on their strong heads
so it sounds like thunder blasting in the sky.

63.
Young parrots that speak sweet words call in the millet fields,
newborn bees hum in opening flower buds,
flocks of geese call in ponds thick with flowers,
and songs in praise of heroes ring out
from the generous homes of the wealthy.[10]

64.
Bands of valiant hunters in mountains full of pitfall traps
in forests where elephant bulls are bound with thick chains,
separated from their cows and calves,
drive male geese from their mates when they cry out in joy.

65.
People digging for sweet potatoes unearth huge gems as well,
tortoises feast on low-hanging mangoes,
geese that live on lotuses perch on laurel trees to sleep
among flowers round as whirlpools, covered with golden pollen.[11]

66.
Women who plant rice sing songs of the paddies,
frightening the calves tied in front of cowherds' homes
where flutes made from dried cassia fruit play,
while seashore songs of fisherfolk women ring out in the mountains,
distracting the women who protect the millet fields.[12]

67.
Bamboo sways in the wind on immense dark mountains,
cracking open the honeycombs so honey spills like a hanging snake
to pour into ponds filled with red lilies and into the sluices,
where spiralled conches drink it as it breaks colocasia stems.[13]

68.
For men suffering hardship who arrive in Kosala every day
the women with long, wide eyes and brows fine as the crescent moon
are deeply learned and enjoy stable wealth:
what more could a man want
but charity and being honoured as a guest?

69.
Every choultry that offers food is full of heaps of dal,
piles of vegetables sliced on cutting boards
with a prized sickle curved like the crescent moon,
and heaps of rice as white as pearls.

70.
Wooden ships bring endless goods to leading families,
healthy fields give them a bounty of grain,
cracks and caves offer fine gems,
and birth in an honoured line results in virtue so hard to attain.

71.
This land is without flaw, so there is no fear of death,
people are so pure of heart, there is no anger between them.
Because no deeds stray from dharma,
there is no decay, only progress.

72.
The flood overflows its path and spreads through the land
but people do not stray from righteousness,
traced designs are rubbed from arms spread with kumkum
but seals on grain are not broken, and people maintain devotion,
women's waists are tiny, wearing down day by day,
and the flowers in their hair are fragrant,
people are not wild or drunk, and they are never miserly.[14]

73.
The smoke of oudh incense, smoke from kitchens,
and fragrant smoke from the presses
crushing bright, sweet sugarcane,
blend with the glorious smoke from Vedic sacrifices,
spreading everywhere like clouds, pervading everything.

74.
Peacocks shrink before the beauty of the women from that land,
sunshine dims compared to the jewellery on their gleaming breasts,
their dark hair makes clouds conceal themselves in gardens,
and their eyes make carp hide in the water
that soaks the fragrant fields.

75.
Waists are so slender they seem to break,
and water churns as it crashes in waves
when the kataiciyar women bathe and red lilies blossom like lips,
geese roaming the canals mimic their delicate gait
and lotuses bloom like their faces.

76.
Women's keen eyes mock Brahma,
their gait mocks the sway of an elephant cow,
their full breasts mock lotus buds,
and their faces mock the full moon.

77.
All sorts of ornaments fight with the sun,
golden tender coconuts fight with women's breasts,
sea foam like ambrosia fights with their sheer clothes,
and majestic drums of honour fight with the rainclouds.

78.
Thriving gardens match the clouds,
in the fields, stacks of threshed paddy match Meru's peaks,
full lakes surrounded by bunds match the brimming sea,
and towns full of wealth match the world of the gods.

79.
Where paddy is not heaped high as a mountain
pearls are stacked in tall rows,
where women do not converse

ambrosia is born of the deep milk ocean,
where there are no fine mountains
there are treasures from the rivers,
where there are no mounds of gold
there are islands of coral and pearls.

80.
The place where young women join together to play ball
does not look like a sandalwood grove, but rather a champak garden.
The place where men like Skanda riding his peacock practise for war
seems not like a flower garden, but a fragrant jasmine forest.[15]

81.
Cuckoos speak women's sweet, childish words,
peacocks practise their dances,
young female conches, shining brightly,
yield pearls like the teeth that shine in a woman's smile.

82.
Toddy sellers have delicious aged toddies in their homes,
plowmen keep tools for tilling the fields in theirs,
the sound of wedding rituals rings out from young men's homes,
and bards' homes contain curved lutes to play any kind of tune.

83.
Garlands drip with sweet, fresh nectar,
routes over land and sea yield sacks of gold and gems,
the fresh breeze scatters raindrops that give bodies life,
and ancient lore brings joy to the ears when sung to music's heights.

84.
Peacocks fanning their trains see the great beauty
of women with long, dark hair and necklaces on their breasts
who pick flowers in vast gardens, and the peacocks follow
like the thoughts that possess young men.

85.
There is no hint of poverty there, so charity is never seen,
no enemies challenge the land in war, so bravery is never clear,
lies are never told, so the value of truth is never plain,
the heights of learning are so complete, wisdom is not striking.

86.
Carts laden with sesame, foxtail millet,
sorghum, proso millet, and horse gram
and carts bearing loads of salt scraped from full salt pans
make their rounds and crowd together at each stop,
so heavy they have to be pushed to roll forward again.

87.
Just as selves without refuge are born on many paths,
changing and changing along with karma to raise them high,
rock candy, honey, syrup, toddy and cowherds' curds
all mix together, changing locales as they go.[16]

88.
Rivers and rivers of people pour in together
on roads where songs and flutes ring out in many places
as a host of people gathering for a festival for the gods
mixes with all who come to attend marriages.

89.
The blare of large conches brought directly to the mouth,
the pounding of drums beaten with short, straight drumsticks,
and the sound of catgut thongs twanging on frame drums
are all overwhelmed by the warriors' manly roar.

90.
The red hands of nursemaids who pour milk from conches
till it dribbles from the mouths of children
onto chests adorned with a pendant, Vishnu's five weapons,
are lotus flowers closing in the white glow of moonlight.[17]

91.
Looks and good conduct endure as inner beauty,
justice endures because no one ever lies,
dharma endures because of women's love,
and their chastity ensures the rains will never end.

92.
Has anyone travelled through that vast land filled with gardens,
all the way to its border and then back again?
Though it branches over and over,
even the Sarayu River has never seen its edge.

93.
I have spoken of the glories of the flawless country Kosala.
Its perfections will last forever, even when the doomsday winds
pound the sea across its banks so it overflows the land.
Now I will turn to a description of its city.

The City

94.
The grand city called Ayodhya is celebrated by all poets
who craft sweet words in proper verse
evoking pure emotion, full of subtlety, splendid in meaning,
and the sages who rendered the Ramayana in Sanskrit.
Every being in all the worlds who has ever done penance
and everyone in Vaikuntha,* the land that all souls crave,
prays to be born there next time.

95.
Is it the face of the earth goddess?
The tilak on her brow? Her eye?
The pearl necklace on her breasts, shining with gems?
Her splendid marriage thread, better than all jewellery?
The vital seat of her life? The lotus where Lakshmi joyfully dwells?
Vaikuntha, even finer than the gods' heaven?
The gold box filled with jewels like Vishnu's kaustubha gem?
Vishnu's stomach, which swallows all lives at age's end?
What should I choose to describe it?[1]

96.
Shiva who is half Uma,
Vishnu, husband of Shri and the earth goddess,
and Brahma, filled with an endless wealth of patience,
know of no other city that compares to it.
Irresistible desire overtakes them and drives them on.
The sun and moon roam through the sky, never blinking their eyes
so they can look closely at what they have never seen before.
If not that, what makes them wander as they do?

---

*Vishnu's heaven, 'Unassailable'.

97.
Brahma created Alaka* and Indra's city Amaravati
as practice for Ayodhya, his famous masterpiece.
Maya and other divine craftsmen forgot their mindborn works,
for they were overcome with shame!
Who could fully describe this city,
its soaring mansions and turrets that scrape the clouds?

98.
The treasured Vedas declare a basic fact:
meritorious deeds lead to rebirth in heaven.
Who but Rama made ascetic deeds flourish
along with dharma on earth?
If virtuous Rama gladly rules the seven worlds,
name another place finer, where every pleasure is found![2]

99.
Red-eyed Mal,† the refuge for all who practise dharma,
gaining wisdom by mastering themselves
with the discipline that conquers the hostile five senses,
was born in Ayodhya, and with Lakshmi born as Sita,
ruled it for countless years.
What golden city in the land of gods can equal this city on earth?[3]

100.
All kings were there, all jewellery was there,
all the rarest gems were there,
haltered elephants, horses, chariots, and others were there,
sages, gods, yakshas, vidyadharas, and divine beings gathered there,
praising the city: what else can compare with it?

---

*Capital of Kubera, lord of yakshas.

†Vishnu.

101.
Ayodhya's golden walls have no equal,
built in a square as architecture dictates,
they are higher than a snowy mountain range, firm as the truth.
Built on the mason's chalk line, surrounded by a moat,
their power clear to masters who know the goals* of scripture:
they should indeed be called higher than height.

102.
Boundless and unchallenged, the walls are like the Vedas,
because they reach heaven, they are like the gods,
because they protect, they are Durga on her stag,
because they restrain the driving senses, they are like sages,
because they hold the trident, they are like Kali,
because they are so hard to approach, they are like almighty God.[4]

103.
In order to see if the world of gods is as fine as great Ayodhya
full of soft-spoken women with arms round and smooth as bamboo,
breasts like golden tender coconuts, waists thin as lightning,
feet red as lotuses, and nails like moons dipped in red paste,
the city walls seem to soar up to heaven.

104.
Since other people gauge them with measuring rods
the way kings rule the earth with their righteous sceptres,
since they face crowned foes, ready to take their heads in war,
since they are built according to rules just as Manu's,
since they offer full protection, protecting the city from view,
because of their strength, repelling spears, swords and bows,
the means of fighting they offer, dazzling the enemy,
because they are full of defensive strengths,
and their discuses look like their sphere of command,
the walls are like kings of the solar line.

---

*The human goals of dharma, wealth, pleasure, and spiritual liberation.

105.
If these walls subdue the roaming wind, the minds of the ruthless,
and the countless weapons of war—
furious spears, murderous swords, bows,
battle axes, maces, discuses, darts, iron clubs,
terrifying slings that can kill everything
from swarming mosquitoes to Garuda, lord of birds—
what more need be said about them?

106.
The foremost kings of the solar line guard all lives perfectly,
shining with a light that drives off darkness everywhere,
firmly set in the belief that fame far surpasses jewellery.
Though their decrees, straight sceptre and command protect the city,
surpassing heaven, surpassing measured space,
Ayodhya's walls were built for beauty.

107.
My tongue now turns to the moat around these walls
as the wave-tossed sea surrounds
the Cakravala Mountains at the edge of the world.
Like the heart of a courtesan bought for gold,
its depths are as murky as feeble verses.
Like the five senses that drag one from virtue,
it has vicious crocodiles.
Like the broad love-mound of a virgin,
it has protection no one can touch.

108.
Clouds cannot see its edge and mistake the vast moat,
deep as the underworld, for the forbidding sea.
Joining their fellows as they draw near,
they sip its water, then rise again,
but their bodies ache when they press against the walls,
and mistaking them for mountains that soar to heaven,
they pour down sheets of rain.

109.
Lotuses cover the moat outside the mighty walls
and spread their lingering scent,
overcome by the shining faces of the city's noble women,
they regain their former strength and lay plans for battle:
surround the vast walls as if ready to lay siege.[5]

110.
Lying in the immense moat dug deep in the earth
to surround the walls that circle the city, secured by arrowslits,
crocodiles that surge from the water are like elephants in musth,
plunging into the sea traversed by wooden ships, then rising again.[6]

111.
Shaking their sawtooth tails, their mouths open wide,
their teeth snap and glitter, a host of crescent moons.
Sparks fly from burning eyes as furious crocodiles follow each other,
eager for battle like furious rakshasas hungry for blood.

112.
The geese that rule the water are hosts of white parasols,
the rare crocodiles are elephants big as Meru circled by the planets,
the waves that bear lotuses swaying on their stalks are horses,
the fish are swords and spears:
the moat is a veritable army.

113.
The moat's rim is made of crystal blocks sealed with gold strips
and a corniced lip of silver that makes it truly splendid.
I know the difference between the water and the crystal tile,
but how does it look to the gods themselves?

114.
If we think of the gardens full of dense groves
lying next to the moat I describe, a vast enclosing sea,
they form a mass of close darkness,
a further enclosure, lingering and heavy,
like a dark blue dress wrapped around tall golden walls.

115.
The four tower gates to the city are like the four Vedas,
which explain righteous paths so every life on the fertile earth
has principles in line with morality.
Soaring even higher than Mal's feet
when he measured the world of the gods,
they stand like royal elephants, symbols of triumph,
stationed at each entrance.[7]

116.
She calls to her mate as dear to her as life,
but he does not come and embrace her, instead staying behind
next to the sculpture of a dove on the tower.
The female dove sulks and flies off to hide in the world of the gods,
in a garden of wishing trees that drop their flowers
on the ascetics beneath them.

117.
Built high with crystal blocks cut to measure
and joints covered with beaten sheets of gold,
soaring high, inlaid with many gems to make them gleam,
fronted by diamond pillars and crossbeams made of silver.

118.
Diamond blocks cut to perfection sit on capitals of emerald,
the joints filled with gold, and then, above a row of carved lions,
a row of sardonyx blocks form the cornices
studded with a row of varied jewels that flash like lightning,[8]

119.
They stand seven stories tall, as if crafted
for all beings living in the seven worlds,
well built in accordance with the architect's chalk lines,
then covered with gold leaf
and topped with jewelled pots at their dazzling peak:
the gateway towers are a crown for Ayodhya,
the glory of the line of the earth goddess.

120.
So bright they make the moon seem dark,
mansions whitewashed with dazzling lime
are like waves on the broad milk sea, looking up as they surge,
churned by an attacking storm that blows in with cruel speed.

121.
Mansions covered with bonded sheets of gold,
which offer fine homes to charming spotted doves,
are shining white mountains made bright
by the perfect rays of the dawning sun.

122.
Millions and millions of mansions are there,
so dazzling the gods mistake them for their own,
with flawless capitals and emerald beams set on fine diamond pillars,
and paintings so real they seem to be alive.

123.
Millions of mansions have floors made with moonstone,
sturdy walls built out of sapphire,
and rafters of gold placed on capitals of coral
set on sandalwood pillars arrayed in a row.

124.
The bases of pillars are carved as lotus blossoms,
like the feet of women with red mouths as waists fine as thread,
they are finely crafted, with pristine interiors,
where some women embrace young lovers while others are dancing,
so sturdy that everyone wants them,
their foundations deep in the underworld,
both mansions and women are countless, and have a golden hue.[9]

125.
Those who enter them look like gods, never blinking their eyes
when the mansions' gathered light bathes them so they glow.
Mansions soar like sky chariots moving faster than thought,
brighter still than the heavenly world.

126.
Women with fine jewellery and brave men wearing garlands
live in these mansions that never stray from dharma's path.
Apart from the gold and jewels used to adorn them,
the mansions are not made with earthly things
and shine brighter than the sun.

127.
As tall as the sky, they possess endless wealth
and are as white as righteous fame.
They are splendid because of the families they hold,
countless good people as true to dharma as the king.

128.
Ropes of pearls hang from them, swaying like a waterfall,
banners shine as one like a spreading range of clouds.
They hold great piles of gold and heaps of massive jewels,
and many peacocks rest there:
mansions are like mountains.

129.
They are surrounded by dense clouds of oudh smoke,
amid long banners made of fine cloth, no different from the clouds.
Their metal tridents are flashing
as if dazzling bolts of lightning are striking in series.

130.
On mansions where women like peacocks wear anklets on their feet,
and their large breasts oppress waists
tiny as the centre of an hourglass drum,
the hanging ropes of pearls amid countless banners
make them a garden of wishing trees.[10]

131.
On the mansions, rows of wide banners stand tall on their staffs
like groves of banana plants on immense mountains.
As the banners rub together, it seems the moon has stopped,
to wane and lose its lustre there with every passing day.

132.
Where there are no grand halls roofed with gold,
there are huts thatched with creepers,
and where there are no courtyards,
there are multistoreyed mansions.
Where there are no gentle hills,
there are hillocks made of gems,
and where there are no empty spaces,
there are canopies strung with pearls.[11]

133.
Flashing like lightning, glowing like lamps, blazing like the sun,
the light from fine Ayodhya
filled with well-wrought gold,
swept out to make the land of gods into a golden world.

134.
Since its rays lengthen with the rising dawn,
shorten at noon, and disappear when night falls,
the round sun shines as if it were the shadow of Ayodhya,
the golden city with flashing gems on its walls.[12]

135.
Dark clouds of oudh smoke surround the golden mansions
as women light incense, treasured girdles on their waists.
If the sea absorbs their fine scent when the clouds head off to drink,
what need be said about the rain they later pour?

136.
The melody of babbled words from young girls with short hair,
the prattle of young women with long tresses, sweet as the flute,
the dulcet speech of gorgeous women and the sweet music of the lute
join the sound of dancers singing in the toddy sellers' streets.

137.
Groups of young men with swords practise fighting skills,
and the bull elephants nearby spew fire from their eyes.
They cut up the ground with their feet, digging deep holes,
but scented powder from the men's chests spills over to fill them.[13]

138.
Young women scatter pearls as they play ball,
and countless maids gather them in heaps.
They glow with so much cooling light
they shine brighter than the moon.

139.
Women dance on the stage, and glances from their dark eyes
are spears that strike young men and eat away their hearts.
Their lives waste away like the waists of those women
as their passion grows.

140.
New blossoms in the gardens pour nectar,
and the bee and southern breeze, both hungry, slip inside.
They cause so much pain to women parted from their lovers
their burning breasts start to fade away.[14]

141.
The sweet tones of the veena, rising from the base note,
are even better when a voice sings out above the music
and the drum kept tight with leather straps keeps time:
parrots speaking with women will close their eyes and sleep.

142.
Women with mouths like ivy gourds and brows like well-made bows
use their flawless feet like newly blossomed lotuses
tinted with the soft hue of red-cotton paste to kick young men
and make their strong arms burn.[15]

143.
In this peerless city where night and day seem the same,
perhaps the portraits never blink since they always want to see
the glowing, perfect beauty, like a burning lamp,
of the bodies of women revered by everyone.

144.
In mansions where Lakshmi shines, seated on her cool lotus,
what keeps the light spreading so it drives off the darkness?
Lamps burning with ghee, or the jewels on gem lamps?
Neither, it is the women's own bodies!

145.
Dancing women move their feet in classic steps
to match the beat marked by cymbals, drum and song.
Their anklets show the different types of rhythm,
and if not, look at the feet of prancing horses!

146.
Smiles bloom on the dancers' faces
and their triumph comes from the torment they cause in hearts.
Their waists are exhausted, worn down day by day,
as their soft breasts swell under necklaces of pearls and gold.

147.
Endless joy is all around, in the geese's gait,
in lotuses as nectar, in carp as muddy shallows,
in bees and their mates as toddy, in drunken elephants as rut,
and if none of these, in women's eyes as dark kohl.[16]

148.
Bull elephants are like mountains
where lions prowl, eyes burning like fire,
seeking caves at their bases to live in with their mates.
Rut pours from the elephants' eyes and loins,
turning the ground into muddy pits
where sturdy chariots with banners slide and become trapped.

149.
Men and women throw off their garlands
which catch the hooves of tall prancing horses,
once women stop sulking and make love to their men
sandalwood paste from their fine breasts makes runners slip and fall.

150.
Horses hack at the earth tirelessly with their hooves
and the rising dust covers gems fallen from riders' jewellery.
Garlands on the shoulders of young men drip nectar
which washes the gems so they sparkle again.

151.
The rut from fevered elephants smells like kino tree blossoms,
the mouths of noble women look like red water lilies,
their ornaments shine with endless rays of light,
and the scent of flowers drifts from their long tresses.[17]

152.
In all the ways its treasures shine, Alaka rivals Amaravati
but it loses to Ayodhya once it sees that city's market streets.
What can be said about the design of the city of the gods?
If Ayodhya is kept in mind, it isn't worth the mention.

153.
In places where young men meet,
anklets ring with a menacing chime,
spears gleam, jewels shine like the morning sun,
deer musk spreads its potent scent,
pearls shimmer, and bees hum.

154.
The roar of conches, the blare of horns,
the arpeggios of the lute, the beat of the drum,
the tone of flutes, the sound of the high-toned lute
all playing together, joined by rhythm instruments,
spread over the city to surpass the ocean's roar.

155.
There are halls for counting the tribute offered by kings,
halls for dancing women with the gentle gait of geese,
halls for chanting the Vedas, infinitely great,
and halls for scholars studying the many precious arts.

156.
The cardinal points are dwarfed by the city streets
where gateways shine with gems that sparkle like the sun.
The floods of rut pour more heavily than a distant mountain stream,
and the rows of horses are vaster than the ocean.

157.
In mansions decorated with jewelled archways
and open terraces so high they trap the rainclouds,
women's glowing faces bloom, their blossoming eyes are arrows,
which plunge into the chests of young men as brave as lions.

158.
The sound of kings' anklets rivals the horses' jingling harnesses,
and the sound of bells on chariots trimmed with gold.
Anklets chime on women who smile while bathing at the ghats,
and from their lotus perches, the geese call in response.

159.
Some women in that ancient city spend their time
quarrelling with their lovers, then reconciling and making love,
singing sweet songs, listening to women sing,
dancing, bathing in wide pools, and wearing flower chaplets.[18]

160.
Some men in that wonderful city spend their time
taming mighty rutting elephants then riding them,
driving chariots yoked to horses with prancing hooves,
and giving generously to the needy to relieve their hunger pangs.

161.
Some men in that vast city spend their time
staging fights between elephants, practising archery and swordplay,
racing horses with white plumes on the track,
and mastering the varied arts of war.[19]

162.
Some women in that shining city spend their time
frolicking like does, picking flowers in charming gardens,
gambling, playing in the water together with their men,
and drinking toddy until their crimson lips grow pale.

163.
Like white clouds changing shape as they race across the sky
to go and sip water from the sea that reeks of fish,
banners soar high above, flapping on the terraces of old mansions,
laughing in jest as they drink the heavenly Ganga dry.[20]

164.
The gateway towers built with sturdy arches
and the three rings of city walls trimmed with fine gold
shamed the gods, soaring so high that nothing could be taller,
like the fame built up by kings with shoulders like mountains.

165.
In the forests, in the hilly pastures,
by the moat wide as an ocean, on the mansions' roof terraces,
by the tanks where women bathe,
on mountains graced with pools and streams,
under canopies trimmed with gems and pearls,
and in the groves where bees hum like lutes,
there are beds made of flowering boughs.

166.
In the great city where drums tied with leather thongs roar every day
terrifying the wave-tossed ocean and the clouds that pour clean rain,
wealth is not locked away, for no one is a thief
and there is no charity, for no one needs for anything.

167.
Since no one is singled out as unlearned
there are no masters of knowledge, and no one there to judge them.
Since everyone possesses every treasured wealth
no one goes without, and there is no class of owners.

168.
The seed of knowledge sprouts and grows here, and from it
countless strong branches of learning flourish,
leaves of rare ascetic deeds grow, buds of friendship appear,
flowers of dharma blossom, and the fruit of pleasure ripens.

Governance

169.
The ruler of this glorious city is the king of kings,
his true sceptre rules the whole earth amid the seven worlds.
The embodiment of dharma, he gave Rama to the world,
the lord with warrior's anklets who is the hero of this tale.

170.
Compassion, dharma, tranquillity, a grounded knowledge of truth,
dominant heroism, generosity and commitment to justice:
consider all these, and other kings had only half
but they serve Dasharatha in full.

171.
Dasharatha's hands, intent on giving gifts, poured so much water
that no hands remained dry on the ancient, sea-girt earth.
He performed sacrifices required of kings devoted to the Vedas
that had not been fulfilled by any other king.[1]

172.
In love, he is a mother, in the good he provides, self-discipline,
since he makes people guide others on the righteous path,
he is like a son,
since he relieves pain, he is like medicine,
in his penetrating thought, he is like knowledge and subtle learning.

173.
He crossed the ocean of beggars by lavishly giving,
the ocean of wisdom through his limitless knowledge of texts,
the ocean of enemies by killing with his sword,
and the ocean of pleasures wealth can bring by enjoying them fully.

174.
That magnanimous lord named Dasharatha, his fame undying,
the king of kings whose honed sword rests in his leather scabbard
ruled so well that all travelled their true path:
flooding waters, birds, creatures, and the hearts of courtesans.

175.
The Cakravali Mountains* were like the king's city walls,
and the vast sea beyond them was like the surrounding moat,
the mountains were like elegant mansions adorned with many gems,
and the earth itself was like the grand city Ayodhya.

176.
The spear in his mighty hand had been worn down,
sharpened time and again to kill those who opposed him.
The golden anklets on his red feet had been worn down,
rubbed away by kings wearing jewelled crowns.

177.
The noble king's parasol is a moon, always growing, never fading,
it offers cool shade to every life, and drives away their darkness,
the moon that fades from the sky, they say,
is really quite irrelevant.[2]

178.
His anklets set with diamonds, Dasharatha was forceful as a lion,
he kept every life on earth safe as if it were his own.
In his perfect world, all lives moving and still
were like a single body alive with its life-breath.[3]

179.
The ruling sphere of command of the king whose strong arms
are round and rise taller than mountains
stands firmly above all, like the sun with his burning rays
forever protecting each life under his unique procession.

---

*See v. 107.

180.
Since no foes would arise to fly at him like arrows,
The king with arms round as drums, itching for war,
ruled over the entire world with such gentle care
he seemed like a poor farmer tending his small field.

The Holy Avatar

181.
One day, Dasharatha touched the feet of wholesome Vasishtha,
a sage equal to Brahma himself, and said,
'You mean more to me than the fruits of my austerities,
more than my father and mothers in my ancient family,
more than the gods I reach through my devotion,
more than everything else.[1]

182.
'Through your favour, the noble kings in my line
ruled the earth so that they outshone the sun itself,
and again through your favour, I have protected the boundless earth
so no one can say I have erred in any way.[2]

183.
'I have protected the earth for sixty thousand years
having driven off every enemy around me,
and I lack for nothing, but for a single torment
that will cast the world into confusion after I pass on.[3]

184.
'Brahmans and sages who endured hard austerities
have lived good lives without any distress at all.
My heart grieves, though, for after I am gone,
they will suffer in chaos, and their pain will never end.'

185.
The emperor who wears a fine crown set with pearls,
master of the royal gate where the drums pound,
finished speaking, and honoured Vasishtha, son of Brahma,
reflected on what he had heard:[4]

186.
'The stormcloud Vishnu, like a blue mountain, immersed in yoga
on his serpent Ananta on the milk ocean where waves crash
once promised the gods, who were suffering greatly,
"I will end the savagery of the murderous rakshasas."

187.
'The gods in heaven sought Shiva, his throat dark with poison,
and explained they were tormented by vicious rakshasas,
but Shiva refused them, for he knew about the matter,
and he joined them, saying, "I am not the one to kill him."*[5]

188.
'The gods went to four-faced Brahma, and worshipped his feet
in a hall made of flawless gems on northern Meru's peak.
They described the savagery of the rakshasas
vicious as lightning bolts.

189.
'Back when Indra was taken to Lanka
by mighty Meghanada, who dragged him there in fetters,
Brahma told Shiva who is half Uma, lovely as a peacock,
that he would be responsible for getting him back.[6]

190.
'They resolved it was vital to kill merciless Ravana,
the rakshasa with ten heads and twenty hands,
but it was not something they could do.
Only Vishnu, the sea of compassion, dreaming on the sea,
could end the gods' suffering by confronting him in war.

*Ravana, the ten-headed king of rakshasas.

191.
'As the gods meditated on the god who sleeps
on the milk ocean where waves leap and flow,
and pressed their hands like red lotuses together in worship,
Vishnu, an emerald mountain, who saves those who understand him,

192.
'The bright stormcloud who guards the twin lights of sun and moon
which shine a great distance, causing lotuses to bloom in abundance,
mounted his vehicle Garuda accompanied by Lakshmi in her lotus
and appeared before them as if ascending a golden mountain.[7]

193.
'Indra, king of gods, and Brahma who dwells in the lotus stood up
and approached him along with the other gods.
They fell before his feet, and were overwhelmed with joy
every time they revered him.

194.
'They sang and danced, running here and there
unable to understand, drunk on the liquor that is joy.
They were ecstatic, sure the rakshasas were now destroyed
and threw heavenly flowers at the feet scented with holy basil.

195.
'Like a cloud settling on a golden mountain, our beautiful lord
descended from the shoulders of Garuda, who takes me as his slave.
He went within a towering hall that soared into the sky
and sat regally on the golden lion throne, his body shining bright.

196.
'When Brahma and the sages, Indra and the other gods,
and Shiva with the battle axe who wears the crescent moon
were seated near Vishnu, overwhelmed with joy,
they described the cruel rakshasas who wield ferocious spears.

197.
'"Husband of Lakshmi!" they despaired,
"Heaven and earth have spent their good karma on the rakshasas
led by the ten-headed Ravana and his younger brother Kumbhakarna,
and there is no means to destroy them.

198.
'"Because of the great boon we granted to Ravana," they said,
"the rakshasas have been assaulting the three thriving worlds.
If they are not finished off now, lord with red eyes,
they will swallow up the world in a second!"

199.
'They shivered with misery as they spoke,
then touched his feet and revered him.
The lord with a garland of holy basil replied,
"Please listen, one thing concerns you all:
You will no longer suffer, for I will relieve the earth's misery,
and slice the heads off deceitful Ravana."

200.
'The lord who is a sea of compassion
spoke again, saying, "All you gods
need to be born as an army of monkeys
in the forests, on the mountains, and in the fragrant groves.[8]

201.
'"I will come to earth as the son of emperor Dasharatha,
who has a sea of elephants, chariots, cavalry and infantry,
and use my peerless arrows, which fly true, tasting blood,
to burn the boons given to those rakshasas,
their lives as fleeting as a ghoul's chariot.*

---

*A mirage.

202.
'"I will go and be born in Ayodhya, city of grand walls,
and my discus, conch, and vast serpent couch
whose poison burns like the doomsday mare's fire
will serve me as my younger brothers."[9]

203.
'They leaped and danced when Vishnu spoke,
and sang rousing music filled with exquisite meanings.
"Now Vishnu, adorned with a fragrant garland of basil,
has told us how he will grant his divine favour!" they cried.

204.
'Indra was overjoyed, and said, "Our fear is at an end!"
Pure Brahma, Shiva wearing the lustrous moon,
and the gods in heaven said, "Our subservience is over!"
Vishnu, the master of the entire world, then returned to Garuda.

205.
'After the lord who has taken me as his slave left on Garuda,
Brahma, the grandfather, spoke to the assembled gods.
"I earlier gave birth to Jambavan, king of bears,
and you must be born on earth as monkeys," he declared.[10]

206.
'Indra, king of the heavenly land of wishing trees, said,
"I will be born as Valin, menacing as lightning to his foes,
as well as his son Angada."
The sun said, "I will be born as Sugriva, brother to Valin."
Agni said, "I will be born as Nila."[11]

207.
'Vayu said, "I will be born as Hanuman." The rest of the gods said,
"We shall help by going to earth to be born as fierce monkeys."
Shiva, destroyer of the triple city, said,
"I shall merge myself in Hanuman, son of Vayu."
Aren't countless other gods born everywhere?[12]

208.
'As red-eyed Vishnu who favours his devotees ordained,
Brahma who dwells in the lotus, dark-throated Shiva,
and the rest of the immortal gods were born as they described,
as monkeys on the land and in the mysterious forests,
then the two gods who give boons to devotees went home.'[13]

209.
The sage Vasishtha pondered these past events, then said,
'Do not grieve, king with shoulders strong as a mountain!
If you can perform a perfect sacrifice that will produce sons
who will master the seven worlds above and the seven below,
your worries, noble lord, will be over.'[14]

210.
When he heard this, the king of kings leapt from his throne with joy,
touched the feet of the great sage, and exclaimed,
'How can I suffer when I have you as my refuge?
Please tell me all I need to complete this sacrifice.'

211.
'The son born through the favour of Vibhandaka,
equal to his splendid father Kashyapa in the virtues of his birth,
his good deeds and great knowledge of the shastras,
praised even by Shiva who wears the Ganga in his hair,
who gave birth to the perfect gods and all other creatures,

212.
'An extraordinary ascetic who has a head with a single deer horn
and knows nothing about the nature of different people in this world,
equal to four-faced Brahma in his knowledge of the varied arts,
righteous Manu's laws, and the Vedas that declare life's goals,
needs to come here.

213.
'This peaceful sage with the deer horn is a man who must be praised,
a mighty ascetic who thinks everyone alive is a simple creature
because they were born on the many heads of Adishesha,
a Brahma ruling from his lotus throne in the depth of his thoughts,
a Shiva who destroyed the triple city,' Vasishtha said.
'Once he completes the sacrifice, then there will be sons.'[15]

214.
The emperor of kings on this earth heard the ascetic's words,
touched his red lotus feet and praised him, saying, 'Master!
Where can I find this sage, righteous and untouched by vice?
Please tell me,' he appealed, 'so I may bring him here.'

215.
'There is a good king named Uttanapada, who wears a shining crown.
He frees the land he rules from its cruel pains
and the crimes that can send one to hell.
No one can best this lord of Manu's line, he is love and compassion,
and his son now rules this land, his name is Romapada.[16]

216.
'The land that Romapada rules suffered cruelly for many years
since no thunderclouds had come to give it rain.
The king called brahmans steadfast in the Vedas,
but though he gave them gifts, the rains still did not fall.
He appealed to them again, and they replied,
"If the sage Rishyashringa comes, the rains will follow."

217.
'As they pondered how to bring this innocent ascetic
so pure he saw people on the sea-girt earth
as nothing more than harmless creatures,
women with shining brows, long, dark eyes,
coral lips, teeth like pearls, and full, soft breasts
arose to honour the king, and said,
"We will go and bring this awesome sage back."

218.
'Romapada was delighted by their words, and he offered them gifts,
jewellery, clothing, and other choice things,
then ordered them away, saying,
"Go, women like spring creepers, your brows like the crescent moon,
arms round as bamboo, with full breasts and failing waists,
hair dark as night, childlike eyes, and lips like the silk cotton flower."
They revered him, then set off in their chariots.

219.
'The women adorned with gold travelled many miles,
and when the pure ascetic's hermitage was three leagues away
they built a hut of leaves and dwelled there
as if they themselves were perfect ascetics.

220.
'The women with dark eyes saw Rishyashringa's father was away
and they went to meet the boy who had mastered Vedic learning.
When they approached, he did not think they were mere animals
but saw them as great ascetics to be offered rites of welcome.[17]

221.
He invited them in with great warmth, asking them to sit.
They did, and after they had exchanged a few pleasant words,
the women with lips red as the palash blossom
raised their pressed hands to the sage,
then swiftly returned to their own leaf hut.

222.
'After several days had passed, the women with tasteful jewellery
brought fruits such as mangoes, bananas, jackfruit,
delicious coconut, and many sweets more tempting than ambrosia.
They offered them to Rishyashringa,
saying, "Please eat these, great ascetic."

223.
'The days passed, and then these Lakshmis with fine brows
asked the virtuous ascetic, "Won't you come to our own home?"
They raised their pressed hands in worship before him
and the boy set off with them at once.

224.
'The women looked as bewildered as were their hearts inside,
absolutely delighted, but also rather troubled.
"Here we are," they said, "look!" and off they went
on the long road ahead while the pure ascetic followed.[18]

225.
'Before the sage had even reached the wealthy city,
clouds spread out and turned as dark as Shiva's poisoned neck.
Pattering drops fell, and the tanks and rivers filled
as clouds poured down the rain in driving sheets.

226.
'The tanks and rivers looked splendid filled with so much water
and the sugarcane and paddy crops grew beautiful and lush.
The dark clouds spread across the sky, drenching the land with rain,
and Romapada knew Rishyashringa must have come.

227.
'"Has he arrived here," Romapada thought,
the sage who has transcended delusion, anger and lust,
drawn by the crafty schemes of women
with blooming lotus faces, lips red as ivy gourd
and soft hair perfumed with oudh smoke?"

228.
'The sturdy king set out surrounded by his army
accompanied by brahman masters of the Vedas.
After six leagues, he met Rishyashringa, a mountain of ascetic deeds,
surrounded by the women with scented hair.

229.
'"I have been blessed with every success!" cried the king,
and his eyes filled with tears from the bliss within his heart.
He touched the sage's feet, then to the women before him
he said, "What you have done has rid me of my pain."

230.
'When the king arrived with brahmans the gods were afraid,
for the righteous sage would soon realize he had been fooled.
But the king pleaded, and Rishyashringa was like an ocean
where the waves crash inward but do not destroy the coast.

231.
'When the king armed with a honed sword hard as diamond
knelt before the perfect sage again and again, appealing to him,
and explained how he had eased the drought no one else could end,
the sage's inner fury ebbed away until it disappeared.

232.
'The sage beyond delusion, a granter of boons who knows truth
was filled with compassion, and gave the king his blessings.
He mounted a swift chariot and quickly drove towards the city,
followed by brahmans who teach the truth of reality.

233.
'The king entered the flourishing city with the sage
met by crowds who had adorned it with decorations.
They entered the palace, went into his magnificent court of gold,
and Romapada bid Rishyashringa sit on a raised lion throne.

234.
'The king offered him the time-honoured gifts of welcome,
attending to him with such delight no slight could be imagined.
He then gave the sage his daughter Shanta,
her lips red as a palash blossom,
following the proper marriage rites, with all the needed mantras.[19]

235
'The land was freed from its agonies, for the rains had come
and driven off the plague of famine as they soaked the earth.
Rishyashringa, the omniscient sage and mighty ascetic,
lived there, my king, as his lush-haired wife Shanta tended to him,'
Vishwamitra ended his tale.[20]

236.
Dasharatha touched the feet of the glorious sage, and said,
'I will leave right now and ask him to come back with me.'
Many crowned kings wearing heavy anklets worshipped his feet,
Sumantra and other wise ministers pressed their hands before him,
and as the king mounted his chariot adorned with splendid jewels,
the gods poured down a rain of flowers, crying,
'This means our trials have ended!'

237.
Horns and many instruments roared louder than a stormy ocean,
minstrels sang songs of praise, brahmans chanted Vedic mantras,
and women like peacocks sang blessings from sweet red lips.
The fourfold army* surrounded him, swelling like the sea,
as he travelled like the blazing sun over gruelling roads
to reach Romapada's kingdom.

238.
When his spies reported that the emperor had arrived,
his fame spreading like fire,
Romapada resolved to go and meet him, warrior's anklets on his feet.
He travelled three leagues joyfully, mighty bow in hand,
as his jewellery flashed, his army poured forth like the sea,
and his minstrels sang in praise.

---

*Infantry, cavalry, chariots and elephants.

239.
The emperor saw the mighty king coming and leapt from his chariot,
a golden carriage that roared to fill thunderclouds with shame.
Romapada approached and fell at his feet,
but Dasharatha raised him up and embraced him,
expressing a long-held love that he could not keep contained.
Romapada was overjoyed, and offered words of welcome
to the emperor holding a spear that shone like the sun.

240.
King Romapada with mighty arms and a spear hungry for flesh
looked at the emperor by his chariot, flowers on his crown.
'My king, whose blazing spear secures the world of the gods,
something has brought you here!' he said.
'Perhaps my many ascetic deeds, or those my land has done?'
He ushered Dasharatha onto his jewelled chariot,
and together they drove happily into the city.

241.
They entered a splendid golden hall in Romapada's palace
and his guest, holding his garlanded spear, was asked to take his seat
as women with jingling anklets on their feet sang in praise.
Wearing a fresh garland, Romapada offered the rites of welcome,
and Dasharatha, who once returned heaven to the gods,
sat cheerfully on the golden throne.[21]

242.
Romapada gave him fragrant sandalwood,
then asked the king with the victorious chariot,
'Please tell me, what has brought you here?'
The emperor told him what happened, and Romapada replied,
'I will send for the great ascetic who has gone beyond envy
and have him go to Ayodhya, good king with a splendid crown.'
Dasharatha then went home in his chariot, surrounded by his army.

243.
The emperor left, and Romapada went to the sage equal to the Vedas
and kneeled until his crown touched Rishyashringa's lotus feet.
Rishyashringa received the king's courtesies,
and asked, 'Why have you come?'
The king replied, 'Master! I beg a boon of you, as your devotee.'
'What is it?' asked the sage.

244.
'Please go to Ayodhya, city of mansions, home to Dasharatha
whose sceptre's fame rises and whose heart preserves dharma.
Born in the famed line of Shibi, who sat on the scales for a dove,
his keen spear once swallowed an asura's power.
After you have gone there, come back home.'[22]

245.
'I grant this boon,' said the ascetic, 'bring me a chariot now.'
Romapada, his spear honed with a sturdy file, bowed low,
and knew the emperor now stood supreme, his pain at an end.
'Master of the learned arts!' he called.
'Please take this chariot with Shanta, your Lakshmi with a fine brow.'
Both climbed in and took their seats.[23]

246.
The heroic king with a curving bow raised his pressed hands
and then, as tranquil sages followed after him,
lustrous Rishyashringa, like the holy Vedas embodied,
set off with his wife Shanta on the road to Ayodhya.

247.
Dharma and the other gods knew that this sage had the power
to bring the Supreme Being, the Truth, down to earth
where he would destroy foul karma that burned like a rising flame,
so they pounded divine kettle drums and scattered perfect flowers.

248.
Messengers reached Ayodhya and approached the king of kings
whose arms had triumphed in war everywhere they turned.
When they informed him that Rishyashringa had come,
the emperor plunged into an endless sea of love.

249.
He quickly got up and took to his chariot
as a rain of flowers poured down, blessings flowed,
drums pounded, many instruments played,
and evil karma was ripped out by the roots.[24]

250.
The king of kings whose drums rumble like thunder thought,
'The mountain of my harrowing pain has crumbled into dust!'
He travelled nine leagues, his heart filled with delight,
and met the sage Rishyashringa, powers had now ripened.

251.
He glowed, as if to demonstrate
that all of his ascetic deeds had taken perfect form.
Clad in tree bark wrapped around his waist,
he was a man like a deer with a luminous body,

252.
A master of shining sacrifice
that ends the gods' troubles and keeps rakshasas at bay,
he carried a staff, a water pot and eating bowl
in his broad hands as the texts prescribe.

253.
The king of kings stepped down from his chariot,
fell before Rishyshringa's feet and offered his sincere blessings
to the sage like a blooming branch
covered with the budding creepers that are the ancient Vedas.

254.
The king raised his pressed hands generous as the clouds
to the sages who had also come, and they offered their blessings.
He asked the master of the learned arts to sit in his chariot
with Shanta, whose eyes bright as fish rained joyous tears,
and invited them respectfully to come into the city.

255.
The crowned king accompanied the sage
as women with shining lotus faces sang out in praise,
and in an hour they reached the grand city Ayodhya
where the drums beat, roaring like thunder.

256.
Vasishtha, who drains the powers of the five lowly senses
that wander as thieves committing foul deeds,
together with brahmans who never stray from the holy Vedas
sat in the royal court, making it shine.

257.
The king entered the hall bright with splendid jewels
and asked the lordly sage to sit on a throne set with fine gems.
Delighted, he offered him the courtesies of welcome,
and then he began to speak.

258.
'Noblest of the noble! Pure sage,
you shine like dharma, like great austerities!
My ancient, righteous line has a regal future
and my good deeds were not wasted, due only to your favour.'

259.
Once the king had spoken, the sage gazed sweetly at him and said,
'Listen, king of kings! With the mighty Vasishtha as your guide,
no other king on this earth can equal you,
you have achieved incredible heights.'

260.
After offering many other polite remarks, he said,
'You have invited me here, king with shoulders broad as mountains,
will you tell me why?
Will you perform the horse sacrifice to gain its reward?'

261.
'I have been entrusted with rule for years beyond count,
so that no distress befalls the land. Yet I have no children,
and I ask you now to give me sons, who will bring splendid fame
as they protect the earth out to the wave-tossed sea.'

262.
'Fear not, king!' Rishyshringa replied. 'Is this world the only one?
Now make haste and prepare everything for this grand sacrifice
that will grant you sons who will have the awesome power
to protect all fourteen worlds.'

263.
The essentials for the rite were swiftly brought
and the supreme king bathed in the Sarayu's pure waters,
then he entered the perfect hall of sacrifice
built as prescribed by the revealed Vedas.

264.
The priests* quickly kindled the three fires and offered the oblations,
then, after a full twelve months had passed,
the divine drums roared as the gods gathered so closely together
no space was left in the glossy sky.

265.
As the omniscient sage poured the oblation
in the sacrificial fire kindled to produce sons,
the gods' lotus mouths blossomed, they thronged together,
they rained down flowers, and cried out with joy.

---

*Rishyashringa, Vasishtha, and other attendant brahmans.

266.
Then, in the midst of the fire,
a goblin with crimson eyes and hair red as fire
burst out from the flames
bearing a ball of pure white rice on a golden plate.

267.
The goblin placed the rice on the edge of the plate
and disappeared back within the flames.
The ascetic ordered the king, 'Give that rice ball, pure as ambrosia,
to each of your queens in accordance with their rank.

268.
The emperor did as the great sage directed,
and as the auspicious conches roared,
he placed a radiant portion in the hands of his queen Kausalya,
her mouth red as ivy gourd, her hair fragrant with oudh.

269.
The king of kings, lord of Kosala where the geese swim
in the tanks, rivers and wooded groves,
gave the next portion to Kaikeyi, daughter of Kekaya's king,
and the gods roared out their approval.[25]

270.
Dasharatha, born in the outstanding line of Nimi
a triumphant king who terrified his enemies,
next offered a piece to Sumitra in turn
making Indra, king of gods, roar out in joy with his fellows,
sure his enemies were now destroyed.

271.
After that, the distinguished lord gathered the scattered remnants
and gave them to Sumitra,
so the right side of all righteous people in the world
and the left side of his enemies trembled.[26]

272.
After the horse sacrifice done with a prancing mare
and the various fire sacrifices lit to produce sons were finished,
watched over by Rishyashringa,
Dasharatha, guardian of the world,
joyfully left the sacrificial field as everybody praised him.

273.
After the sacrifices prescribed by the Vedas were finished,
the drums and splendid instruments pounded and blared,
the entire world was released from darkness
and King Dasharatha entered his chambers to take his royal throne.[27]

274.
Fulfilling his prescribed duties, he worshipped his family gods
in their proper order according to the law,
sacrificed to the other gods according to their right,
and showered a rain of gold on the illustrious brahmans there.

275.
Next he gave realms to rule, wealth, chariots,
horses, and fine garments to the gathered kings,
then departed as musical instruments played
and took his royal bath at a ghat on the Sarayu River.[28]

276.
The gathered kettle drums pounded
and the assembled white parasols decked with pearls gave shade,
many kings circled around him, then assembled in his audience hall,
praising him so much even Brahma was ashamed.
Dasharatha bent down to touch Vasishtha's feet,
and then he stood forth, glorious.

277.
Then, as directed by the supreme ascetic Vasishtha,
he worshipped the feet of the mighty sage with a deer horn,
and offered fitting words of respect. 'I have been saved!' he said.
'What could I receive that is better than this?'

278.
'I am your devotee, master, due to the favour you have shown.
My suffering is over, and now my life will flourish.'
The radiant ascetic blessed the king, his heart filled with joy,
then drove home with the ascetics who had joined him.

279.
After that the king, his pain at an end,
touched the feet of the other sages and praised them.
They blessed him, overjoyed, and then they set off
and the lord of the earth felt peace.[29]

280.
After a few days had passed,
the king's three wives suffered morning sickness.
Their faces and their stunning bodies
seemed equal to the moon.

281.
When the time of birth arrived
the glorious earth goddess was overjoyed,
Punarvasu, called Vey,* and bright Cancer praised by the gods
rose and sparkled in the sky.

282.
Siddhas, yakshas and their wives,
masterful sages, gods, and those who dwell in Vishnu's heaven
assembled in rows and roared out their approval:
ancient dharma lost all hesitation and rose supreme!

283.
Virtuous Kausalya bore the man who is the fortune of the worlds,
the Pure Light, the perfect one who has realized the holy Vedas,
who swallowed all the worlds at the time of cosmic dissolution,
and shines with a beauty like the stormcloud and the darkness.[30]

---

*The seventh lunar mansion, 'The Two Chariots'.

284.
The flawless daughter of Kekaya's king* bore a son
as the gods spread across heaven roared out.
Indra and the other kings glorified her,
and Pushya† and rising Pisces both shone.

285.
As Indra, master of wishing trees, who raged against the mountains
and the other gods crowded in the sky, celebrating and dancing,
Sumitra, the youngest queen, gave birth to their younger brother‡
as Ashlesha,§ shaped like a dark snake entering an anthill,
and Cancer offered good fortune.[31]

286.
As the earth held by the many-hooded serpent¶ danced with joy,
and the Vedas resounded all over the land,
Sumitra, her eyes dark as poison, once more gave birth
as Magha** and Leo rose up in glory.[32]

287.
Celestial women danced, kinnaras sang songs sweet as ambrosia,
all sorts of instruments played,
and the gods ran about and paraded,
overwhelmed with joy because the rakshasas were surely dead.[33]

288.
Women ran to serve the king
and danced, proclaiming the joyful news.
The counsellors gathered, surveyed the constellations and planets,
and proclaimed, 'Now the world knows no sorrow!'

---

*Ashvapati.

†The eighth lunar mansion, 'The Nourisher'.

‡Lakshmana, held to be an embodiment of Vishnu's discus.

§The ninth lunar mansion, 'The Embrace'.

¶Adishesha.

**The tenth lunar mansion, 'The Bountiful'.

289.
The emperor bathed in the Sarayu's sweet waters,
and gave lavish gifts of paddy seeds and delightful wealth.
Then, as white conches blared, he went with the sage Vasishtha
and gazed upon the lovely faces of his sons.

290.
The emperor had the drums beaten to pronounce his command:
'Taxes shall be defrayed over the entire earth for seven years,
treasure houses filled with wealth shall be unlocked,
and the poor shall receive everything they need.

291.
'Warriors shall relinquish their weapons,
crowned kings shall be freed to return to their own lands,
the obligations of brahmans who chant the Vedas shall be fulfilled,
and festivals shall shine across the land, performed with ceremony.

292.
'You shall go out and enter the temples,
and accomplish what you need
in the brahmans' quarters, junctions and crossroads.
You shall give lavish offerings of camphor, incense and garlands
to adorn the gods in morning and evening worship.'

293.
When Dasharatha gave these orders, the drummers he sent forth
hoisted their drums on elephants and went out to proclaim the news.
In the city, young men and women with waists like lightning
plunged into an ocean of joy because of their delight.

294.
Everyone gathered row by row and called out their devotion,
they broke out in sweat and their bodies shivered with joy.
They rained wealth on everyone as they shared the news,
but could the people truly know their redeemer had arrived?

295.
As joy surpassed all limits in this vast, holy city,
groups of noble ladies, their gathered maids,
crowds of highborn men and their servants
threw sandalwood paste, perfumed oils,
musk, and scented powders on the streets.

296.
For twelve days, the entire city
expressed its joy in these ways,
and people did not know themselves.
Then the faultless sage Vasishtha thought of the princes' names.[34]

297.
He gave the name Rama to Vishnu who is the true goal,
who saved a mountain with a trunk from a crocodile
when it cried, 'God who rests dreaming on your serpent couch!'
and that very day gained the lord's favour.[35]

298.
The sage who grants boons, and understands the true paths,
the meanings of the Veda that prescribes religious practices
so clearly they look like a fruit held in the palm of the hand,
gave the name Bharata to the king's next shining son.

299.
'The name of this child who has the form of light
and the indomitable power to kill the scheming rakshasas,
let the gods triumph, and free the earth goddess from pain,
will be Lakshmana,' said the sage.

300.
Meditating on the pearl taken form, a light so beautiful
red lotuses seem to have bloomed within him
and the fact that all enemies would die by his hands,
the sage gave him the name Shatrughna.

301.
When the sage who never errs gave these names
along with Vedic mantras that offer renown,
rivers that are treasures in the king's land
overflowed the ocean full of the truth
of brahmans who chant the Vedas and are expert in the shastras.[36]

302.
The king of kings, master of the world,
loved no life-breath and body more than Rama,
who was beautiful as a painting,
blue lilies and shining lotuses joined as one.[37]

303.
During the days when the princes grew up
speaking childlike, sweet words,
and taking their first charming steps,
like the sun that comes to drive off darkness
like the four Vedas flourishing with light,*

304.
The sage equal to the lord who wears the crescent moon
oversaw the rites of tonsure and investiture with the sacred thread,
taught them the learned arts along with the holy Vedas,
which, having no border, can never be measured.[38]

305.
They mastered elephant handling, chariots, horses,
and other fields of knowledge as appropriate.
They practised archery and the use of many combat weapons
as Rama, incomparable lord of gods, grew up with his brothers.

*The Vedas' three chanted tones.

306.
Sages, gods, the earth goddess, and Ayodhya's people
would have joined them there, and would not have wanted
to stop living there even for a moment, sure that the princes
would end both types of karma and any hardship they endured.

307.
Noble Rama and his younger brother Lakshmana
wandered the land like a single thread drawn through oiled hair,
roaming among the rivers, the misty gardens, and the ponds,
showing that the earth goddess had performed great deeds.[39]

308.
Bharata and his younger brother Shatrughna
never parted for a second when they travelled by horse or chariot
nor when learning to chant the Vedic texts.
They were always together,
like Lakshmana and Rama who takes me as his slave.

309.
Rama and his three younger brothers
went among the sages who dwell in fragrant groves,
returning to the city when the sun had set.
Those who saw them were overjoyed,
like crops that flourish when the rainclouds arrive.

310.
Every woman in the city and the strong young men
who caressed their large breasts
prayed like Kausalya and Dasharatha to the gods in their hearts,
'Long may these princes live!'

311.
When people saw them, they said,
the supreme lord Rama whom the Vedas do not fully know
and his brother Lakshmana who is always at his side
are like the ocean and rainclouds that cause lotuses to bloom
walking together with golden Mount Meru.[40]

312.
My lord Rama's face shone like a lotus
filled with tenderness when he saw anyone before him.
'Is there anything you need?' he would ask. 'No trouble to be found?
Our women and fine men are superb, are they not?'

313.
'It is just as you say, lord, we have you as our king!
There is nothing that we need.
You will rule the thriving world and every life it holds
until a day of Brahma passes.'[41]

314.
The best of the three greatest gods lived happily
as everyone in the grand city
offered him their praise,
and his brothers revered him, touching his perfect lotus feet.

Taking in Hand

315.
As Dasharatha, king of kings, lived happily,
the entire universe flourished under his single parasol,
the drums of victory pounded,
and the sages praised him.

316.
He entered his court that soared up to heaven,
an audience hall adorned with gems
crafted with skills Maya himself did not possess
when he built the golden city in heaven* where wishing trees bloom.

317.
He shone there on his esteemed lion throne
and divine messengers who roam the heavens wondered,
'Is he our own king Indra?'
but decided, 'No, he is not that thousand-eyed god.'

318.
Kaushika, the imposing sage, who once thought
he would create anew all lives, all worlds,
and the gods before them, four-faced Brahma at their head,
stepped before the king mighty as a lion.[1]

319.
Once Kaushika came forward, the king arose,
his necklaces brighter than the sun in heaven,
like Indra seeing Brahma approach in his fragrant lotus,
and he kneeled to touch the sage's feet.

---

*Amaravati, Indra's capital.

320.
After rising and revering him, the king returned to his throne,
a superb work of craftsmanship adorned with gold and gems.
He offered flowers to the sage's lotus feet with heartfelt love,
saying, 'The bonds of my karma have been cut free!

321.
You are a boon to my palace, great one,
and you have come so freely
so I can walk around you filled with reverence,
is this because of my people's good deeds?
No, and nor is it due to my own karma,' he said politely.
'This is the karma of my ancestors.' The sage replied,

322.
'Your spear relishes the taste of your enemies' flesh, great king,
but the gods and sages like me are being hindered.
But for the snow-capped silver mountain, so much finer than others,
Brahma's own world that he rules from his lotus,
the milk sea, the superb capital of heaven,
and Ayodhya itself with its gem-studded mansions,
is there any other refuge?[2]

323.
'From his royal throne in the cool shade
where the wishing trees drip scented nectar,
Indra left and came to you, king, wanting to discuss his problems,
taking shelter under your parasol that alone protects the earth.
You understood, and killed Shambara, jewelled bands on his arms,
along with his line, and recaptured heaven.
Does Indra not now rule the kingdom you returned to him?'

324.
After Kaushika spoke, the king whose palace gates
roar with the three pounding drums
rolled on a sea of joy that no one could measure.

He gazed at the sage, raised his pressed hands,
and said, 'I have achieved the rewards of rule,
please tell me what to do.' The sage responded,[3]

325.
'Among your four sons, there is one noble boy with a dark body.
Send him with me, and urge him to stand in battle and protect us,
so the rakshasas do not obstruct the sacrifice, like desire and wrath
which rush up and torture the ascetics who fear the passions.
They hinder my grand rite in the forest's penance grove.'
The king despaired at his words,
for they were as cruel as Yama who seeks lives.[4]

326.
When the words of this disciplined master reached his ear
like a flaming torch thrust in a gaping wound
made by a spear driven into his chest,
the king whose spear is Death felt nothing but despair,
and his precious life reeled back and forth, swinging in the balance
like a man blind since birth who gains his sight
then loses it again
because of the misery gripping him.[5]

327.
The king wearing a fragrant garland that dripped nectar as he moved
said, his misery somehow allayed, 'Rama is so young, great one,
he has never been in combat. If this is what must be done,
I myself will come, and guard your grand sacrifice
where Shiva, who wears the cool Ganga in his matted locks,
Brahma, and Indra themselves have come—I will set out now!'

328.
As soon as the king finished speaking,
the sage who once began to create the world rose in anger.
His eyebrows creased high on his brow, he gave a harsh laugh,
his eyes burned red, and poured smoke to darken the world.
The sun disappeared, things spun off their axes,
and the gods feared the world would end.

329.
Vasishtha pondered the mind of the irate sage
and declared, 'Please calm yourself.'
He turned to Dasharatha and said,
'When your son Rama gains unique powers,
are they to be denied?[6]

330.
'Like the forceful sea, which surges
when a flood is fed by the pouring rains,
the time has now come, noble lord,
for Rama to achieve total mastery.'[7]

331.
The king deferred to the advice of his guru
and commanded, 'Summon Rama, Lakshmi's own lord,
and bring him to me.'
The messengers asked the thoughtful prince to come
and he presented himself before his father.

332.
The king pointed out Vishwamitra, master of the four ancient Vedas,
to the prince, who came with his younger brother Lakshmana,
and said, 'You too, noble lord, are a father to these young boys
and their perfect mother as well.
I give you them now, please care for them.'

333.
Vishwamitra calmed the fury in his heart, the vice of anger over.
He offered the king his blessings,
then took the princes into his care, saying,
'We shall go, and complete the ongoing sacrifice.'

334.
Rama, sustainer of the earth, strapped on his victorious sword
and on his shoulders proud as mountains
he slung his two quivers, as bottomless as the truth,
and took up his conquering war bow.[8]

335.
He and Lakshmana, also girded for war,
followed the sage Vishwamitra like a shadow,
and left as though their father's own life-breath was departing
to pass beyond the golden walls of lovely Ayodhya.

336.
They set out from the city, unrivalled even by heavenly cities
where ascetics dwell as their reward,
and reached the banks of the Sarayu,
its flowing waters home to geese that chitter
like the anklets of women who dance on the stage.

337.
The three spent the night in a grove so thick with bees
they seemed like the silken hair of women with budding breasts
who work the fields where honey pours from areca palms
when honeycombs are broken by winds fragrant with sugarcane,
and flows out over the bunds.

338.
As the seven green horses of the sun ran up the soaring crags
of the grand Udayagiri mountain, where low-lying clouds
turned it into a caparisoned elephant as they drifted across its peak,
they travelled on, and crossed the river.[9]

339.
The lord Rama saw a grove shrouded in dense smoke
rising from a sacrifice where gods enjoy the taste of their share.
He bowed to the holy ascetic Vishwamitra,
and asked, 'What is this place?'

The Killing of Tataka

340.
'When he fired on the lord with the crescent moon in his hair,
Desire stood here, and in the rage that burst from the lord's third eye
his body burned away like a silk cotton flower spitting flames.
He became the bodiless god that day, known from then on as Ananga.[1]

341.
'My son who dwells in the Vedas,
when the lord who wears the elephant skin
burned Madana and stripped him of living flesh,
his ashes drifted here.
This region is therefore called Anga, or "Body",
and this place is called Kamashrama, "Home to Desire",
so named for the same reason.

342.
'To rip attachment and desire out by the roots
and bring an end to rebirth,
the ones who strive to reach pure knowledge of the real
keep their thoughts on Shiva, and he practised yoga here!
Could words ever describe the holiness of this place?'

343.
The brahman finished his tale, and the brothers were amazed.
They left that place and met sages whose wealth is the righteous way
who, filled with joy, invited them to spend the day together.
The next morning, they approached a scorched wasteland
as the sun with his blooming rays climbed over Udayagiri.

344.
There is no season but summer there,
the sun god always roams, holding his banner of triumph
as he drinks every trace of moisture from the land,

so that even Agni, god of blazing fire,
feels his eyes burn if he sees it,
his heart burn if he thinks of it.[2]

345.
Just speak of the heat in this place,
and the tongue that speaks will burn away.
The vault of the sky burns there,
so too the night that covers the world,
the sunlight burns from the break of dawn,
the rainclouds burn, thunder and lightning burn,
is there anything there that does not burn?

346.
It never grows cool,
like the heart of a man who has been humbled
though he raged on the battlefront with perfect courage
while spears and arrows poured down
like rain from great stormclouds,
by losing the jewel that was his honour*
to the schemes of corrupt rogues.

347.
Throughout the barren forest, rich treasures lie scattered,
rubies that fell when cobras' poisoned mouths split open,
white pearls that fell when leafless bamboo stems split open,
dark pieces of oudh that fell from the trunks of milk bushes
when they withered and split open like the bodies of ghouls.[3]

348.
The world will not cross it, for nothing would live long,
even the frightful goddess Kali can only run away.
The sun's chariot will not cross it when it climbs the arching sky,
the clouds will not cross it, not even wind will cross it.

---

*Manam ani, a grand ornament emblematic of a man's honour.

349.
Like dazzling bursts of lightning that split apart the clouds,
scarlet light flows from cracks in the scorched ground
as if blood pouring from wounds in the earth goddess' body,
it streams from the rubies on the hoods of serpent lords
who have fire in the poison they spit
to rip eyeballs clear apart.

350.
Burned by the cruel heat that beats down from above,
the trumpeting elephant searches for a place to hide.
A huge cobra writhes with hunger that makes its mind stew
so it draws near and rises up, ready to swallow prey,
and the elephant comes racing in, right into that open mouth!

351.
In the wasteland the god of blazing fire claims entirely for himself
elephants and crows lie dead, their bodies charred and black.
They are scorched clouds fallen to earth,
torched by that fiery doomsday mare*
the sun blazing in the sky.

352.
Mirages, the chariots of ghouls, shimmer in the forest
as if Varuna† had come racing in to cover the land with floods.
Were the heat to rise back up after everything was charred,
the heavens would catch fire, and he has pity for the gods.

353.
The mirage that rises from that deeply rooted fire
is itself a throne of crystal set on feet of refined gold.
Made for the king named summer, it is his seat of triumph
as he rules that awful forest which bakes under the sun.

---

*See v. 202.

†Lord of the waters.

354.
There is not a drop of pity to be found in this land,
like the minds of women who sell themselves for gold,
like the minds of the wise who are set on liberation
scaling the walls of the three relentless foes
as they crush the source of pain, karma of both types.[4]

355.
As the parched gravel on it crumbles, the land turns to dust
and splits down to the depths to open cracks so wide
the rays of the sun can pass down below
and shine even on the land of the serpent lords
who have rubies on their hoods.

356.
This is the cruel wasteland, alive with leaping flames.
They entered, and the great ascetic thought to himself,
'The great power possessed by these two knows no bounds,
but they are delicate as flowers and may suffer a bit.'

357.
Sensing their plight, the sage gazed at their two faces,
and the princes bowed at his feet, for they realized his intent.
He taught them two mantras that four-faced Brahma had created,
and the two princes took them and committed them to heart.

358.
Once they possessed the mantras,
the cruel wasteland that had burned with leaping flames
to make the doomsday fire a trifle
cooled so that they seemed to move through clear, fresh water.
The generous lord bowed before the sage, and spoke.

359.
'Tell me, sage, what has happened to this land?' Rama asked.
'It lies ruined, like the country of a king destroyed by crime.
Did Shiva, who has the swirling Ganga and fine garlands in his hair,
burn it with his third eye, or was it something else?'

360.
'Listen well,' the sage replied to Rama, 'There is a woman
who leads a roaming life of murder, ending sweet lives.
She looks as foul as death, and still more she is strong,
like a thousand rutting elephants joined together as one.

361.
'A man was born of the yaksha race, ruthless as fire,
his power so stunning it was praised throughout the worlds.
A champion with a sober mind, his name was Satcara,
and to him was born a righteous son, the indomitable Suketu.

362.
'Suketu had no sons and his heart was pained,
so he worshipped the grandfather Brahma, magnified by praise,
the god who dwells in the enduring lotus blossom,
and performed brutal austerities for an age of passing days.

363.
'The grandfather known in the holy Vedas appeared before him,
and asked, "What desire would you have me fulfil?"
Suketu said, "I am wretched, for I have no children. Bless me!"
Brahma replied, "There will be no sons, man of subtle learning,
but you will have a daughter.

364.
'"This daughter will be born with the enormous power
of a thousand elephants frenzied with rut, and she will be lovely
like the simple, sweet peacock, the goddess in the lotus.
Now go," said the unborn god, and then he disappeared.

365.
'Born as Brahma's favour had ordained, this girl with fine jewels
seemed like rosy Lakshmi, and when she became a woman,
Suketu noted her beauty and searched for a proper husband.
He gave her to a yaksha named Sunda, a lord among their kind.

366.
'Seeing this woman like a goddess and the yaksha with each other
was like watching Kama and Rati embrace.
They plunged into a sea of utmost pleasure
that seemed like it would never end as days passed into nights.

367.
'They passed many days like this, and then from her womb
the woman with the shining beauty of Lakshmi gave birth
to Subahu, a brawler of enormous power,
and Maricha, who made the earth wail with his immense arms.

368.
'When they grew up, with sorcery, duplicity and power
that friends, indeed their own mother, could not fathom,
the yaksha with a seething temper who had fathered these sons
grew haughty and reckless with pride.

369.
'Sunda went to an ashram, home of the mighty ascetic Agastya,
a sage who had taken the entire crashing ocean in his hand
and sipped it dry to halt the hateful asuras' evil,
and he uprooted the tall trees there, tossing them aside.[5]

370.
'He took the lives of bucks, does and blackbucks,
creatures loved by sages who delight in the self-discipline
that brings them what they cherish,
and he broke down all the trees, such as the towering gamboge.
Agastya glared and his eyes streamed fire, burning Sunda to ash.

371.
'Tataka heard of Sunda's death, and erupted in a fire of fury.
The woman with golden bracelets cried, "I will finish off the sage!"
She raced to Agastya's ashram together with her sons,
and entered the place where the great ascetic lived.

372.
'They closed in on the ashram, and roared out for the sage
with screams to terrify thunder, hurricanes and doomsday fire,
to strip the lustre from the gods, to frighten the sun and moon,
to make clouds and lightning tremble, to rip the universe apart.

373.
'The sage who gave the boundless ocean called Tamil to the world
let out a roar that would humble lightning
and from his eyes poured hissing fire.
"Because of your murderous deeds," he cried,
"you shall become rakshasas, and live as those low beings!"

374.
'Instantly, the yakshas were consumed by fire
which seemed like molten copper as it hissed from his eyes.
They became rakshasas, crude beasts intent on slaughter
who roam and kill all living things,
striking terror in heaven and on earth.

375.
'Transformed by the sage's wrath and the curse he inflicted
the two brothers fled, powerless to strike back.
They sought refuge with Sumali, a rakshasa in the underworld,
and made a show of kinship, saying, "We will be your noble sons!"[6]

376.
'The two sons of that foul woman stayed with Sumali
living for ages down in the underworld,
but later they left to roam the world like the doomsday winds,
storming and killing as uncles of Ravana, the ten-headed ascetic.

377.
'Tataka's heart seethed like fire, obsessed with the thought
of the fury of that sage who showed such ascetic power.
She left her mighty sons and headed off, at last to make her way
to this forest, where flames leap high from the constant blazes.

378.
'She wanders now in the shape of a woman
as if every sin were gathered together beyond measure and form.
Should she want to rip out the earth in fury or drink away the sea,
or hate the heavens and pull them down,
this is a woman who can!

379.
'If an ocean could walk, endowed with two mountains,
a poison born within it, a roar the equal of thunder,
the fire that burns on doomsday, and a pair of crescent moons,
that is what her body is like, her appearance causes terror.[7]

380.
'Young prince with shoulders that make men want to be women
when they see you with their own eyes,
this evil woman's name is Tataka, she lives in this forest,
and her trident is as close to hand as her serpent bangles.

381.
'As the single trait of greed destroys every virtue
when it never loosens its grip on the heart,
this unspeakably foul rakshasa has transformed this place
destroying farmers' vast fields where the land was always fertile.

382.
'She serves the king of Lanka, raincloud adorned with a garland!
This woman with the strength of a mountain disrupts the sacrifice,
she has ruined my own! She roams the whole land of Anga
taking kill after kill, finishing off whole lines of beings.

383.
'Every creature wise Brahma made when he created the worlds,
is nothing more than food to her.
In a very short while, young prince,
every being alive will end up in her gullet!
What more must I say?'

384.
The lord who wields the bow and holds the conch in his hand
listened to the tale that the great sage had told him,
then nodded his head wrapped with a fine scented garland
and said, 'Where does she live, this woman who does such things?'

385.
The sage who keeps the five senses within his control
heard the words of the young man bold as an elephant.
'Noble lord,' he replied, 'she lives there, on that mountain—'
and as he spoke she came, a dark mountain crowned with fire.*

386.
The anklets wrapped around her feet
had mountains inside the jingling bells,
each step she took pressed in the earth
so the sea poured into the holes.
Even Death, bold as fire, grew frightened
and ran off to hide in the underworld,
when Tataka ran at them, uprooting mountains behind her.

387.
The filthy rakshasi glared at them and her eyes sparked flames
as if the doomsday fire had split in two and flared on the sea.
A tremble of fury appeared on her brow
and her mouth was a cave baring fangs,
which curled out like the tips of crescent moons.

388.
Her breasts shook under the garland she had made
from huge, rutting elephants tied together trunk to trunk.
When she gave out a roar that would terrify lightning,
the land of the gods, the cardinal points, the seven worlds,
and everywhere else lurched and trembled with shock.

---

*Tataka's red hair.

389.
She roared like a raincloud booming with thunder,
stared at the three before her, then broke into a smile.
She ground her teeth, looked over at cruel Death,
her trident with bladed tips that all the world fears,
then broke open the cave of her gaping mouth, and spoke.

390.
'I defend this land as my own, no one can best my strength!
I have destroyed everything in it to exterminate all life.
Now you have come here, and you shall tell me why,
did your fate push you forward to fall by my hand?
Or maybe you think I need juicy meat?'

391.
She glared at them, and her look burned clouds to ash,
her heart seethed, and one kick turned a mountain to dust.
She gnashed her long fangs, two strong halves of the moon,
grasped her trident and screamed at them in rage,
'I will hurl this right in your chests!'

392.
Even though he knew what the sage wanted him to do
and she had begun her work of death, making living souls tremble,
the lord did not aim his arrow and instruct it to end her life
for the thought she was a woman lingered in his noble mind.

393.
As the woman with white teeth and wild red hair rushed at them
crying, 'I will hurl my spear and kill you!'
Rama paid her no heed, and the brahman who knows the four Vedas
grasped the thoughts of the prince, and spoke.

394.
'All her deeds towards us have been evil, prince adorned with gems,
she has not killed us only because she believes us dried-out husks.
A female so vicious, what do you think she is?
Do you think her a woman?

395.
'She has harmed modest women, so hold her in contempt.
If she can crush all strength in the arms of mighty men,
experts with the sword, as fast as you can say her name,
who better would this quality called manliness describe?

396.
'Her arms are like Mount Mandara, Indra has submitted to her,
and kings and gods, their armies lost, have run off in defeat.
Now given all this, when it comes to manliness
what difference could there be between her and young men?

397.
'Noble son of the solar line, whose kings protect the earth
by turning the strong wheel of command that surrounds it,
she fights with the great and has taken many lives on this earth.
Must this woman who blights dharma have a man's body too?

398.
'Think of days cut short for those given life,
look to dharma, young man with a spear like death.
Let alone the thought that you would send her to heaven,
is there another like her, a death that loves feasting
as soon as it catches the scent of life?

399.
'What else can be called evil if not this vile feasting,
snatching many stable lives and tossing them in her mouth?
There is a lack in her, noble lord, of that quality called woman,
an innocent simplicity and a long braid at the back.

400.
'I tell you this after pondering the endless true dharma.
I do not say it because I hate her,
there is no dharma when one gives in to anger.'
The brahman said to Rama, 'Kill this rakshasi now.'

401.
The noble prince listened to what the sage had told him,
and replied, 'Since a breach of dharma is near at hand, true one,
and since you order me to do it, what path is there for dharma
apart from taking your words as Veda and carrying them out?'

402.
The rakshasi, pure evil that had taken woman's form,
sensed what the lord of the sweet waters of the Ganga had decided,
so she took that cruel fire, the trident in her red hand,
and hurled it at him along with the fire in her eyes.

403.
That fierce doomsday fire, the shining trident
that the woman like a new death threw in her rage,
came at him like the planet Rahu comes at the full moon
but Rama stood fast, poised to fulfil the sage's command.

404.
No one saw Mal instantly set his fine bow to foot,
bend it and string it, then fire off an arrow.
They saw pieces of the trident, now shattered,
hurled by the fierce woman who had stolen it from Death.

405.
In the time it takes to say a word,
the rakshasi dark as a cloud passing in the night
rained down a hail of stones that could fill the whole ocean
but the hero brushed them aside with a rain of arrows from his bow.

406.
The lord with a dark body shot a lethal arrow
that raced towards the black rakshasi with the speed of a word.
It did not lodge in her chest hard as diamond
but went clean through her back,
vanishing like advice the wise give to rude oafs.

407.
As soon as that young man like a soaring golden mountain
attacked with his heavy arrow, a windstorm that rages on doomsday,
she fell, like a cloud that soars in the sky at the end of time
to rain down heavy stones, and then falls low
crashing with thunder and lightning.

408.
Tataka fell, her mouth open, teeth smeared with flesh,
and rivers of blood gushed over the dusty wasteland.
She seemed like a victory banner hewed down,
fallen to the ground that day
as a menacing sign of a day to come
for the rakshasa crowned on each head.*

409.
The torrent of blood that poured from the arrow
deep in Tataka's rugged chest
turned the woods into a sea, as if the sweeping crimson
had lost its hold on the evening sky
and fell down to wash over the vast wasteland.

410.
In this first battle of Kakutstha who wears gold sparkling with gems
and did not spurn the words of the sage great as Brahma,
even Death who roamed with hunger,
afraid to swallow the lives of rakshasas who wear fearsome swords,
relished his own small taste.[8]

411.
'We take our rightful place,' said the gods to the sage,
'and nothing hinders you now.
You shall give divine weapons to the prince.'
They offered their blessings and showered flowers
on the young man like a cloud holding a rainbow,
then they all departed.[9]

---

*Ravana, who has ten heads.

The Sacrifice

412.
Once they had left the forest cooled by the gods' rain of flowers,
the sage made great by his forbidding deeds
gave weapons that equal the word of Cataiyan, lord of Venneynallur,
a man like medicine for the disease of famine
to the people on this earth.

413.
The wise master of his senses taught Rama all the divine weapons,
clear in the lord's mind as soon as they were conferred.
They were overjoyed to unite in him,
as though the fruit of all good karma
had come seeking to join him in the next rebirth.[1]

414.
The divine weapons exclaimed,
'We have joined you, hero, and we shall never leave!
Like your brother, we shall always be at your just command.'
'Very well,' replied Rama, and the weapons revealed their forms
to the lord the colour of the blue kaya blossom.

415.
Afterwards, the three travelled for two leagues
and then they heard a thundering sound before them.
'What is that, lord?' great Rama asked,
and the sage who had destroyed all effects of karma replied.

416.
'That is the sound of two rivers meeting,
The Gomati and the Sarayu, revered by the gods,
named for its source, the Manasasaras.'*
They went on, and reached a holy river whose waters end rebirth.

---

*The 'mind-produced lake', said to have been created through a mental act of Brahma.

417.
Rama asked the mighty sage, 'What river is this,
so pure the gods themselves must praise it?'
'Long ago,' said the sage, 'Brahma sired a king named Kusha.
This champion had four sons, as perfect as the Vedas.

418.
'Their names were Kusha, Kushanabha,
blameless Adhurta, and Vasu, famed for his valour.
Kusha ruled Kaushambi, Kushanabha cool Mahodaya,
Adhurta pristine Dharmavana, and Vasu ruled Girivraja.[2]

419.
'Kushanabha had one hundred daughters, their lips red as coral.
One day when they were growing up, speaking sweetly,
they went to a garden with their maids.
Vayu came there, and when he saw them, he was enthralled.

420.
"Kama with the sea-monster banner has shot me with his bow,
and I suffer, women with keen, broad eyes. Marry me!" he said.
The women with lustrous gold bangles replied,
"We will place your request at our father's holy feet.
We will only be yours if he assents."
The wind god cracked their spines, and they all collapsed.

421.
'Vayu left the distraught women, who crawled to their father
and told him what had happened with stuttered, sweet words.
The king calmed his hundred daughters with long braided hair
and married them to Brahmadatta,
a man free from the darkness of ignorance,
who was the son of a mighty ascetic, the sage Culin.

422.
'The moment Brahmadatta touched their lotus hands,
the women stood straight and regained their full beauty.
Since Kushanabha, ruler of the earth, had no male heir,
he made an offering for sons in the sacrificial flames,
and a commanding man named Gadhi, master of swift horses,
arose like the sun from the middle of the fire.

423.
'In time, Kushanabha passed the kingdom and crown to Gadhi
and attained the golden world of heaven.
My older sister* and I were born to Gadhi, king of kings,
who long ruled the famous city of Mahodaya.

424.
'Gadhi gave his daughter in marriage to glorious Ricika,
a man whom even his father, the sage Bhrigu, could not equal.
Ricika, master of the Vedas, fulfilled ethics, wealth, and pleasure,
then performed splendid ascetic deeds and joined Brahma,
who rules his heavenly world from a blossoming lotus.

425.
'When her husband took the path to heaven,
Kaushiki could not bear it, so she became a splendid river
and followed him to the sky. Ricika saw her, and said,
"Descend to earth in this river form, and put suffering to an end."
The lord of ascetics then attained Brahma's world.

426.
'This broad river,' said the sage, 'is my own older sister,'
and great Rama and his younger brother were amazed.
The three travelled a bit further, then Rama asked,
'What is this grove veiled in darkness?' The great ascetic replied,

---

*Kaushiki (Satyavati).

427.
'This place is pure, like the hearts of women
who think of no other god but their husbands.
Listen still further! Mal with red lotus eyes,
whom no one, not even the Vedas or gods, can know
stayed here and did penance for the good of the world.

428.
'He is called by his own holy name when prayers are recited
to cut through karmic bonds on earth and in heaven.
They describe him by asking who can ever fully know
the ways he warps reality through the power of his illusion?
He is the pristine form, we cannot know his aims,
and he performed great ascetic deeds here for a hundred aeons.

429.
'When he dwelled here, an asura named Mahabali
so powerful he seemed like another Varaha,
who made the entire earth yield to his tusks,
seized control of heaven and earth.[3]

430.
'The forceful asura had every confidence
and began a sacrifice where ghee stoked the flames
that the gods themselves could never have performed.
For payment, he would give the world and its wealth to brahmans.

431.
'The gods learned of his largesse and came here
where they revered the lord of illusion.
"End the foul work of this evil man!" they prayed,
and the lord decided to do what they asked.[4]

432.
'Noble, dark-hued Vishnu took mortal form as a child
born of the omniscient sage Kashyapa and his wife Aditi.
Like the seed that contains the banyan tree within it,
he became a tiny dwarf.*

433.
'The miraculous one put on the three-stranded sacred thread,
the waistcord made of reeds, the ring of darbha grass on his hand,
and his pure tongue recited mantras and the Vedas.
He then went to the sacrifice, his little body equal
to the realm of his knowledge that only the wise can know.[5]

434.
'The conqueror of worlds learned that he had come,
and when he went to greet him, he stood there amazed.
"There are no brahmans like you, magnificent one!
Given that, can anyone can be higher than me?"

435.
'The dwarf was grateful for the manly asura's praise,
and responded, "Your generous hands offer limitless gifts,
even finer than what your supplicants request.
All who have come are now distinguished men indeed,
and anyone who has not come merits no regard."

436.
'Delighted, Bali asked, "What may I do for you?"
"Mighty lord," the brahman responded, "if you grant me a favour,
I would like all the earth I can cover in three steps for a gift—"
but Bali cut him off. "Consider it given..." he started to say,
but his guru Shukra stopped him from finishing.[6]

---

*Vamana, Vishnu's fifth (and first human) avatar.

437.
'"The person we see before us is an illusion," he warned,
"you must not believe he is this dwarf as dark as a raincloud.
You need to know that in a previous age
he swallowed the whole world and the universe beyond!"

438.
'"The way he approached me makes that impossible," Bali replied.
"I stretched my hands out to him, and he brought his below mine.
Don't be foolish! Nothing could be better for me
than if the dark, perfect hands you describe were actually his.[7]

439.
'"If respected masters of the texts that prescribe dharma
come forward and teach noble people who receive them,
they should not distinguish between friend or foe.
Who could be more noble than this man standing here?[8]

440.
'"You have spoken out of ignorance! Noble men are generous.
Does anything at all lie beyond their own largesse?
It is wrong to beg for anything, even one's own cherished life,
but to give? That is true delight.[9]

441.
'"Everyone dies, but not all of them are dead, father.
The dead, they say, are beggars
who cheat death with outstretched palms.
And who but the generous live, even though they die?

442.
'"People do not become enemies even due to horrid crime,
true enemies confront the generous and tell them not to give.
They degrade themselves,
and there is nothing as foul as that.

443.
'"Principled lords give gifts when they are rich,
and thus they gain fame. For those who strive for such merit,
greed is a cruel foe that corrupts from within
and it must be dismissed," Bali challenged his guru.

444.
'"Preventing me from giving even before the gift is chosen,
is that an appealing trait in you? Unworthy Shukra!
Know that the families of the wicked who oppose largesse
will perish without food or clothes."[10]

445.
'Bali vented his anger like this, taking nothing to heart
from his counsellor's warning that his guest would do him harm.
"You will have all you can cover in three steps," he told the dwarf,
and he poured water over the towering god's tiny hands.[11]

446.
'Like repayment for help a person offers to the noble,
the instant the consecrated water touched his hands
the dwarf slighted by his own parents grew tall as the sky,
astounding all who watched and filling them with terror.

447.
'His firmly grounded feet spread out to cover the earth
but did not stretch further, as if the world were still too small.
His first step spanned the worlds above, conquering the heavens,
and with emptiness beyond it, retreated to stay there.

448.
'His next step covered all the worlds,
and since the earth had no room for a third step,
he placed his foot on the head of his devotee Bali.
And so, young prince with a bow at your shoulder,
that tiny dwarf was the true lord crowned with holy basil![12]

449.
'"These belong to Indra," said the dark god, and he gave him the worlds.
Then he went to the milk sea, where he rested on his couch,
and those feet that had measured the worlds
turned red when Lakshmi caressed them with her hands.

450.
'Because of its history, this place will end the stubborn karma
of those who behold it with love, and they will not be reborn!
There is nowhere else like it, noble prince,
it is the best place for me to sacrifice as the Vedas command.[13]

451.
'I will perform my sacrifice here,' he said,
and entered a blossoming grove
to obtain everything necessary for the rites to follow.
He then began the sacrifice, and told the princes to keep it safe.

452.
For six days, the sage conducted a sacrifice fit for the gods
that no one else could have imagined or performed,
and the two sons of the emperor who rules the whole world
protected it as eyelids protect the eye.

453.
The older of the two young heroes who were guarding the rite
approached the omniscient sage, and asked,
'Great one whose virtues are praised by all, when will they come,
those savages you described, known for their foul deeds?'

454.
The sage remained silent and offered no response.
The prince revered him, then went outside, ready for war.
He gazed up at the sky, and in swept the rakshasas,
thundering and roaring, horrific as lightning.

455.
They poured down like fire and rain, launching arrows and spears,
ripped out the mountains and hurled them below.
They screamed curses, bellowed threats, and flung axes,
and cast every treacherous spell that came to mind.

456.
As if a stormy ocean had risen in the sky, filled with gleaming fish,
the encroaching rakshasa armies overwhelmed the grove
and the weapons they threw smothered it
like the rain in a monsoon.

457.
Shimmering swords advanced, weaving in and out,
as legions of rakshasas roared, beating drums with short sticks.
They closed in as fast as a gathering rainstorm
booming and pounding on doomsday.

458.
Rama pointed them out to Lakshmana, and said,
'These are the monsters the sage with matted locks described!
Rakshasas with red hair and sparks that fly from their rolling eyes,
gnashing their lips with their split fangs.'

459.
Lakshmana gazed at the sky, then at his bow,
and fire danced in his eyes.
He raised his pressed hands to Rama, and said,
'Lord of gods, you will see the rakshasas swarming above
fall to the earth, their bodies in pieces.'

460.
Wary that flesh and blood from rakshasas with smoking spears
might fall into the sacrificial fire kept pure for offerings,
the lord with red lotus eyes used his arrows
to thatch a roof above the royal sage.

461.
Like the gods who quaked with fear when the lethal poison arose
and sought refuge with the god whose red, matted locks
are graced with the moon, its crescent perfect for a single day,
the ascetics were terrified of the vicious rakshasas
and appealed to the lord dark as night,
crying, 'You are our protection!'[14]

462.
'Do not worry,' Rama said, and made the gesture of safety,*
then drew the divine string of his bow back to his ear.
The surface of the earth was soon flooded with blood
as he built up a mountain of rakshasa heads.

463.
The husband of Lakshmi fired an arrow
at the two sons born of ghastly Tataka:
it knocked Maricha back into the sea,
and dispatched Subahu to the palace of death.[15]

464.
The lord with a flower garland fired arrow after arrow
and instantly they covered the sky.
'They tread on our heaped corpses,' the rakshasas cried,
'they will leave none of us alive!'
and they ran over each other to make their escape.

465.
The cruel arrows kept coming,
dreadful as lightning to the fleeing rakshasas,
and headless bodies jumped up to begin their rigid dance.
Many ghouls came and sang Rama's praises
while a canopy of crows spread out above.[16]

---

*The right hand brought to chest level with the palm facing outward.

466.
A torrent of flowers poured through the crowded birds
while kettle drums and other instruments roared like thunder.
Indra and the other gods arrived and offered praise,
honouring Rama as he lifted his elegant bow.

467.
The saintly ascetics showered blessings like flowers,
and even the trees offered flowers of their own.
Vishwamitra brought his sacrifice to its proper end
and complimented Rama, filled with delight.

468.
'You created all the worlds, and later you protected them,
swallowing everything living and still in your great stomach.
The world will say I am blessed because you saved my sacrifice,
but I think of it differently, I know you are far more.'[17]

469.
After saying this, the sage whose virtues are firm as a mountain
spent the day happily in the flowering grove with his fellow ascetics.
Then the son of Kausalya approached and asked him,
'Please tell me, how may I serve you today?'

470.
Vishwamitra said, 'I may say things are difficult, lord,
but nothing can be difficult for you.
Great challenges lie before you, but first
we shall visit the king of Mithila, city of lush fields,
and witness his sacrifice. Let us go!' And the three travelled on.

Ahalya

471.
They reached the river Son, a fine woman,
her ornamented breasts, flowing with goodness,
are the sandbanks graced with oudh, sandalwood,
and great gems cleansed by her waters,
her waist, the newly grown cane,
her jingling girdle, the day's blossomed flowers,
her dressed raven hair, the black sands,
and anklets are wrapped around her feet
like the river's side channels flow around mountains.

472.
When they arrived at the river, the sun plunged into the ocean,
his chariot pulled by bridled horses so fast they outrun Aruna's gaze,
as if to ease the heat that seethes in his own form
and give them a fresh, cool dawn.

473.
They rested in a grove filled with sweet-smelling flowers
where joyful bees sleep with their wives,
quitting lotus ponds when the petal doors have closed
on temples that hold fast to their dharma:
scented flowers, newly bloomed, on long stalks
that rest in cool, murmuring waters.

474.
'A garden like this, what is this place?' Raghava asked,
and the sage who endures pain to end his karma explained,
'Kashyapa's wife did penance here,
long ago, out of anguish for her sons.[1]

475.
'A vidyadhara woman once found her way to the lofty world
beyond the cosmic sphere of the storm-coloured god who rules me,
and worshipped there, praising the goddess on her lotus throne.
Lakshmi was pleased, and offered a garland that bees never leave.

476.
'The lady tied the garland to the bridge of her lute
and came back from unborn Brahma's world.
Durvasas, the sage in stained clothing, saw her return
and perceived she had sung to the goddess who rules him.
He bent low to touch her two feet in worship,

477.
'And she said, "Your greatness knows no bounds, good sage,
please take this garland that once crowned the goddess
who wears a tilak on her brow, and gives birth to all living things
as she rests on the god who creates, sustains, and destroys the worlds,"
then she gave it to him out of kindness.

478.
'"All the unthinkable penance I've done," he thought,
"for this garland that crowned the gods' queen!"
The fierce sage danced, and wrapped it around his head,
"Deeds are gone," he realized, "this is the path of liberation!"
and rejoicing, he attained the land of the gods.

479.
'A vast storming raincloud on a silver mountain
blossoming with a thousand red lotuses,
Indra shone on the elephant Airavata with a body so bright
he seemed to contain the condensed rays of the sun.

480.
'Rambha, Menaka, Tilottama and Urvashi drew near him,
dancing on the street, singing songs full of longing
with voices that made even sugar seem bitter
refined by the anklets they wear on their feet,
flower buds in the bodiless god's quiver
for him to rain down as arrows.[2]

481.
'The chowries rolled like waves, brushing him on both sides
as the moon's thick rays might sweep past a vast dark mountain,
and his supreme white parasol shone like the moon itself,
full and unfading, alive with light as it soars high above.

482.
'The conches, cymbals, woodblocks and pounding royal drums
made such a din, they engulfed the auspicious hymns,
and like the roar of the powerful ocean
the four Vedas thundered out to swallow up the world.
Durvasas saw the majesty of the lord in procession
and his heart was struck with wonder.

483.
'In his joy, the peerless sage held up the perfect garland
to place it in Vasava's hand, but Indra took it with his goad
and draped it on Airavata, a beast of sudden power.
With a trunk as thick as a palmyra tree,
the elephant snatched it and ground it underfoot.

484.
'As the great sage watched, hot rage flowed from his eyes,
and the gods feared the whole world would turn to ash.
They quit their places and fled, the sun and moon stopped shining,
the eight directions went dark, and the worlds spun out of true.

485.
'Smoke rose with each breath, and he gave a thin smile
like the one Shiva wore when he shattered the fortress.
His eyebrows arched high on his shining brow
and the jets of flame that arose from his eyes
were enough to stagger lightning. "Hear me," he raged,
"lord of a hundred sacrifices, so swollen with pride!

486.
'"I was given that garland by the lady who won it,
a gift to cherish given to her by the goddess
who reigns sweetly on her throne, the chest of the lord,
lord of all beings, lord of the earth goddess,
the incomparable lord of the Vedas!

487.
'"I saw you just now in all your splendid beauty, and in my joy,
I offered this fragrant garland to you, but you spurned it.
All your great treasures, and the riches you alone hold
will enter the sea and lie there hidden.
You will become feeble, and you will suffer pain."

488.
'The celestial women, the divine wishing trees,
Surabhi with her ambrosial milk, Indra's prancing steed,
his rutting mountain of an elephant, and all the rest
quit his retinue, leaving nothing of value behind.
They ran off in terror, to enter the sea and lie there hidden
like the enemies of Kannan, who lives in Venney.[3]

489.
'All the worlds suffered famine from heaven on down
because of the wrath of the furious sage.
Indra, who once clipped the wings off of mountains,
four-faced Brahma and the rest of the gods
approached the god with a mole on his chest,
the abode of Shri who dwells in the red lotus.

490.
'The grandfather in the blossoming lotus and the other gods
described what the furious sage had done through his curse.
"We have no safe haven, we take your feet as our refuge!"
"Do not fear, do not fear, no need to be troubled,"
said the god who had once measured the worlds.

491.
'"Make Mandara the churning pole, Vasuki the rope,
and the full moon will be the balance weight.
The gods and the asuras, split into sides,
will take both ends and grab hold of the rope,
then add the herb,* and churn the crashing sea
so the ambrosia will emerge from its roiling waters.

492.
'"I too will come, so arise, be quick now, go,"
and as soon as the immortals received his favour
they worshipped him and offered their praise.
"We have nothing to fear," they cried, "our hardship has ended!"
and they trembled with ecstasy, rousing them to dance.

493.
'They ripped out the mountain, wrapped Vasuki around it,
set the moon on top to weight it down, and poured in the herb.
Then they churned the ocean until it surged with waves,
the surface of the earth began to sag, and Ananta† uncoiled below.

494.
'Vishnu became a mighty tortoise, Mandara whirled on his back,
and he stretched out a thousand hands to pull the churning rope.
All that was hidden by the sage provoked to anger
came back again at the command of the noble lord
who never reaches the hearts of those who stray from dharma.

---

*U. Ve. Ca. identifies the herb as amritavalli, celestial creeper.

†The world serpent held to support the earth.

495.
'After all that had fled and passed beyond
was born anew when our lord showed his favour,
the gods and asuras fought with each other,
but because of the gorgeous woman Mohini
the asuras gave up their struggle and died,
and the immortals savoured the rare ambrosia.[4]

496.
'When it happened, Diti was consumed with grief.
She went to Kashyapa, touched his flower feet,
and said, "My sons were all killed by Indra and the others.
Bless me, and give me a child,
a son who will crush them all."

497.
'As soon as she finished, he replied, "I give you a son.
Now go, and live on the earth until a thousand years have passed,
and if your ascetic deeds are great, your intention will be realized."
She went and practised hard austerities.

498.
'Vasava heard of this and went to see her in the guise of a disciple.
He sensed a moment when her practice faltered
and destroyed the son within her womb,
splitting the child into seven fragments.
She cried out in anguish, her tears rained down,
and he pronounced a name, "The Maruts."*

499.
'This is where it happened,' the sage explained,
'And that place over there is called Sharavanam, a stand of reeds
where the child born of the ascetic who wears the moon
grew up in Uma's womb, his power too vast
for hoary Vayu or Ganga to raise him.

---

*The Maruts are fierce storm gods who serve as attendants to Indra.

500.
Driving off a darkness as black as Yama's body
the god who sustains the world appeared, brimming with light,
as his chariot emerged from the roaring blue sea
like the first cause* in the primal lotus that grew
from Mal's navel to burst into bloom.[5]

501.
The three travellers who seemed like the trio led by the unborn god
rose from their stay, and saw a holy river breaking its banks,
the Ganga, equal to the Golden River[6]
since its currents drag off cassia flowers, swollen with thick nectar
from a forest, the matted locks of the god with the red-eyed bull.

502.
'Tell me, father, what are this river's merits?' Raghava asked.
The sage replied, 'There was a king in your holy line, my son,
Sagara, who raised Lakshmi in his triumphant arms.
He lived in the great city of Ayodhya, and he protected the world.

503.
'This valiant king had two wives, a princess from Vidarbha
who gave birth to Asamanja and his son Amshuman,
and gentle Sumati, younger sister to the lord of birds,
who bore sixty thousand sons, men of strength true to dharma.[7]

504.
'Sagara commanded power, aware of his sons' loyal service.
He performed the final horse sacrifice, but the gods were furious
and told of his deed to Vasava, whose garland swarms with bees.
Indra stole the white stallion, and hid it where Kapila dwells.[8]

---

*Brahma.

505.
'Amshuman went after the galloping horse
and searched the whole earth, leaving nothing unseen.
He was baffled, for he did not know the king of gods had hidden it,
so he went to tell his grandfather whose heart was set on the sacrifice.

506.
'The king despaired when he heard this, and shared it with his sons.
They were crazed with anger, like the submarine mare,*
and hot rage poured from their eyes.
They probed the four landscapes,† then dug into the earth
scraping it up with their hands to reveal the underworld.

507.
'They shovelled away in the northeast
digging a hole nine hundred miles in depth and width, they say,
and then they saw the horse standing behind Kapila,
the sage whose austerities grow ever greater.
They rushed at him, full of contempt and hissing like fire,
hurling curses as they assailed him.

508.
'The great ascetic was outraged,
for the wrath they had kindled burned cruel.
He opened his eyes, they streamed fire, and in his smile
which had once appeared on the god crowned with silk cotton buds,
the fortress seemed razed once more.
Sixty thousand royal sons were reduced to ashes,
and the good king, set on sacrifice, learned this from his spies.

509.
'The king was tormented, crushed beyond feeling,
he saw no release from his pain.
He asked his grandson, not knowing the answer,

---

*See v. 202.

†The landscapes of classical Tamil literature; see v. 29.

"All of them are dead, the sacrifice is in progress,
how can it now reach its end?"
The prince then set forth to the underworld, where Kapila lived
and where his austerities bloomed.

510.
'One look at the mountain of silvery ash and those lifeless bodies,
and Amshuman's mind stood as still as a post.
He fell down before Kapila and worshipped his fine lotus feet,
then rose again and offered words of praise.
The sage said, "Go, you may take the horse."

511.
'Amshuman was delighted to hear this from the perfect sage,
he worshipped him again, and returned with the galloping steed.
The king then completed the sacrifice in full,
giving the ritual share to the gods, and he finished his life,
my son whose fame will last in written words,
after giving his grandson the throne.

512.
'Because the sons of Sagara dug it, sagara means "the ocean",
that excellent realm of sea monsters.
Sagara's peerless grandson ruled the whole world
and in his long line there appeared a king,
Bhagiratha, who rose up like the sun.

513.
'In the days when this shining king turned the wheel of command
and the entire earth was delivered from common hold,
when the ancient sage Vasishtha taught him his genealogy
the king knelt before him, placed his forehead on the ground,
then rose and asked a single question.

514.
'"Tell me, teacher," he said, "what austerities I must perform
to end the utter subjection in the broad expanse of hell
of my ancestors whom the furious sage Kapila crushed."
The brahman then replied.

515.
'"You cannot be soft, king of kings, ruler of the earth,
you will endure long ascetic deeds to redeem those slain men,
meditating on the grandfather in the red lotus blossom
for a full aeon, with no respite," announced the flawless sage.

516.
'He handed over the entire world to his chief minister
then went to the Himalayas, the proper field for austerities.
For ten thousand long years he performed hard ascetic deeds
until the first cause, grandfather Brahma, arose in the primal lotus.

517.
'"Your ascetic deeds delight me,
and your vast host of ancestors slain by Kapila long ago
will obtain the highest path once their bones are washed
by the river in the sky, should it come pouring down
to reach the broad, open range of the earth.

518.
'"Yet if the high river among the stars comes down to earth,
who but Shiva on his bull could bear her and slow her down?
So continue, meditate on the lord who is half gleaming beauty,"
said the creator of all worlds and every life in them,
and then he disappeared.

519.
'Bhagiratha meditated on the god who is half woman,
resolute in his austerities for ten thousand more years.
The god the colour of fire came to him and said,
"I will realize your intention," and then he withdrew,
and the king spent five thousand years worshiping the Ganga.

520.
'She came to him as a lithe young woman and asked,
"What is the use of your asceticism?
If the surging train of water comes down
who could really bear her force? What Hara* said is pure folly!
You now understand, so perform worthy austerities."
Then the lofty river went off.

521.
'He was bathed in pain, and reflected on Shiva, the pristine flame
whose golden knotted locks are filled with basil leaves,
datura flowers, cassia blooms, bilva leaves and crown flowers,
for twenty-five hundred years, performing great ascetic deeds
until he started to glow. The lord of Uma the mountain girl[9]

522.
'Came before him, and said, "Tell me your thoughts."
He worshipped, then said, "The Ganga made me tremble,
she told me what you would do, my lord."
"Fear not," said Shiva, "I will prevail. The river will not escape."
He vanished, and for twenty-five hundred years
the king continued his austerities.

523.
'He consumed nothing but dust, wind, withered leaves,
flowing water and the sun's hot rays, later refusing this last,
then for thirty thousand years the king endured hard austerities
filled with a ripening love.

524.
'She appeared, a lofty river pouring down with a roar
that terrified the world of Brahma
who emerged from the lotus in Vishnu's navel,
the worlds of Indra and the other gods,
and then the husband of the mountain's daughter
veiled her in his perfect knotted locks so that not a drop escaped.

---

*Shiva.

525.
'Like a dewdrop on a blade of grass,
the heavenly river concealed herself
to hide in the pure lord's matted crown.
The king worshipped him, stunned, and the god replied,
"Do not be concerned, the heavenly river rests in my matted locks."
He released a bit, and down she flowed,
spilling out over the earth.

526.
'The king ran ahead of the plunging Ganga
so the dead kings of old* would gain their path to heaven.
Down she raced, her current so fast
it laid waste to a sacrifice the ascetic Jahnu was holding.
The sage burned with a rage that leaped up in flame
and trapped her in the palm of his hand.

527.
'Jahnu drank it up with pleasure as the sages around him laughed;
the king saw it happen, bowed low, and told him the whole tale.
"Take it," said Jahnu, and released the Ganga through his ear.
The river poured out with a start, at last to merge
with the ashes of the scattered bodies of the dead.

528.
'Sagara's sons who had languished in hell ascended to heaven
as the assembled gods cheered and rained down fragrant blossoms.
King Bhagiratha went back as the royal drums pounded
and a full array of strings and horns sounded forth in return
when he returned to Ayodhya, the city with beautiful walls.

529.
'Thus this great river, which arose beyond the universe
at the lotus foot of the highest god when he measured the worlds
and which Brahma carried as sanctified water,

---

*The sons of Sagara, previously reduced to ash by the sage Kapila; see vv. 502–12.

was brought down by Bhagiratha's austerities, my son,
to reach the surface of the earth.[10]

530.
'Since Bhagiratha brought the Ganga down for Sagara's sons
doing stern austerities for ages, it is named the Bhagirathi.
Since it passed through Jahnu's ear to flow over the earth,
this peerless river has another name, the Jahnavi.'

531.
The sage finished his tale, and the brothers were filled with wonder,
they worshipped the Ganga with joyful hearts, then forded the river.
Vishala's king approached, his arms broad as mountains,
and touched the sage's feet.
They lingered to enjoy conversation, then continued on their way.

532.
They entered the land of Videha, rich with tilled soil
where the heron rises from its lotus bed
in a flooded rice field as women pull strong weeds,
and the reflections of their wide eyes, those bright, faithless swords,
appear to it like fish, and make it ashamed
when it snaps at them with its beak.

533.
In the gardens, the wide gates of sluices drummed in rhythm,
ashoka trees in full blossom lift the lamps high,
the lutes are scented flowers, streams of honey are their strings,
and bees sing the melody while peacocks stage the dance.[11]

534.
In the flooded rice fields, the blue lilies seem like eyes
as sturdy field hands toss them aside on new lotuses
that have grown round and full in the sun,
they torment desirous young men with glances sent as love notes
by women whose brows catch the water's light.

535.
In the reservoirs, women who prattle like warbling cuckoos
are followed by geese in full plumage, which see their hips sway
and mistake them for their own kind.
Diving birds that plunge in the cool waters turn on each other,
dyed red by the lasting stains of women's saffron paste.
They will not rest, even when flowers close in a sleep of their own.[12]

536.
In the rivers, there would be no rush of cool water
without the unfailing floods of sweet sap from crushed flowers,
the milk that pours from the teats of nursing water buffalo,
juice that pours from the sweet fruit of mango trees on low banks,
and the ambrosia churned from cut lengths of smooth sugarcane.[13]

537.
In the creeks, the scabbard fish leap high into palm spathes
as the massive young water buffalo start in alarm,
spooked by the beat of musicians' drums on the dancing stage
where women with dark, liquid eyes have breasts like soaring peaks
which press so close together they could crush a single thread.

538.
In the tanks, graceful women dive to swim in open water,
putting swords back in their sheathes as they close their long eyes.
When they rise, they look like Lakshmi emerging
from the churning waters of the milk sea long ago.
Their white bangles clink, ringing out like calling waterbirds,
and bees swarm together to dive in fragrant flowers.

539.
The three travellers were charmed by such sights
as they journeyed through the land,
and made their way to Mithila, secure behind its ramparts.
They rested beyond the outer wall, its banners high above,
and there on the open plain

they saw a large black stone, towering and solid,
a great ascetic's wife* who had ruined the honour of her home.

540.
As soon as the dust from Kakutstha's feet swept over the stone
she was freed from the spell that had robbed her of thought.
She took her own form, and stood there in full beauty
as if one with the ankleted feet of the lord who knows the truth.

541.
The great sage said, 'Noble heir of Bhagiratha
who brought the Ganga to earth from the vast sky above,
the woman who stands humbly before you,
splendid as lightning, with joy in her heart
is Ahalya, wife of the sage who gave a thousand red eyes
to Indra, king of gods, when he acted on immoral desire.'

542.
When he heard these words of the sage with golden matted locks,
the husband of the earth asked him to explain.
'She seems as proper as a mother!
How could something like this have happened in the world?
Was her stone form due to karma,
or something she did in this life itself?'

543.
The sage turned to Rama and replied,
'I have heard, my gifted boy,
that Indra, lord with a dazzling thunderbolt,
once lusted for the breasts of Gautama's doe-eyed wife,
and waited for the sage free from envy to leave home.

*Ahalya, wife of the sage Gautama.

544.
'Peerless Kama's arrows, and the glances women throw as spears
rained down over Indra and overwhelmed his mind,
reason lost to the throes of lust.
Seeking to end his pain, he coaxed Gautama away from home,
then took the form of that truthful sage and went in.

545.
'He entered, and they made love together,
drinking the clear, sweet liquor
that is the passion of a wedding night.
She sensed the truth, but even so,
she lusted too deeply to know she was wrong.
Right then, the sage rushed in
with the power of the three-eyed god.

546.
'When the sage entered, he had no bow to fire arrows
but he had the power to launch invincible curses.
His wife froze in terror, caught in the act of a crime so great
it will remain in the world for all time, and can never be erased.
Purandara* cowered there, then became a cat and tried to steal away.

547.
'The restrained sage knew what had happened
and fire rained from his eyes as he turned to Indra,
and cursed him with words like arrows shot by your own hand.
"You shall bear the mark of a woman, one thousand times over!"
In an instant his curse covered Indra with vaginas.

548.
'Purandara felt endless shame and he fled away, bound to his crime
so that anyone who saw him would give a sneering laugh.
Gautama then turned to his gentle wife and said,
"You are like a whore to me, you will become stone."
She collapsed, transformed into black rock.

---

*Indra.

549.
'"We say the great have a duty to tolerate mistakes!" she cried,
"Give my plight an end, sage like Shiva streaming fire!"
"When you touch the dust from the foot of a man named Rama,
the son of Dasharatha, whose cool garland buzzes with bees,
you will be delivered from this form of stone."

550.
'When the gods saw Indra,
they came to Gautama with Brahma at their head
and begged him to relent.
The rage had ebbed from the sage's thoughts,
so he replaced the vaginas with a thousand red eyes.
The gods then returned to their own worlds,
but the woman remained there as stone.

551.
'The deeds that shape the present were made in the past,
and now, for all worlds, what is there to suffering?
Nothing but gaining salvation!
Lord dark as a raincloud, in your fight with black Tataka
I saw the nature of your hands,
and now your feet have shown me their own.'

552.
The lord with a dark body, whose perfect granted healing,
understood the full meaning of what the sage had told him.
'Come with us, mother,' he said, 'give no thought to your plight.
Obey your mighty husband, he will honour you in return.'
She bent to touch his golden feet, then they all walked on together.

553.
They approached the hermitage of Gautama, the masterful ascetic,
and when he saw them, his heart trembled with wonder and delight.
He greeted them warmly, and brought them into his home
offering perfect hospitality with all the rites of welcome.
The lordly son of Gadhi turned to Vishwamitra and said,

554.
'This woman with a waist thin as a vine appeared in her own form
when the dust from the foot of this dark-hued man touched her.
Welcome her with kindness, for she holds no error in her heart.'
The sage like the lotus-born Brahma accepted what Kaushika said.

555.
The lord exalted by his virtues touched Gautama's lotus feet,
circled the sage, offered his praise,
then led that sacred woman made great by her perfect chastity
and brought her to Gautama's hand.
The young men left the fragrant grove with Kaushika,
and Mithila soon came into view, shielded by its fine walls.[14]

Beholding Mithila

556.
That grand city seemed to call the noble man with red lotus eyes,
saying, 'Quickly now, come,' as it reached for him
with banners for its hands richly adorned with jewels.
'Shri,' the town called, 'has left her lotus,
and due to my good deeds, she has come here to live.'

557.
They watched rows of sparkling banners fly on the busy palaces
like celestial women staging dances in the sky.
The flags knew he had come, sending Dharma as his envoy,
to marry a woman of infinite beauty,
for all of them recognized no other man was right.

558.
They saw long white banners on the palaces of Mithila
so closely set they hid the sun, forming a shining milk ocean.
They grew damp in the mist as they touched the clouds above,
but soon they were dried by swirling clouds of incense.

559.
They entered Mithila through its shining golden walls,
and the city seemed like Shri's home, a budding red lotus,
for it had borne Sita, so perfect even Kama could not paint her.
He dipped his brush in ambrosia to begin, but was overwhelmed
when he could not capture a single perfect limb.

560.
They walked down a broad street lined with palaces,
and the way was not easy, for golden ornaments lay scattered
where young men and women, brows curved like the new moon,
had cast them off in their quarrels.

The street was a seabed of gems,
dry after the sage who shaped Tamil* drank it away,
or like the night sky whirling with stars.

561.
Streams of rut became a river that poured
from fierce-eyed elephants that break their riders' goads,
and met the foamy river from horses' bridled mouths:
muddy, dark, light, then turning to dust
as chariots rolled past on the restless road.

562.
They walked down a long street that flowed with nectar
from garlands swarming with bees
that sweet-voiced women had cast off in quarrels,
each flower was as tender as a woman twisting in the war of love
with the passion that makes two hearts one.

563.
They saw women dancing on stages in golden halls,
their waists too thin to be real.
As music soared from drums and lutes, joining together,
eyes followed hands, hearts moved with eyes
and melodies from greased strings were as sweet as a baby's words.

564.
They saw women swinging from emerald areca palms,
their fruits red as coral, bees roaring in pity for all those fragile waists,
they were rising and falling like birth after sullied birth
as the minds of young men swayed with them.

565.
Gemstones, gold, sandalwood branches, white yak-tail hair,
and from deep in the jungle, oudh, peacock fans and elephant tusks
had been piled high by strong plowmen who tend the fields

---

*Agastya.

and now filled the market streets they saw,
like the golden Kaveri, which spreads endless treasures on its banks.

566.
They saw bridled horses racing past, minds absorbed in speed
coming into the turn like a potter's wheel as he spins it hard.
They turn too fast for the eye to see them singly
and become a constant whole
like the insight of sages, or the friendship of the noble.

567.
They saw, like lovers who are life to each other,
quarrelling when they meet, goaded on by Kama's arrows
which roil the mind like a churning pole,
elephants with tusks white as diamond,
their minds full of rage, red eyes bursting with fire,
clash against each other like mountains, refusing to break apart.[1]

568.
They saw the moon rise in every high window of jewelled mansions
which revealed well-honed spears, the bow of the mind-churner,
a piece of red pith, and a curl of sapphire, swarming with bees,
though not the dark spot that marks the face of the moon.[2]

569.
They saw red lotuses break into open smiles
and ramble drunkenly on with empty words
after drinking fresh, fragrant liquor in crystal cups,
showing their joy as they reveal their lovers' quarrels
which they cannot keep hidden, however hard they try.

570.
They walked happily, listening to the honey that is music's call
as women hurt their hands, flower buds tipped with nails,
by turning the lute pegs, tightening the strings that run like nectar
to offer a feast for the ears, joining minds to hands,
and showing white teeth with their smiles.

571.
They saw many women playing with balls that shine like mirrors
like the hearts of women with love-mounds like cobras' hoods
who share in the body's joys and then take their price.
The balls turn black as they pass kohl-streaked eyes,
then turn red again as they touch the women's hands.[3]

572.
They saw many ponds where women swam with pleasure,
their bodies' virtues so pure no likeness can be found.
Other things must suffer then: lotus, blue lily,
red lily, leaves of the bindweed creeper, blue lotus,
red sholapith, waves, carp and the spawning snakehead murrel.[4]

573.
They saw gambling sessions where women threw dice,
their eyes like weapons, garlands loose in their hair,
betting bangles, earrings, jewellery, necklaces, fine dresses,
blouses made of the choicest cloth, and carved lutes,
holding the crystal gambling chips that glow red in their hands.

574.
They saw many places where handsome youths fenced with swords,
their arms marked with sandalwood traces of lovers' breasts,
moving as if to show a mind gone wild, whirling and pausing,
as the bolting senses, overwhelmed, drag it here and there.

575.
They saw young men wandering with fine bows in their hands
as if the lord's eye had never stripped Kama of his body.
They had soothed angered women, so their hair was dyed red,
and they looked like a mortal sun, whose heart would offer anything.[5]

576.
They saw groves where women who would shame heavenly dancers
were picking flowers and speaking to green parrots with sweet words.
They seemed like flower boughs or peacock fans,
and the bees hummed to cheer them
when the geese trailed behind, ashamed of their own gait.

577.
They saw a moat as deep as the Ganga, surging with waves,
surrounding the golden walls of King Janaka's palace,
and the reflection of mansions fit for the gods played on its surface
revealing the beauty of the gods' world, now visible on earth.

578.
They saw a crossing where geese swam happily with their mates
and they rested there, by a tower reserved for young women,
the home of a princess who made things seem like light:
the lustre of gold, the fragrance of flowers,
and the savour of poetry composed with honeyed words.

579.
When Brahma on his lotus, or anyone else
speaks of a beautiful woman, they speak in similes
searching the cosmos for her likeness, and find no one but Shri.
But now she herself has appeared here on earth,
so can I somehow, somewhere, find a different likeness
and render it in words?

580.
Like blossoming creepers who wear anklets on their soft feet,
necklaces on their breasts, and girdles on their perfect waists,
her maids all around her saw the beauty of her body,
and she stood there as a queen of lightning
while a hundred million lightning bolts bowed to her in service.

581.
The body of that woman, bearing virtues from patience on,
would cause women fine as Uma to raise their hands in praise.
Those who beheld her could not take it in, for their eyes had to blink
and the gods in heaven wished they had more than two eyes.

582.
Her flashing eyes outshone the does' eyes, the leaping carp trembled,
the honed deadly spear and the murderous sword fell back in defeat.
She was like ambrosia rising on the palace heights that day,
not from the milk sea when the lord churned the mountain.

583.
If gods who eat nothing but ambrosia beg for a woman like her,
a woman whose words are as sweet as fine honey,
what cure but ambrosia can the sea full of gems provide?
Four-faced Brahma creates, but could he make her again?

584.
Women with glittering eyes, Menaka and other heavenly dancers,
charm gods like virtuous Indra, who governs the heavens above.
Yet their hearts burned when they saw the body of that woman
for they knew their faces, cool moons, had faded in the daylight.

585.
Who performed austerities for aeons, their bodies withered,
so this woman would leave her red lotus to live in this world?
The truth lies beyond me, was it countless brahmans?
Dharma himself? Earth, heaven, or the gods above?

586.
Her companions, women of unrivalled beauty, called out to her,
'Gentle doe with flower bud hands!' 'Mother!' 'Honey!' 'Rare ambrosia!'
They approached her politely, and spread a thick bed of flowers
before her every step to honour and protect her feet.
She walked on those blossoms dusted with pollen
and bloomed with shining light.

587.
Her eyes had such richness they routed and crushed
all murderous things, from spears to lethal Yama.
Mountains, walls, granite and grass
all flowed with love when they saw her standing there:
words cannot describe it.

588.
Women give so much joy when they share a glance,
their lush, alluring eyes are a festival to see.
And she, sweet to all women, a healing, pure ambrosia,
must have been so much more when our lord first saw her.

589.
Young women with eyes like cool rain have always worn
large jewellery like necklaces and small jewellery like earrings.
They all have beauty, but when this perfect woman wore them,
each one realized its nature, a beauty made complete.

590.
There she stood, her virtues beyond comprehension.
Their eyes met, seized each other, consumed each other,
and their hearts passed from within them to join and become one
as the lord looked at her and she looked at him.

591.
Her eyes as they watched him were two sharpened spears
that sank into the arms of that strong, well-built man,
and the red eyes of the hero who wore ringing anklets
bored into the breasts of the girl as lovely as Shri.

592.
Bound together by their eyes as they drank each other in,
their inner selves pulled and drew each other close.
The lord with a sturdy bow, and the girl with eyes like swords
felt their hearts travel out to become one on their shared journey.

593.
The girl with no waist and the man beyond reproach
became a single soul, two bodies uniting,
two beings set apart, pulled from their union in bed on the sea,
once more joined with each other: what need is there for words?

594.
Her long eyes seemed to have no end, and since they never blinked
that woman with gold bracelets stood like a figure in a painting.
When the young man went with the sage and disappeared,
her thoughts, composure and beauty followed him.

595.
What use was being female for this woman with a moon-like brow?
As soon as the man with the fragrant garland had left her sight,
the hooked goad called composure for the elephant called the mind
straightened right out and became completely useless.

596.
She felt great desire, and as it overwhelmed her
her mind and body trembled like her waist as thin as thread.
Lovesickness flowed in her eyes as she watched him go
and spread through her body, a drop of yogurt curdling milk.

597.
She stood mute, she could not voice the pain she felt,
and she sobbed as she felt it deep within her mind.
Then Kama drew his arrow and fired it at her heart,
as if tossing a log of wood into blazing flames.

598.
Her eyes were like spears never tempered by flames,
they reached back to her earrings, which sparkled in the light.
Her braided hair and dress fell loose and tumbled about her,
and she burned like a flower garland tossed into the fire.

599.
She lost her shining girdle, her bangles, her composure,
her swirling heart, her reason and the lustre of her body.
Left bare and empty, she was like the sea of milk
which gave up all it had when churned by the gods.

600.
Her jewellery came loose and fell away, her modesty left her,
her wholesome beauty faded, and as life was poised to fail,
she suffered like a wounded doe struck by an arrow in her breast.
Her friends struggled to hold her, a peacock with gold earrings.

601.
They laid her on a flower bed misted with cold, fine spray,
spread thick with flower pollen, tender leaves,
and blossoming boughs soft as the feet and hands
of the girl whose sidelong glances strike the earrings on her ears.

602.
She lay on the bed of perfumed flowers newly picked that morning,
and it faded like the moon when the cruel serpent swallows it,
a pond thick with lotuses on long stalks, all dried and withered,
or silk cotton flowers hit by a storming blast of sleet.[6]

603.
Like raindrops falling from clouds on mountain peaks,
tears like pearls fell from her eyes and spilled onto her breasts.
Thick beads of sweat on her curving brow were dried
by breath hot as smoke from the blacksmith's forge.

604.
She seemed a fine peacock gravely wounded by an arrow
shot from the bow of a forest hunter whose cruelty knows no mercy.
Fire burned hot within her fevered heart, and she faded away,
growing dry on her bed like a delicate blooming bough.

605.
The fragrant flowers on her bed burned up and pricked her,
her cooling creams on her body flaked off like parched grain.
The threads strung through her jewels snapped and fell apart,
and flower boughs blackened as fire leapt with searing flames.

606.
Her servants, her nursemaids, foster mothers and their seniors
were tormented by her agony, and overwhelmed with fear.
'What is happening?' they cried, but did not discern the reason
so they whirled flowers and damp rice to drive pain from her heart.[7]

607.
Her friends stood close by her side and fanned her
but the breeze from the fans only strengthened the flames.
Her necklaces and garlands blackened, smouldered and burned,
as if she were a melting doll of gold.

608.
She imagined a forest* thick with flowers, peaceful in the night
imagined his two arms as emerald mountains, or strong iron bars,
imagined his eyes as red lotus blossoms,
imagined a storm cloud diving down with a rainbow.†

609.
'He forced his way into my heart, and carried off my feminine ways
along with my life, shaking loose my self-control,
yet the bow made pure and holy by those arms that rival mountains
was not made of sugarcane, so this man cannot be Kama.

610.
'If I had to say, he is not from the world of the gods
for he blinked his eyes, those lotuses rich with scent.
He carries a sturdy bow in his broad hand,
and also wears the sacred thread, so perhaps he is a prince?

---

*Rama's hair.

†Rama's dark body holding a war bow.

611.
'The beauty that moves in women, the shyness I've had since birth,
the thoughts that cross my mind, I cannot find them anywhere.
He has gone away, wounding his feet as he moves over the earth,
yet he has entered my eyes. He is a remarkable thief!

612.
'Not hair dark as sapphire, long arms, or face like the moon,
nor his shoulders like mountains of emerald,
it was his smile more than anything
that swallowed up my life!

613.
'Not his shining chest, which drinks up lives, nor his lotus feet,
it was his walk, like the gait of a proud elephant
joyous as rut pours from its broad cheeks
that still stays trapped in my heart.

614.
'The prince crushed the wall of virginity that surrounds me,
and its counter-siege weapon, the composure I've had since birth.
To see him with my own eyes once more, to know that it is him,
will it rip my life clean away?'

615.
She said these things, and as she wasted away,
the ardent passion in her burning heart
'He stood before me—he is gone'
kept her thoughts from making sense.

616.
The ancient, blazing sun shook his slender hands
and hurried off to plunge deep in the western sea,
as if he too could not stand the fire of passion
that burned in this woman with a goose's soft gait.

617.
Death revealed himself to that perfect woman when he appeared
as evening twilight, which stokes the fire of longing.
The noose he threw was the southern breeze, perfumed by flowers,
his red hair was the fiery sky, his dark body the night.[8]

618.
The birds that call from high above are a drum,
the sea that rings below an anklet, the bloody sky the hair,
and the sinful night that tortures lovers is a dark coat.
Evening has all these things, they make him into a goblin.

619.
Bathed in the fire known as lakes,
smeared with the poison of fragrant new blossoms,
the southern breeze swept into wounds from Kama's arrows.
Weakened as her suffering mind and virtues melted away,
Sita saw evening come with powers of madness
and cried, 'Is this the face of Death?'[9]

620.
'What captures the lives of women who suffer?' she wondered,
'The sea? A sapphire mountain? A fragrant kaya blossom?
A blue lily bud, glowing bright? A blue lotus? A water lily?'
The evening turned as dark as the lord with the blooming garland.

621.
'Night, you hooded cobra, your dark hue spreads in the sky!
The stars are your fangs, your breath is the northern wind,
your mouth that drips poison is the spreading crimson.
Kama the archer does not stay his hand,
I have but one life, and now it is leaving me.
You wrap yourself around me, keeping me from fleeing;
what hatred do you bear me, inciting hatred in return?

622.
'This darkness, is it the sea risen high,
or has the halahala poison been smeared across the world?
Because everyone thinks of his blue colour, does it fill all space?
Has Death's own black hue been mixed with kohl
to spread across the earth and the heavens above?

623.
'Yet this lord who appeared is lost from view
and I see no one to stop him.
Manmatha shoots arrows into me in the darkness of night.
He has no mercy for one like me, a woman to be pitied.
I deserve compassion!
Has he taught you magic, you sins of my past lives,
and now you come as the krauncha bird?'[10]

624.
This woman suffered there, her mind immersed in painful thoughts,
on a terrace made of cool moonstone in a palace so tall it scraped the sky.
Her friends removed the lamps lit with ghee, for they burned too hot,
and instead turned night to day with gems, lamps that never need trimming.

625.
The full moon arose, like the gold pot of ambrosia in the sea
when Vishnu, proud and mighty, once churned it
so the goods could drink their fill.
The mountain was the churning staff, a serpent was the rope,
and gems and droplets filled the sky to glitter there like stars.

626.
Long ago, the hungry lord who ate the worlds and the seas
lay on a banyan leaf, and a red lotus bloomed from his navel
while unborn Brahma hummed the four Vedas like a bee.
Then a new lotus, the white circle of the moon
bloomed from the dark, stormy ocean.

627.
As the night grew full, veiling the sky where all the stars bloom
as if setting the points that map out its bounds,
like a young palmyra spathe placed in a silver pot,
sheaves of moonlight rose in the east to lap at the darkness.
What did they do to the woman who speaks sweetly as a parrot?

628.
Darkness besieged the world, sending evening as its vanguard.
Sheaves of light appeared as the cool moon rose,
intent on eating it all, and spread everywhere
like the fame that swallows heaven and earth
of Cataiyan in Venneynallur, where sweet water floods the fields.

629.
The grand craftsman the moon who rose over the flooding waters
felt the universe had grown too old since it was born long ago
from the stalk of a fine lotus, the navel of Vishnu the guardian.
He raised his hands to restore it, using moonlight as the plaster.

630.
As the lotus blossom shrinks, draws its petals in and closes,
and swarming bees leave along with Lakshmi
who had come to rest in it with love,
the red lilies are weak lords from hamlets, who only stand tall
once the king who ruled the world with his sceptre has fled.

631.
'White fire, you rose in black fire, the darkness called night
that kept growing stronger, coming to swallow the world!
You confront us as an enemy, me and the pounding sea,
run off by the hue of the lord whose magic will not leave me.

632.
'Moon who rose from the sea, you are not evil,
and you will not kill anyone. If you truly appeared
with the goddess who walks gently as an elephant cow
and the sweet, perfect ambrosia, why must you burn me so?'

633.
The rays of the white moon that rise thickly above
were a horsewhip slashing at her soft breasts,
and she writhed on a couch strewn with blooming flowers
like a goose trapped in searing fire.

634.
The moon's rays attacked, sparing nothing as they spread,
she was burned, she wilted, she collapsed,
then the woman who spoke as sweetly as a mynah
withdrew into herself like the red lotuses on her bed.

635.
They spread fragrant salve on her, over and over,
but she burned, and it dried up as it baked.
They fanned and fanned her, but her soft breasts smouldered.
What medicine is there for the sickness of love?

636.
The bed of soft flower buds and blossoms spilling pollen
was blackened and charred by the fire on her body.
Her maids, whom she cherished more than her own mother,
brought a thousand things twice over and piled them high.

637.
The woman charming as a goose suffered like this
on a bed of scented flowers in the grand home of the women.
Now I shall speak of the state of the lord who, as I was saying,
had seen the body of this woman as radiant as lightning.

638.
The three travellers went onward and visited the king
who welcomed them with pleasure and invited them to stay.
They rested in a palace that soared up to the sky,
like golden homes in the heavenly city that pleases the gods.

639.
A sage came to meet them there, Shatananda, son of lovely Ahalya
who had been returned to her true form by the beautiful lotus foot
of the hero with a power so ideal, all deeds ever done
now seemed to walk embodied in his own living form.

640.
The two princes went to greet the approaching sage
and as they bowed to revere him with devoted hearts,
the sage with countless virtues lifted them both up
gave them his blessings, then went on to see Kaushika.

641.
The royal sage born of Gautama saw Kaushika
and gazed at the mighty ascetic's lustrous face.
'This land must have done such austerities,'
he exclaimed, 'for you to come here now!'

642.
Kaushika, his thoughts ever immersed in honoured texts,
looked at the noble face of that famous ascetic Shatananda,
a friend to all, the equal of Brahma on his cool lotus throne,
and the great sage began to speak.

643.
'Listen, good sage whose austerities are refined,
This noble youth beside me finished off the creature Tataka,
her voice harsh as thunder! He allowed me to end my sacrifice,
he ended the curse on your mother, he ended all pain in my heart.'

644.
After Kaushika spoke these words of praise
the master of countless austere deeds replied,
'Is anything impossible for this triumphant prince
if he enjoys the honour you offer him? Also,

645.
'Listen, young lord with a garland of fragrant blossoms,
I will explain something to you.
This great ascetic has been seasoned by true royalty,
guarding the world as its upright king for aeons beyond count.

646.
'While he was steeped in dharma, committed to his rule
he once entered a dense forest, eager for the hunt.
He came upon a sage always glorified with praise,
yes, the great one named Vasishtha, famed for his austerities.

647.
'Arundhati's husband welcomed the hunter with proper ceremony
and asked him to bless his home, to which the king agreed.
Vasishtha said, "Let us prepare a grand feast for you,"
and called Surabhi the wishing cow.*
He told her, "Let your milk flow in the form of fine food,"
and the cow poured it out before them.

648.
'"Take this food, king," Vasishtha said, "and enjoy its range of tastes,
together with your army." He served them the meal,
and once the king and his men had wiped their leaves clean,
received garlands and sandalwood, and they felt restored.
Kaushika studied the cow with a careful eye, and he began to speak.

*See v. 488.

649.
'"You did not even have to get up, austere sage!
This cow offered a perfect feast to all, to everyone in my army.
Now given this fact, and given as well
that masters of shastras and the Vedas, supreme in perfection
hold that the finest things, whatever they are, are proper to a king,

650.
'"It is not right for a cow so impossibly rare to remain here,
You must give her to me."
The sage was silent for some time, but at last he spoke.
"As for me, with my bark clothing, I have nothing to give.
But, good king who plows with your deadly spear,
if the cow comes with you may keep her as your own."

651.
'"I shall do as you say," said the king, and greedily
he leapt up with haste to tie a rope around Surabhi's neck.
When he left she slipped her halter, crying,
"My lord, master of all the Vedas!
Did you give me to this man with strong, fine arms?"
The sage who knows the Vedas and their disciplines replied.

652.
'"I would never give you to anyone.
It was that king with jingling anklets who stole you away."
Seized with rage, the cow cried out,
"Watch as I take this king whose war drum pounds like thunder
and destroy his army!" With that, her hair bristled, and

653.
'Yavanas, Chinese, Shonakas, warriors from Pappara and more
arose from the tawny hair of the cow, brandishing weapons
and they slashed apart the king's brave army,
but then the king's fierce sons came through their blades
and they rushed at the sage, blazing with fury.

654.
'"This is not the power of Surabhi at work," cried the princes,
"The deceit of the sage who knows the shrutis made us come,
and now we will slice off his head!" They rushed at him in anger,
but sparks poured from the sage's eyes and burned them away.

655.
'The king watched as his hundred sons died, and his anger blazed,
burning like fire when ghee is poured.
He drove up his chariot, and shot an arrow from his bow.
"Resist!" cried the sage to the staff in his hand.

656.
'Kaushika fired every missile he could, using all the gods' weapons,
but the staff of the sage devoured them all.
The king watched it glow, then prayed to Shiva,
worshipping the god who raises Meru as his bow.
The lord gave him an incredible weapon, and with this new power,

657.
'The king launched the weapon. The gods trembled with fear,
for they thought he would burn up the worlds,
but the sage stood fast and swallowed it when it came.
Fiery sparks shot from his body when the vicious weapon hit him,
and he shone as the weapon's power dimmed.

658.
'The king saw it all unfold before his eyes and thought to himself,
"In courage, might and lustre, no one surpasses brahmans,
nor has he the power to rule the entire world."
He committed himself to penance
and set out to the east, home of Indra, king of gods.

659.
'Obsessed with his defeat at the hands of the mighty sage,
this king became an ascetic, and set himself to the same trials.
When Indra saw him there shining, his heart shook with alarm,
and he sent down one of Rambha's kind,
the famed doe-eyed woman named Tilottama.[11]

660.
'One look at Tilottama, and Kama's arrows broke the king's resolve.
He plunged into an ocean of lust, and after countless days with her,
he understood the merit of ethical texts admired by mature minds.
"This is poison," he thought, and turned from her in sheer disgust.

661.
'He grew angry, for this was the work of the king of heaven,
and he cursed simple Tilottama, crying, "You will become mortal!"
His lotus eyes red, his heart dark with wrath, he stormed away
to the southern realm of Yama, mightiest of the eight lords of space.

662.
'Once Kaushika went south, to spend his days in proper austerities,
Trishanku, a dominant king who lived in Ayodhya,
approached his guru Vasishta, the sage who aided his efforts.
"Bless me," he said, "and send me to heaven in this living body."
The sage replied, "I have no idea how."

663.
'"If you cannot do this, noble brahman, I will search the broad earth
to find a man who suits my mind, whoever he might be.
I will perform this sacrifice!" he said.
"You scorn me," cried the sage, "your own family preceptor!
I have served you so long, yet you seek someone more agreeable.
May you become a loathsome, vile man!"

664.
'Vasishtha, son of Brahma in the lotus, raged at Trishanku
and this king of kings, whose lustrous body shamed the sun,
became black, and his face grew dark like a lotus at sunrise.
He then assumed a detestable form, hated by all who saw him.

665.
'His gold necklace, his crown and his jewellery turned to iron
and his clothes, garland and sacred thread turned to leather.
His foul body was black and filthy, and once he returned home
he was shocked when everyone drove him away,
so he made his way to the forest.

666.
'After a few days in the forest, Trishanku entered a grove
where the great king Kaushika was absorbed in brutal austerities.
Kaushika said, "Who are you, vile man? Why are you here?"
Trishanku bowed low, and explained all that had occurred.

667.
'"Is that all?' Kaushika laughed. I will perform a grand sacrifice,
and you will enter heaven in the living body you have now!"
He invited ascetics, and many came, but Vasishtha's sons spoke up.
"We have never learned what to put in the fire
for a royal sacrifice on behalf of an outcaste!

668.
'"We do not accept this!" they said, and Kaushika was enraged.
He cursed them, "Be hunters, condemned to their foul work."
They became hunters and ran off to roam throughout the forest.
Focused now, the sage said, "Come, partake of the oblation,"
inviting the gods to eat as the sacrifice continued.

669.
'"What's this?" the gods mocked him. "How very fine!
A king offers to the fire on behalf of an outcaste?"
Kaushika responded, "I will command it myself.
Good king with haltered, mighty elephants,
you will enter heaven through my ascetic power!"
Trishanku then rose into the sky, soaring high above.

670.
'Once he reached heaven, the gods were enraged.
"What's this?" they cried. "You want to come here?
You are a loathsome outcaste, fall down to the earth!"
Down fell Trishanku with nothing to hold him,
and he called, "You are my refuge, sage!"
Kaushika raised his arms and roared, "Stay, stay where you are."
Then he broke into laughter.

671.
'"I will remake the realm of the sneering gods who scorn me
and all the other heavenly worlds!" he stormed.
The sun, the moon, the planets and the asterisms will still shine,
but let them change course as I turn north to south.
I will make all things new, be they moving or still."

672.
'King Indra, the lord of fragrant wishing trees
four-faced Brahma, Shiva, his throat stained with poison,
and the other gods approached Kaushika, and called,
"Accept our way, good sage. You follow the path of dharma,
protecting a man who comes to you for refuge.
Let him remain among the stars.

673.
'"You shall be a royal seer among sages,
and five asterisms will descend to the south
to illuminate your majesty," they said, and departed.

The ascetic famed in all quarters then hurried off to the west,
the realm of Varuna, lord of the broad oceans.
And while he was there, immersed in fierce austerities,

674.
'King Ambarisha, lord of armies, sword, and a sturdy bow,
a glorious man, his words sweet as ambrosia,
the true life for all lives in this world,
sought to buy a young boy to offer in sacrifice.
He drove his chariot to many wild places, carrying much gold.[12]

675.
'He reached a flowering grove, home to the ascetic Ricika,
and after Ambarisha had stated his purpose,
the ascetic's three sons offered themselves.
But their mother said, "The youngest is mine,"
and their father said, "The oldest stays."
The middle child Shunahshepa laughed, and turned to the king.[13]

676.
'"My father gave me life and raised me," he said.
"Give him the gold he needs to end his grinding poverty."
He touched his father's feet, then got into the king's chariot.
As the two steadfast men travelled off,
and the dazzling sun reached the summit of heaven,

677.
'The king got down from his chariot to fulfil his daily rites,
and the truthful, virtuous boy went off to perform his own.
There he saw Kaushika, the sage who had conquered his passions,
and placed his head at the sage's lotus feet, overcome with anguish.

678.
'The sage looked tenderly at the boy who lay trembling before him
and asked, "Why are you so upset?" Shunahshepa replied,
"Master of the subtleties of dharma, my mother and father
handed me to King Ambarisha in exchange for a fortune in gold."

679.
'The noble sage heard how his older sister and her husband
had offered their son. "Rest easy," he said, "I will protect you."
He asked his sons which of them would go with the king,
but they refused, and as he watched them leave,

680.
'His heart seethed, sparks flew from each pore in his skin,
and his eyes burned so red that the rising sun was shamed.
"Because you have no compassion in your hearts," he cried,
"You shall be aimless hunters who wander the forest in torment!"

681.
'Kaushika cursed his four sons who had survived Vasishtha's fury
and off they ran as wretched hunters.
He turned to his fine nephew, whose mind quaked with fear,
and said, "Cast worry aside! I will offer you two mantras."
He taught them to the boy, and said,

682.
'Go with the king, young man, wearing your garland,
and when you are bound to the sacrificial post
recite the mantras, then Brahma, Vishnu, Shiva on his bull
and the other gods in heaven will come
and you will not die even when the rite is finished."
Shunahshepa praised his uncle and continued on his way.

683.
'On the field of sacrifice, the boy invoked the sage's mantras
and in rode the gods, on eagle, goose, bull and other mounts
to meet on the field and surround him.
They watched over the young boy's life during the sacrifice,
and then the sage headed north.[14]

684.
'Once in the north, he placed his lotus hands at his nose
and pondered the one syllable in the heart* for many long years
as the ida and pingala channels grew still. Because of his inner fire,
the crown of his head split open, and clouds of smoke black as night
streamed out to form an unbroken cover, shaking all the worlds.[15]

685.
'Like the fine cloak of Shiva, destroyer of the triple city
who covers his body with a flayed elephant hide in his unique way,
or like the rainclouds that spread out as they rise,
the thick smoke rose ever higher, veiling the earth beneath it.

686.
'As the darkness gathered close and spread over the worlds
even the crowding rays of the sun disappeared.
The eyes of the elephants who bear the earth were masked
along with the eyes of the patient guardians of the quarters.[16]

687.
'As the smoke suffused the cloudy heavens
all things moving and still on earth grew afraid.
The burning rays of the sun turned back
and the gods trembled in its light.

688.
'Brahma who dwells in the lotus, Vishnu who flies on the bird,
Shiva who rides the bull and Indra who wields the thunderbolt
all travelled to the northern quarter with the other gods
to face the ascetic they esteemed above all others.

---

*Om.

689.
'Great Shiva who is crowned with the crescent moon,
shining Vishnu who wears a garland of fresh basil,
and Brahma, born from Vishnu's perfect lotus, all offered praise,
saying, "No one has mastered the Vedas like you, great ascetic!"

690.
'The brahman Kaushika appreciated their words.
He bowed, pressed his two fine hands together
and rejoiced, as the gods departed for their realms,
knowing, "The good deeds I have done are now fulfilled!"

691.
'This is what happened long ago, and there is no one else
made great by fierce austerities who is the equal of this sage.
You are blessed with the favour of this master of true principles.
Is anything beyond you?' said Shatananda, sage of boundless power.

692.
After the beloved son of Gautama had finished his tale
the two valiant heroes were awed, and filled with delight.
They rose and touched the feet of this consummate ascetic
who blessed them when they stood, then travelled on his way.

693.
After Kaushika and Lakshmana went to rest on their sweet beds,
Rama, his body a ripe darkness,
felt the nightfall, the moon, his solitude and his being
become the woman he had seen.

694.
'The flash of lightning that vanishes in the sky
must have taken the form of that sweet girl.
If I think, I think of nothing but this,
I see her with both my eyes, inside my thoughts.

695.
'She has eyes that shine like the flooding ocean of milk
where dark Vishnu sleeps on his grand serpent couch.
Could she be the goddess Lakshmi, dwelling on her lotus?
For now she lives within me, in the lotus of my heart.

696.
'She may never have me, but my eyes have swallowed her
to end the harrowing pains caused by my desire.
In this world where nothing is clear, all that moves and is still,
everything alive has become her golden form.

697.
'Even if her breasts like golden pots, adorned with swaying gems
never touch my own plain chest, when will that perfect time come
when I see her face like the moon, her mouth red as ivy gourd,
and that gentle smile, shining like the moonlight?

698.
'Her waist a chariot dais ringed with a girdle,
she has two eyes long as swords, two heavy breasts,
and that one smile that eats up my life.
She is Death intent on me, why do I need her so much?

699.
'If Kama sets his sugarcane bow to his foot and strings it
to destroy me as he shoots a rain of flower arrows
binding my thoughts to that golden woman,
who is really the master of this thing called strength?

700.
'The moonlight spreads like deep floods on the milk sea
as it surges in anger to take me as its own.
It enters my heart, burns away my life
but if it is white, could it truly be poison?[17]

701.
'A place away from the good path that rewards?
Would my heart ever go there? No, love is the sure cause.
This girl with gold bracelets, her words sweet as syrup,
she must be a virgin, there can be no doubt at all.'

702.
The moon sank down into the sea
as if the reigning king Night saw his parasol fall,
or the perfect gem that adorns a woman's brow
vanished from his queen, the western quarter herself.

703.
When the lord called the moon disappears,
the directions, his beloved wives, feel so much grief
they rub off the soft sandalwood cream
that makes them shine with beauty.

704.
As the lord with a garland grew weak, pained by ardent love,
light healed his scattered mind and made his lotus face bloom
when the sun appeared like the third eye that split the brow
of the god that is the eastern mountain,
who wears a cloak of elephant hide, the night that covers him.[18]

705.
The quick hooves of the sun's green horses trample the ground
and dust spreads over the eastern mountain, becoming red paint
as brahmans pour water and flowers from their hands at dawn.
As his new light touches the peaks, the hot sun slaps vermilion
on the face of a rutting elephant, the guardian of the east.

706.
The flower ponds bloom from their depths and burst into colour
when lotuses open their faces and blossom.
They are like faithful wives who saw their husbands off to war

with dim hopes of wealth and a promise to return grown old,
but who now glow with joy, their low spirits forgotten,
when their men, dear as their lives, ride home in fine chariots.

707.
As kinnaras sing, pairing their music to the infinite Vedas,
the world gives praise, and gods, sages and brahmans worship,
the sun's rays spread like the golden, matted locks
of the three-eyed god who dances on the heavenly stage
as the ocean pounds, the earth its drumhead paste.

708.
Rama, who put down the discus to bend the bow he wields,
did not sleep on the ancient sea, lying on his serpent
under a thousand ruby lamps.*
Instead this dark raincloud slept in a deep sea of pain.
But the sun in his one-wheeled chariot stroked the lord's feet
and Rama awoke to reach the shore of his dark ocean of night.

709.
When the night had somehow passed as if a cosmic age had turned,
Rama arose like a caparisoned elephant waking from sleep,
and finished the morning rituals enjoined since ancient times.
He bowed to the great ascetic, to him the living Vedas,
and went with his dear brother to King Janaka's hall of sacrifice.

---

*Rubies set in the hood of each of the thousand heads of Shesha, Vishnu's serpent couch.

The Noble Genealogy

710.
King Janaka fulfilled the rite, ending his grand sacrifice
while the drums roared from every side, pounding like thunder.
This lord grand as Indra returned to his palace
and its towers so tall they scraped the moon,
then rested with the brahmans in a splendid royal hall.
The prince with a garland and fine curving bow in hand,
his brother and the honoured sage Kaushika sat at Janaka's side.

711.
Janaka looked at the two princes next to him
and both of his eyes seemed to drink in their beauty.
He bent to touch the great ascetic's feet, and said, 'Master,
who are these two? Please tell me all.' Kaushika replied,
'These guests of yours are the sons of the noble Dasharatha.
They came to witness your sacrifice, and would like to see the bow.

712.
'Is there anyone who has not heard of Manu, first of the solar line?
Next came Prithu, the noble ruler who wielded his mighty bow
to make the earth goddess offer milk from her breast
so the agony of hunger would not pain the world's creatures.[1]

713.
'King, your splendid crown glittering with the nine gems,
who has not heard of Ikshvaku, who performed austerities for aeons
worshipping Brahma to dispel karma and call down the Pure Light
so we may behold him as he lies on his grand serpent couch?[2]

714.
'Next, Kakutstha, who long ago rode Indra as a mighty bull
after the king of gods told him of his plight, and appealed to him,
"Can you save my heavenly world, killing the asuras I cannot best?"
He agreed, and went with bow in hand to triumph over the enemy.

715.
'I cannot list all the triumphs of those who followed, king,
but consider a lord of this noble line, his fame too vast for words.
He used a tall mountain to churn the roaring milk ocean
and offered ambrosia to the gods so they would not die,
nor grow old with grey hair and withered limbs.[3]

716.
'Many followed after, king whose spear remains sheathed.
Their descendants are innumerable, men gleaming with fame,
rulers who turned the wheel of command to rule the three worlds.
I note one of them, Mandhatr, who ruled the earth so well
a tiger and a deer could drink from the same stream.

717.
'Once, lord, your anklets worshipped by conquering kings,
when the asuras warred with the patient gods
who wear garlands and crowns set with time-honoured gems,
Mucukunda, an ancestor, ruled heaven on his own
as though the god Dharma himself had arrived with bow in hand.[4]

718.
'As if I were able to praise each king, anklets shining with gold,
who once ruled this broad earth, the life-breath for all who breathe!
One ancestor, king whose long spear flashes like lightning,
was Shibi,* who offered his life in exchange for an innocent dove.

719.
'There were sons† who changed the earth, shifting hills and valleys,
who dug up the mountains that obstructed their father's sacrifice.
They carved out the salty sea, king whose foes die by your spear,
what more proof of their fame do you need?

---

*See v. 244.

†The sons of King Sagara, see vv. 502–6; 526–30.

720.
'How could I give a full chronicle in a day, king,
your shining spear steadfast in power?
Ananta himself would find it hard to tell.
But one king, Bhagiratha, brought the Ganga from heaven,*
to flow over Shiva's matted locks through his crown of cassia flowers.

721.
'One ancestor subdued the entire world bound by the thriving sea,
as easily as if it were a small fruit in the palm of his hand.
He completed a hundred grand horse sacrifices as laid down by law,
king whose parasol is the moon without its rabbit-shaped stain,
an impossible feat that made Indra suffer.[5]

722.
'Dilipa, who bested the moon in war, the conqueror of Rudramurti,
and Kuvalayashva, whose sharp arrows cut down the asura Dhundu
were rulers in this line, and after them came a man named Raghu
who conquered Indra in the east, then the other directions in turn.[6]

723.
'Aja, who churned the sea of kings with his bow as the mountain,
enriched the beauty of his thick arms, so strong in wrestling,
when he took Indumati to his breast, her teeth like pearls,
just as Hari, dark as night, took his goddess Lakshmi.

724.
'No one has not heard of Aja's son Dasharatha, king,
your palace gates alive with the sound of drums and horns,
and Brahma himself could not list every virtue of his noble sons.
You shall hear me tell them, though, insofar as my skill allows.

*See vv. 512–30.

725.
'Dasharatha takes dharma as his shield, more righteous than Manu.
A sun with a discus as his rays, he treats his foes like morning frost.
He needs only his bow to guard the world so every life can thrive,
but Dasharatha suffered because he had no son.

726.
'He believed he could end his sorrow by appealing to Rishyashringa,
the sage named for his deer horn, who had earlier appeared
and pursued women whose brows curve like a war bow,
who have long, dark eyes, lips like red ivy gourd,
waists like lightning, and love-mounds bought for money,
for he thought their breasts made them horned creatures too.[7]

727.
'"I have protected the earth to the ocean," he said to the sage,
"but since I lack the blessing of sons whose hair is scented by flowers,
my wives, their breasts held tight by bands, are not pregnant.
Grant me sons, so they may guard the world after me."

728.
'The sage heard the king's words, and was delighted to help.
"I will grant you masterful sons," he said,
"fully able to guard this world and all other worlds beyond.
Let all be made ready for sacrifice, so the gods can eat their oblation."

729.
'The sacrificial field was swiftly prepared, and items arranged
for the mighty ascetic to complete the king's offering.
As the sacrifice neared its end, out from the fire
a magnificent goblin emerged at the head of his troop
bearing white rice on a golden plate adorned with gems.

730.
'Heeding Rishyashringa, who knows the truth of the Vedas,
Dasharatha, filled with fine qualities that equal his majesty,
dished out the sweet meal shining on the golden plate set with gems
and gave portions to his three wives according to their rank.

731.
'Kausalya bore Rama, his body dark as the sea,
to set right the bad karma spread by callous evils on the earth
and fulfil the good karma caused by the dharma proclaimed
in the profound and endless Vedas.

732.
'Kaikeyi, princess of the Kekaya clan, gave birth to Bharata
a lord of such beauty, with virtues beyond scorn
he stands equal to Rama, rightly called a brimming sea
fed by the flooding river of morality.

733.
'The junior queen Sumitra bore two men of such power
they terrified vicious rakshasas determined to destroy dharma.
They equalled mountains that walk the land, each holding war bows,
golden Mount Meru and lofty silver Kailasa.[8]

734.
'These princes were like the four Vedas,
even more skilled than Saraswati in their subtle mastery of the arts,
and archery minded their command like any foe who faced them.
They all flourished, like the sea that rises with roaring waves
under the fullness of the moon.

735.
'They are, by virtue of royal name, the sons of tranquil Dasharatha,
whose feet decked with anklets are where lords offer tribute.
But Vasishtha invested them with the sacred thread and trained them,
good Janaka whose spear stays sheathed, to memorize the Vedas.

736.
'I brought these youths with me, good king with fine anklets,
so they would kill the fierce rakshasas who assailed my sacrifices.
I arrived at my home, the penance grove, and when I entered it,
the vicious rakshasi Tataka led those monsters in their attack.

737.
'Look closely, lord, and observe great, virile Rama,
the power of his perfect arms that hang down to his knees,
his body the colour of the wave-tossed sea.
His single arrow pierced the breast of Tataka,
her eyes spitting fire like sparks in a forge,
pierced a mountain behind her, a tree beyond that,
and then sank deep in the earth.

738.
'There seemed no end to the scattered heads,
their red hair like leaping flames rising high like mountain peaks.
And there, too, Subahu, son of this rakshasi,
was killed by an arrow and gained the path to heaven.
As to the other, Maricha, I do not know.
I ended my sacrifice and then I came here.

739.
'Through the might of my austerities, I have crafted weapons
beyond the grasp of seers, which Brahma cannot comprehend.
If they are launched in anger, they will blaze up in fury
so the worlds with their mountains and seas will burn away.
I myself have invested them in Rama,
and they will obey him, striking terror in hearts.

740.
'Behold his feet, wearing gold anklets, brighter than a lotus.
The mere dust upon them restored Gautama's wife to her own form!
I have love for this dark-bodied man, more than I have for life itself.
That is his story,' the sage said, 'and that is the strength of his arms.'

The Bow

741.
'How can I answer?' Janaka asked. 'My heart trembles,
for I have been routed by this treacherous bow.
My daughter's vows of penance will be fulfilled
if this noble youth can simply raise the bow
and lift me out of this sea of pain!'

742.
He made up his mind and called to his retainers,
'Bring me the sturdy bow, unyielding as a mountain!'
'Very well,' they replied, and they bowed low and raced away
to enter the hall of weapons covered with heavy gold.

743.
They came in, and with a pointed glance at the men inside
they declared, 'Our ruler, mighty Janaka himself,
orders us to bring out the bow of three-eyed Shiva
using all our gathered powers.'[1]

744.
Men with bodies to rival mighty elephants,
their hair long and thick, bulging shoulders hard as granite,
sixty thousand strong, with power beyond measure
lashed the bow to two beams and hoisted it aloft.[2]

745.
The broad earth goddess felt her back relax
and even Mount Meru, that proud northern mountain
firm and towering on the earth, felt its own shame.
The whole royal city flowed in like the sea, and the people cried,
'No place on earth can hold it!' when they saw the bow.[3]

746.
'Can anyone alive wield it,' called some,
'except for the lion with the conch and discus in his hands?
He stands before us, and once he strings the bow
our young girl will have her glorious wedding!'

747.
'To call that a bow is a sham,' said some, 'it is the Golden Mountain!'
Said others, 'Four-faced Brahma made it, but not by hand,
he used the might of ascetic power gathered within him!'
'Has a man ever strung this bow,' called some, 'in any age before?'

748.
'Is it rugged, soaring Meru, compressed?' called some.
'Is it the king of serpents,' called others, 'shining and lordly?'
'Is it the churning rod once used to churn the great ocean?'
'Is it a sweeping rainbow that has fallen from the sky?'

749.
'Why has the king ordered the bow brought out?' wondered some.
'What kings would see their honour tarnished?' asked others.
'Perhaps it could be done,' said some, 'given good karma.'
'Just wait till Sita sees it,' said others.

750.
'What is the target for an arrow from this bow?' asked some.
'The king has levelled the bow on his own daughter!' said others.
'The lord with the discus,' said some, 'now he could surely wield it,'
and a few here and there said, 'This is cruelty hatched by fate.'[4]

751.
As the pressing crowd spoke, the men presented the bow,
set it before the king, and sprained the back of the earth.
'Someone comes to face the test!' cried the kings watching,
and they shook their hands in a flourish of disdain.

752.
The king saw the face of the youth strong as an elephant calf,
saw the bow that caused this anguish, saw his own daughter,
and Shatananda,* son of Gautama, looked into the king's mind
and began to tell the story.

753.
'Isha,† who once took the Himalayan mountain for his bow,
felt that Uma, half his own body, had been shamed by Daksha‡
and his fury soared, ripping through his patience.
He seized this awesome bow and drew near the sacrifice
that Daksha, still livid, was holding.

754.
'Teeth and arms were strewn about, the gods took flight,
slipping into hiding places no one had ever entered,
and the fires of Daksha's grand sacrifice faltered and died out.
Then the three-eyed, eight-armed god§ let his anger cool.

755.
'Still holding the sturdy bow, Shambhu watched the gods tremble
as they realized they still were in possession of their lives,
and he gave it to a true king who plowed foes with his sword,
an ancestor of King Janaka, this mighty bull of a man.

756.
'Need I describe to you the power of this bow?
Apart from you, generous sage, like Hara with matted locks,
who else could understand?
Listen, then, to the story of the daughter born to this king,
her love-mound like a chariot dais.

---

*Janaka's preceptor.

†Shiva.

‡The father of Shiva's wife Sati (here identified as Uma).

§Shiva in his form as Virabhadra.

757.
'A yoke was placed on the mighty necks
of a pair of bullocks with horns dark as iron,
which pulled a golden plow inlaid with countless jewels
fixed with a diamond plowshare, to prepare the field of sacrifice,
and so we plowed endless furrows in the vastly powerful earth.

758.
'On the blade of the tilling plowshare,
as though the earth goddess had revealed her true form
alive with the light of the dawning sun
a princess was born, her qualities so splendid
even the goddess who rose from the sea with the clear ambrosia
was humbled, and fell back to worship at her side.

759.
'What words are there to describe her virtues?
They came into new life each vying with the other
when they met that blooming branch of a girl.
Beauty did its penance to reveal itself in her!
After this girl was born, all others lost their wholesome beauty,
as the rivers did when the Ganga descended from the sky.

760.
'A wonder like this, where else has it ever happened?
Be it through the work of fate, or the power of the bow itself,
every king on this earth has travelled to come here,
brought from their varied lands by the deeds of their own pasts.
They lust for this Shri, good sage, as the gods lusted for her before.

761.
'The kings came in like roaring lions on elephants in musth
with armies like booming seas, but when they spoke of marriage,
The bow of the god with a tiger skin and cape of elephant hide
was there to answer, for as we have insisted,
only the bow's master will wed this girl in holy marriage.

762.
'Powerless before the mighty bow, they were powerless as well
before Kama's gentle sugarcane bow, and they challenged us,
for they desired her, good king who protects the world with words,
the girl known to the world along with this rock-hard bow,
and now they assault us in war.

763.
'Like the wealth of kings who, wanting fame, put giving first,
our king's great army has been worn away, even as the other kings
who desire the girl with braided hair that hums with buzzing bees
have seen their forces surge like their own desire.

764.
'Seeing this king with strong, fine shoulders weaken in cruel war
as he protects the bow of Shiva who rides the young bull,
the gods with bright crowns took pity and swelled his ranks
to make kings flee in terror like crows who see an owl at night.[5]

765.
'From that day on, no one has dared to approach the bow,
and the kings who ran off have not turned their chariots around.
Marriage seems hopeless, so if this boy can string it, marvellous!
Sita, her hair full of flowers, will not waste the bloom of her youth.'

766.
The sage Kaushika pondered Shatananda's counsel with care,
nodded his head crowned with matted locks,
and gave a look to the youth like a war bull,
the generous lord, his holy body like art,
who sensed the mind of the great ascetic
and gazed at the towering bow.

767.
He rose from his seat like a leaping flame
surging as the ghee pours down to stoke the fires of sacrifice.
The gods roared out, knowing the bow was conquered
and the vanquishers of the three mortal foes* offered up their praise.

768.
Before Rama obeyed the ancient sage mighty in asceticism
and broke the mighty bow, the bodiless god shot arrows
into the heart of each young woman there who wore fine jewels,
and he broke mighty bows† by the thousand.

769.
'The limbs are so thick on that towering bow!
If his broad, perfect hand fails to take the nurturing hand
of that timid young girl with the shining brow,' they said,
'life will be a waste for her.'

770.
Some clasped their hands in worship as tears gathered in their eyes.
'If this young man, strong like a fine elephant, cannot string the bow,
the girl with musk-scented hair will not die alone,' they said,
'we too will plunge in the murderous fire!'

771.
'If our generous lord was truly eager for this marriage,' said others,
'why doesn't he simply hand her over, and tell him to take her?
To bring the bow of the god who contained the flooding Ganga,
and set it before a boy like this, how ridiculous!'

772.
'This learned sage has no shame!' some said,
'Our king is the cruelest man alive!' said others,
'If this noble youth cannot set the bow to foot and bend it,
our comely girl will never gain a husband!' said some.

---

*Lust, anger, and mental delusion; see v. 354.

†The brows of the young women beholding Rama.

773.
While women like peacocks were saying such things,
the good sages voiced their delight and the gods above rejoiced,
with a stride to humble a mighty lion, a massive bull,
an elephant or the Golden Mountain, Rama stepped up to the bow.

774.
He reached for the bow massive as the Golden Mountain
as though he were slipping white conch bracelets and gold bangles
on the hands of the rare, perfect ruby named Sita,
and lifted it high like a wedding garland.

775.
When everyone saw him take the bow in one hand
their eyes froze wide open, and they watched without blinking.
Yet he was so fast to set the bow to foot and string it
no one realized what had happened, they only heard it crack.

776.
'Whom can we take as our refuge?' thought the gods in despair,
horrified the universe given Brahma's name* had split.
Could anything express the nature of what happened on the earth?
The serpent who rests there as a root to support the world
thought lightning had struck, and lay terrified.[6]

777.
The gods showered down a rain of flowers, the clouds a rain of gold,
the wide oceans all roared and sprayed out many gems,
the companies of noble sages all offered their blessings,
and Janaka, lord of regal, frightening spears
knew that his good karma had now yielded its reward.

---

*Brahmananda, 'Brahma's sphere'.

778.
Garlands, jewels, sandalwood paste, scented powders, fragrant oils,
lustrous pearls from the sea, gold, gems and fine clothes flew high,
trumpets and white conches blew, and instruments rang out,
as the city surged with joy, a sea under the full moon.

779.
While well-crafted lutes played their honeyed notes,
teeth flashed and earrings shimmered when the women danced
with faces like the glowing moon, eyes like resting spears,
as peacocks dance when they see clouds and know rain is coming.

780.
Like drinkers who quench their thirst with liquor,
women with red streaks in their glowing dark eyes
stopped sulking in anger and embraced their husbands.
The needy carried off the wealth of the ruler of the earth
like white clouds coming, again and again, to sip from the open sea.

781.
Sweet music from artists, ambrosial music from singers,
divine music from lutes drawn out like honey by their masters,
gentle music from flutes, notes branching out with talent:
the gods drank it down, and their bodies froze as if in a painting.

782.
Heavenly women wanted to see the lord who broke the bow
so they left their realm and embraced the mortal women
who seemed like them in manner, beauty, dance and song,
but when dark lotus eyes blinked, they jumped back in fright.[7]

783.
'A true son of Dasharatha,' said some,
'He is Vishnu with red lotus eyes,' said some,
'His body is a storm cloud,' said some,
'He is like a deep blue flower,' said some,

'The world has been overwhelmed,' said some,
'This is not a mortal man,' said some,
'Look,' said some, 'he is God himself,
who rests on the ocean teeming with fish!'

784.
'Our princess would need a thousand eyes to see this noble man,
and each time he sees this budding branch of a girl,
the lord would need the same!'
'Look at his younger brother,' said some,
'The world has done its penance,' said some,
'Let us worship the sage who, out of any place on earth,
has brought them to this city!'

785.
This was how things happened here,
but I had started to tell what had happened before
to the trusting girl with gold bangles,
passing the night together with the moon,
with full breasts and tiny waist,
her black eyes like swords streaked with red,
clinging to just a breath of life as she yearned to see him again.

786.
Her life reeling back and forth, she left her soothing flower bed
and went to a palace made of crystal
surrounded by ladies adorned with gold.
There she lay down, exhausted, on a couch of soft flowers
in the midst of a pond filled with pristine lotuses,
its water brought to life by the moon's rays.

787.
'Dear cool, fragrant lotuses,
show mercy to a girl who comes to you like this!
By showing me the dark colour of his body in your leaves
you have ended my misery,
you showed his dark eyes that swallowed my mango-leaf hue
but you fail, for you do not give me the man who is my life!

788.
'Those hands that bend the bow like Meru that shrinks before him
those shoulders like iron bars, the quiver that spills over with arrows,
that chest that wears a victory garland,
crossed by a thread that glows like the moon,
if I cannot see them once more, will my own life ever return?

789.
'He wore a garland in his hair, the bees hummed around it
while the new moon turned above as its light melted in the sky.
A dark raincloud armed with a longbow, he took my soul that day
filling his eyes and drinking it down, this is the truth
in my heart now, to be in my heart always.

790.
'Fierce Kama took my soul when he raised his conquering longbow.
His cruel arrow ripped my heart as flame rips through cotton.
But the man who does not come when women are in turmoil
to tell them, "Have no fear," what kind of manliness is that?

791.
'Firm breasts, you rise up and swell, but what good has it done?
Will I ever hold him close, and caress the chest of that noble man
with a face bright as a slip of moon, never rising to wax in the sky,
who mastered the bow that could not be bent?
Do all the penance you can!

792.
'Where did it arise, this moon?
It showers poison on my breasts that swell from fevered thoughts,
kindled by an arrow that bodiless Kama shot at me,
lodging deep to fill my heart.
Even so, it is not the moon that comes at night,
for its face lacks any stain.[8]

793.
'Bodiless Kama pressed me close and pierced my body with poison,
the arrow that blazes its way through my heart.
Yet my life was not burned,
it emerged from the wound and went off in pursuit,
to take refuge at the feet of the proud young man
like a dark elephant hot with rut.
I cannot understand you, heart, but you found a way to return.

794.
'The raincloud that soars in the heaven and a lightning flash across it
have come to earth as his chest and sacred thread,
a fine man come and gone.
He remains in my thoughts, but I do not know who he is,
he remains in my eyes, but somehow they never see him.

795.
'Born of the giving sea, healing ambrosia in a splendid golden pot
never could have appeared elsewhere,
yet fools let it slip through their hands.
I am the same, I was right there before him,
but I did not embrace that lordly man and go to his strong arms.
He's lost to me, beyond my reach, what else is there to say?'[9]

796.
These thoughts about him possessed her,
and she fell apart, suffering so much,
a girl with breasts covered with gold, sobbing and sobbing,
as she sank down, deep in her pain.
Let me tell you what someone else said,
a woman with kohl-streaked eyes and a face like the moon,
her heart renewed for she knew
the bow like a mountain now lay broken in two.[10]

797.
Nilamalai was her name, a woman with long, wide eyes,
and her necklaces and earrings flashed in a dense rainbow of light,
her flower-decked hair and dress slipped down,
as she ran to Sita, fast as a shimmer of lightning.

798.
She reached her but did not bow at her feet,
declaring her presence with cries,
singing and dancing, a woman filled with boundless ecstasy.
'Tell me, my dear,' said Sita,
'why have you come, your heart so full of joy?'
Nilamalai bowed low before her, and started to explain.

799.
'There is a king with a sea of horses, chariots and elephants,
a learned scholar as well, Dasharatha by name,
the sole ruler to turn the wheel of earth's command.
His broad hands shower down wealth like the rainclouds,
and he has a son more beautiful than Kama
whose flower arrows overwhelm the mind.

800.
'His arms are so muscled they could be oak trees,
his power makes you wonder if he might be
the pristine lord who rests on his serpent couch.
In the company of an esteemed sage and a younger prince
he has come to our city, and Rama is his name.

801.
'They say this man covered with gold and jewels
came to see the bow that holy Shiva once fired,
and it was placed before him at our king's command.
This strong man strung the bow with ease,
and the gods in heaven trembled.

802.
'In an instant, he set the bow to his foot and bent it so fast
you would think he knew its secrets well.
Down it fell, broken in two, so the assembled lords jumped
and the gods sang his praise as they showered him with flowers.'

803.
After hearing this man like a raincloud had come with the sage
and that he had the greatness of the god with eyes red as lotuses,*
Sita's doubts fell away, for this was surely the same man,
and as her lap swelled with desire,
her beautiful girdle broke apart.

804.
Anyone who thought she had no waist would say, 'It exists!'
as her delicate breasts swelled round and full, for she was ecstatic
and knew in her heart that if the proud man her maid had described
were not really him, she would die.

805.
This is how Sita felt, a woman suffering from her desire.
Janaka had never such joy when he heard the loud crack
of the bow made by Brahma, who rests on a leafy lotus,
and turning to Kaushika, he started to speak.

806.
'Tell me, my lord, which would you prefer,
shall we quickly hold the wedding for your young charge
and conclude the rite this very day?
Or shall we send the beating drums to call Dasharatha,
the king with anklets that jingle and armies that roar,
and invite him to come to our land?'

---

*Vishnu.

807.
'Let us send word to that manly king,' replied the great ascetic,
'he will come here at once. That would be best.'
Janaka was overjoyed, and sent out a messenger
with a message on a palm leaf to bring the king the news.

Setting Out

808.
The messengers took to their mounts and rode like the wind,
and the drums pounded like thunder when they reached Ayodhya.
They entered the palace, where crown smashed against crown
as kings rushed forward to worship the emperor's feet.

809.
Dasharatha granted them entry, and they stood before him politely,
touched his feet wrapped in shining anklets,
then arose and praised the magnanimous king.
'After your sons left, king, here is all that happened,'
they said, and offered a full account.

810.
They finished their tale, then the messengers took out the palm leaf,
saying, 'Here is the royal letter, famed king of limitless power.'
At the request of the emperor, the lector took it.
'Read it,' Dasharatha said as both his anklets jingled.

811.
When the king heard what Janaka had recounted in his letter,
how his eldest son Rama had broken the bow,
his rock-hard arms swelled like mountains
until his armbands grew tight and split apart.

812.
'We heard a thunderous crack some time ago,' said the king.
'It must have been the sound of Rama breaking the mighty bow
that the god with a battle axe and a crown of matted locks used
when he conquered the seven worlds at Daksha's sacrifice!'

813.
After the king with shoulders like mountains had spoken,
he had fine garments and gold ornaments heaped up before him.
He ordered that they be given to the messengers, saying,
'These messengers with ringing anklets should take them all.'[1]

814.
Dasharatha then commanded, 'Let the drums be adorned!
Place them on the elephant, then announce the news.
My armies and devoted kings shall march before me
to Mithila where Rama stays, like Kama in summertime,
born to reward the merit of my forebears in the solar line.[2]

815.
'Just as Jambavan* wandered to proclaim the news
when Vishnu with lotus eyes, wearing a crown wrapped in holy basil
measured out the world as was his right,
the pariah will go among my army, a sea full of leaping horses,
to drum and announce my command.'

816.
The moment the sound of the drum reached their ears,
women with round bangles, handsome young men,
foot soldiers, and devoted kings were rocked with joy
like a sea whipped up by the wind.[3]

817.
The army of the king who strides like a bull then departed,
flooding out like the immense sea that overwhelms the land
in the end times when the cosmic age turns,
so no room remained anywhere in the world.

---

*See v. 205.

818.
The earth is too small for every chariot gathered there,
and the kings who ride in them glow like the sun.
With their jewelled caparisons flashing in the daylight
the elephants are clouds lit by rainbows.

819.
The parasols opened wide over their handles
look like endless geese on the wing up to heaven.
The host of war flags rising high up above
makes the entire sky look like strips of flayed leather.

820.
The fluttering banners are white clouds rising up to own the sky,
then looking below to see mountains with trunks, flowing with rut.
They seem to think these elephants are the ocean,
and dip below so they can drink their fill.[4]

821.
All the ornaments there shine like the morning sun,
spreading warmth that robs shade from peacock-fan parasols.
Those peacock parasols bloom more beautifully than rainclouds,
while the war drums roar louder than clouds ever could.

822.
The horses in jingling harnesses ridden by women
are like a river where geese float on the rolling waves.
Women with full breasts graced with gold, their soft hair askew,
look like lightning bolts on rainclouds, the elephant cows.[5]

823.
Everywhere the army goes, people press so close together
kumkum and musk on the breasts of women
and sandalwood paste on the massive arms of men
coat the earth like a bed after love play.

824.
The pearl necklaces on deadly breasts kept covered by clothes
by women with red mouths, their voices sweet as syrup,
shine with the light of the full moon.
The morning sun also shines from rows of inlaid gems
crowded on their jewellery.

825.
The archers and bowmen, young men with scented topknots
and golden arms so strong they put mountains to shame,
walk next to their women with waists thin as vines
like elephant bulls paired together with their cows.

826.
A host of palanquins set with pearls carry women,
their hair so dark they look like rainclouds decked with flowers.
Only their faces are visible, looking like sky chariots
flying past as scores of full moons soar together with them.

827.
The caparisoned elephants, wild in their musth
pour down so much rut they cannot cross the mire.
Roaring like a stormy sea, their trunks stretch out
to seek the elephants that stand at the cardinal points.[6]

828.
The ranks of horses leap, but, like cruel demons,
their feet never touch the earth.
They are like the minds of courtesans with breasts cinched tight,
in their dancing stride and in touching without touching.[7]

829.
Some women sulk and avoid looking at their men.
They sigh with annoyance, their brows furrowed,
and pull the garlands from their hair.
Yet still they follow, as if the men were their own lives.

830.
Fearless elephants, their cheeks flowing with rut,
sparks flying from their eyes at the thought of the goad,
rush forward like rivers, breaking down the slopes they hate,
ripping trees out by the roots and breaking them apart.

831.
Dasharatha, like a flourishing bough that frees all lives from tears,
had not yet set out, but his army that preceded him
had travelled so far, so closely packed a bean could not fall,
the front had reached Mithila's walls, its banners flying high.

832.
Women with hair that hums with bees,
bewitching the men who see them,
go in their own decorated carts.
The crowded faces make them seem like moving lotus ponds.

833.
One young man drives a fine bullock cart
that carries the woman he loves, as beautiful as a portrait.
When he turns to look at her, the kohl on her eyes
is pure ambrosia for this sturdy lord.

834.
One man is apart from his wife gentle as a fawn.
While in the wetlands filled with water and mud,
he sees geese and lotuses, and his heart stops:
he stands there swaying back and forth.[8]

835.
In the vast army filled with many kings who rule the earth,
where the conches and drums roar like thunderclouds,
the surge of white parasols and rippling white chowries
make it the Ganga River.[9]

836.
Women like goddesses who speak so sweetly
have eyes that rip life from those who behold them,
those sharp spears of Death, piercing men's chests
make the army a battlefield.

837.
The infantry is packed together like a pride of lions,
their feet packed together, stepping on each other,
their shoulders packed together like close-set pillars,
their swords packed together like lightning clustered in the clouds.

838.
One man who cannot pull his eyes away
from lustrous breasts pressed together with a breast band
walks as if blind, with no idea where to go,
and slams into a huge rutting elephant.

839.
A woman gorgeous as a peacock rides a favoured horse,
and as it leaps, she slips and falls off.
A good man lifts her back up with arms like iron pillars,
but instead of standing her up to embrace her
he keeps her in his arms.

840.
One young man sees a woman with dark eyes like arrows
suffering as she walks on sore feet soft as lotuses,
and says, 'My chest is nowhere near big enough
to hold her inviting breasts, two elephants flowing with rut.'[10]

841.
One young man marches like an elephant dripping with rut
as the bees hum around his wrapped topknot.
He looks at the eyes of a nearby maid, and says,
'Those are so sharp!' then he looks at the spear in his hand.

842.
A young man sees a woman with long, wavy hair,
small feet like lotuses, and black eyes like swords,
and says, 'Your hands are stacked with bangles,
your full breasts are graced with jewels,
but where have you left your waist?'

843.
A young man sees a woman who does not say a thing
apart from hints she gives with eyes lethal as Death,
and says, 'Someone will take you by your beautiful hands
in a flooding river, and help you reach the shore.'[11]

844.
Camels carry heavy burdens, tiring to unload.
They do not eat sweet budding leaves,
but seek bitter neem so their mouths dry out
like the mouths and hearts of toddy drinkers.

845.
Men from Pappara with red eyes and thick bodies dark as night
march with a loaded yoke over their shoulders,
like rutting elephants that pull up their sturdy sheds by the posts
and carry them with the hitching beams draped over their necks.

846.
A rutting elephant that rebels against its mahout
places its trunk on an elephant cow women are riding.
Terrified, they feel faint and wretched,
for their hands are too small to cover their eyes.[12]

847.
Dwarves ride on elephant cows
so small their tails drag on the ground
in the midst of women wearing beautiful girdles,
like frogs riding turtles in a bunch of new lotus flowers.[13]

848.
One woman fertile as a blossoming branch rides a racing horse,
its legs curving back, while an elephant follows it.
The horse seems to think she is not of the earth,
but rather belongs to the king of gods.[14]

849.
Men spread the joyous news that our father broke the bow,
and women were ecstatic: they ran forward,
not caring their long hair was hanging loose
or that pearls were spilling from their broken girdles.

850.
Many brahmans crowded together and hurried on,
fearful of the maidservants and the rutting elephants.
They walked on tiptoe, carrying their parasols and water pots,
never lowering their right hands that kept their noses closed.[15]

851.
Rama appeared before women wearing fragrant garlands
and tears of joy pooled up in their eyes.
'If you have come to meet us,' they said,
'mount the chariot with us,'
and they raised their pressed hands in worship.

852.
Rumbling chariots, elephants, horses,
and pounding drums were everywhere,
making such noise no one could hear a thing.
People walked on as if stricken dumb.

853.
The crowd of women whose hair hummed with bees
wearing garments so fine that spiders could have woven them
walk with a swaying gait, bells jingling on their anklets:
they seem like a pond where the geese are all calling.[16]

854.
Lovely women like Lakshmi on the wave-tossed milk sea
peer out through holes in the curtains.
Men see their eyes and are captivated;
joyful bees hum in flooding elephant rut.[17]

855.
The jewelled anklets of women who look like haughty deer
with dark, intense eyes that can pierce through a life
ring out like sweet-sounding instruments,
and horses thunder with the roar of soaring rainclouds.

856.
On the faces of women whose feet delight the earth goddess,
some eyes are blissful, delighting Kama himself
as though eyes are little bees filled with delight
resting on lotuses that give the joy of drinking nectar.[18]

857.
The dust spreads everywhere, mixed with fragrant powders
that fall off lustrous breasts, full as golden tender coconuts,
of women with lips red as ivy gourd
and waists too small to believe.

858.
Countless men and women on enormous, handsome chariots
travel on, enjoying thoughtful discussions.
Noble people crowd together with so many others,
calling out to each other joyfully as they make their way to the city.

859.
Chariots, infantry, and bridled horses gather everywhere
and travel so fast, the layer of dust grows thick.
Misty holes in the clouds that pour down sheets of rain are sealed,
and the elephants' temples grow clogged at the cardinal points.[19]

860.
Warriors shift their glittering swords to the shield hand,
and reach out to take their wives with hands adorned with bangles.
Ever so gently, they help them walk over the slippery path
soaked with rut from elephants wearing golden caparisons.

861.
Dark lilies, red lilies and unfurling red lotuses burst into bloom
in the fields, ponds and tanks filled with fresh water
to reveal the beauty of eyes, mouths and hands. Seeing them open,
women beg their husbands, 'Pluck them and give them to me!'[20]

862.
Women on rows of beautiful horses dismount to let them rest
and see elephants drawing near.
They run here and there like peacocks,
fragrant hair hanging loose, precious jewellery spilling,
sheer dresses barely held up with hands as soft as budding leaves.

863.
Nighttime falls as parasols, peacock fans, a host of peacock hangings,
and banners press tight together to block every shaft of light.
The glow of swords, spears, crowns and other jewellery spreads
so day and night exist in the same moment.

864.
Men with bodies that shine like the sun see women's eyes,
well-honed swords on the lotuses that are their smiling faces
showing fine teeth like pearls on lips like the palash blossom.
'Split up! Split up!' the men call, 'Those swords will cut through us!'
and each of them goes his own way.[21]

865.
Women pause, their girdled love-mounds like a cobra's hood,
hindered by the impassable crowds on the path.
Gems and pearls fall down when the knots of their necklaces break,
and scatter over feet like new leaves, bright with jingling anklets.
They stand still, as if they cannot move forward.

866.
The victory drums pound all around like thunderclouds,
making bullocks yoked to carts break away
and dump all the burdens hoisted on them, row after row,
together with the ropes that bound them.
They run free, as women near them hurry off like scared geese,
and like yogis, their suffering was over.[22]

867.
Elephants like mountains see ponds and climb in,
paying no heed to mahouts firing slingshots fierce as the wind.
Like mighty Airavata rising from the milk sea
showing only his tusks, and temples like cinched breasts,
they stay there, refusing to climb out.[23]

868.
Like pairs of kinnaras, bards playing lutes rode on horses
with female singers with eyes like swords,
hair dark as sand, and red mouths dripping ambrosial words.
They rode together as they travelled, to sing and play in turn,
invoking the 'love in hardship' mode as honey for the ears.[24]

869.
A young elephant bull with fierce eyes rushes forward, mad with rut,
like a mountain with a waterfall, making crowds of people scatter.
Bees with striped wings first swarm the flowing rut,
then swarm the women riding elephant cows as the bull pursues them.

870.
While the drums roared as their leather heads were beaten,
and the chariots, elephants, and triumphant cavalry
joined together with men and women in one splendid procession
as if the vast sea watched the rise of the full moon,
the crowned queens of Dasharatha set out on the journey.[25]

871.
Kaikeyi, daughter of Kekaya's king, began the journey
on a palanquin adorned with superb gems,
surrounded by a thousand maidservants
like a gorgeous goose shining in a bunch of lotuses on a pond
while bees hummed sweetly, so that goddesses felt surpassed.

872.
Queen Sumitra, mother of the twins, looked like lightning in a cloud
travelling to lute music on a palanquin inlaid with emeralds
surrounded by two thousand women riding mules,
their wide eyes like dark lilies streaked with red.

873.
Queen Kausalya, mother of lord Rama, travelled on a chariot
and was revered by the gods like gathered stars around the moon,
her face with white teeth and mouth red as silk cotton,
while the bards sang treasured songs played to the cymbals' rhythm.

874.
So many women travelled with them, people said, 'Think about it,
there are no women in the seven continents but for here in Ayodhya!'
They carried peacocks, geese, green parrots,
mynah birds, dolls, and regalia such as chowries,
which lay coiled like conches taken from their wraps.[26]

875.
Bodyguards kept watch, and guarded the feet of queens
as if they were cherished goddesses,
wearing uniforms and holding rattan staffs that assert their strength.
Some rode on horseback, some spread out on foot,
their eyes showering sparks of anger for no reason at all.

876.
Hunchbacks, dwarves, little people, and groups of maids
rode on dappled horses that strode gently as geese,
and women with garlands in their hair rode on elephant cows
swarmed by bees, beetles and dragonflies, a canopy above them.

877.
Sixty thousand women with breasts like budding lotuses
who were even more splendid than the impossibly lovely Lakshmi
surrounded the queens, seated like painted dolls,
in covered carriages inlaid with coral, rubies, gold and emeralds.

878.
Surrounded by two thousand brahmans who offer with their hands
so the gods can enjoy the oblations with their tongues,
and who delight in the Vedas, ambrosia to the ear,
Vasishtha, husband of chaste Arundhati, was on a pearl palanquin
in the shade of a white parasol, like Brahma on his goose.

879.
While a sea of battle elephants, horses, elegant chariots,
and infantry wearing golden anklets surrounded them on all sides
as though circling a forbidding mountain, Bharata and Shatrughna,
divine bowmen, brave brothers with Lakshmi on their chests,
drove in chariots as had their two brothers who followed the sage.[27]

880.
On the auspicious day, at the auspicious hour, the emperor
adorned with jewellery set with diamonds and pearls
finished his ritual duties, then placed his head at Vishnu's feet.
He gave brahmans gold, countless jewels, land, and herds,
and then he set off towards Mithila.[28]

881.
Eight thousand brahmans holding water pots chanted mantras,
poured holy water and darva grass on the king and blessed him.
Ten million women wearing jewelled girdles approached in waves,
glorifying Dasaratha with sweet songs from their red mouths.

882.
Lords of the realm crowded before him, calling to each other.
'The conch roars,' said some, 'the king must be leaving.'
'He has not seen me,' said some, and others said, 'He looked at me!'
'I lost an earring in the crowd, now I can't show myself before him!'

883.
Women with bangles rode horses with jingling golden harnesses
surrounding the king like lotuses on the waves of the deep sea.
Other lotuses, the red hands of lords wielding lethal spears,
were all pressed high in reverence as Dasharatha began his journey
riding in a huge, jewelled chariot like another sun.[29]

884.
Dust clouded the air, striking the heavens and falling back down,
to cover everything out to the edge of the world.
In the crowds, no one could see another, and the dust kept pouring,
filling the stormy sea as if it hated Sagara's sons.*

885.
Conches, flutes, horns, small trumpets, cymbals and drums
roared out, putting thunderclouds to shame,
while peacock regalia, parasols and peacock fans eclipsed the sun.
The moon ran when it saw the white parasol,
the gods were bewildered and fled.

886.
As Dasharatha travelled on, dignified as Indra,
the sound of the chanted Vedas, the blare of right-turning conches,
the roar of elephants breaking their bonds, the pounding of drums,
the voices of brahmans giving blessings and criers calling the hour
travelled out to the edge of the world.

887.
Dasharatha moved, and on every side, hoping to catch his eye,
kings with tight anklets raised their pressed hands, lotuses in bloom.
Dust from chariots, horses, feet and elephants filled the air,
until heaven grew as clouded as earth.

---

*See vv. 502–30.

888.
The elephants, chariots, horses and infantry in the crowded army
had no way to make more room, and no other world to enter.
If the earth goddess wrapped in the ocean felt her back relax,
Dasharatha carried her burden for her, people said, but how?[30]

889.
The king and his army travelled several miles,
until they reached Chandrashaila, a mountain like golden Meru.
Kama's elephant named Night appeared,
and as fragrance spread from breasts, Kama's arrows,
and sandalwood from the southern mountain,*
the army stopped and rested.[31]

---

*Potiya Mountain.

Seeing the Mountain

890.
Countless rutting war elephants nudged by elephant cows
streaked with vermilion on their foreheads, crowded by calves,
were like a herd of forest elephants among the dense trees,
with Chandrashaila shining like the lord of the herd.[1]

891.
The breasts of women with voices sweet as a mynah bird
are held as tight in their lovers' embrace
as elephants tied to cedar and sandalwood trees
that reach up to the sky, breaking tender banyan tree branches.
Covered with necklaces, they are so firm they humble Meru,
renowned by the bowman Kama, they yearn for their lovers' hearts
like elephants seeking watering holes, bearing heroes on their backs.[2]

892.
With the tactics of an expert when mistakes cannot be made
using politics to conquer foes who will not submit in war,
one tethered elephant grasped the beautiful base of a shala tree,
ripped it out by the roots, and left as a walking mountain.[3]

893.
One elephant stormed off with its foot still chained to the post
and broke two huge trees as it walked between them,
like Krishna dragging the mortar when he crawled away
and broke two sturdy arjuna trees with dense, soaring branches.

894.
One elephant was like a king who takes no heed of subtle counsel
informed by every sort of text on political strategy.
Its mahout was like a royal minister seeking to control his charge
by soothing its fury with sweet words, trying to keep it from bolting.[4]

895.
Hooked by the iron goad, one elephant trumpeted like thunder
even though it saw no enemy.
Catching the scent of a forest herd, it raced off like the wind
as black kites flew close behind,
and when it saw a river before it, it ran like a river itself.[5]

896.
An elephant smelled an odour spreading like the scent of rut
that lay heavy in the rows of elephant sheds.
It raced towards it, straightened the controlling goad
then saw a blooming blackboard tree and reduced it to dust,
grinding it into the earth with its feet.[6]

897.
If nobles who have clarity of wisdom mix with lesser minds,
they drive out their weak points, people say.
So too, the golden wheels of chariots wore away
everywhere they rolled, turning black rocks their own bright colour.

898.
A flock of peacocks wandered in the forest
as if coming to see the girdles on women with deer eyes,
and to see the golden beauty of their figures, or perhaps to wonder
if cochineals were crowded on their lips red as ivy gourds.[7]

899.
Young women dismounted their horses, and walked like goslings
to seek shade under a stand of young trees.
Girdles, earrings, and other jewellery glittered on their bodies,
and they glowed like a branch filled with blooming flowers.

900.
Sore from their long journey, women lay down as bees swarmed,
mistaking their faces and tender hands for blooming lotuses.
As they slept, their lustrous bodies were reflected on a crystal rock,
alarming their maids, who took the reflections for real women.

901.
As if lightning flashing in the rainclouds had come down to earth,
women dismounted elephants that knelt by the mountain slope.
Their waists quivering like vines and anklets jingling as they walked,
they entered their lodgings as if Lakshmi with an hourglass waist
had left her own lotus and had also come to stay there.

902.
Champion horses brought to Ayodhya by Arabs
were led into camp, neighing so loudly they were frightening,
then fed the best food by their grooms. Tied in rows in their stables,
they were like the rainbow of gems on Bhudevi's necklace.[8]

903.
Long curtains were hung around the women's quarters
as if ocean waves were arrayed in rows.
Storehouses were built as if the seas were set in rows,
elephants were tied in rows, a string of clouds amid the trees,
horses were hitched in rows as if stopping the swift winds.[9]

904.
Men wielding spears honed to a fine edge wandered
to find women with doe eyes who looked like dancing peacocks.
Kings heard the conches blow, drums pounding loud as thunder,
saw the royal banners flying and rushed to the emperor's pavilion.

905.
Young men saw their lovers' bodies smudged by clouds of dust
and wiped them clean with cloth light as milk foam.
The young women glowed as if the men were painters
who were restoring beautiful portraits.

906.
The kings descended from their elephants like lions
who come down from the mountain and then pounce to the ground.
They went to stay in their pavilions set up in shining rows
as chowries waved back and forth like opening palm spathes.[10]

907.
In each tent with its raised banner, its crest sewn on white cloth,
the faces of women wearing garlands seemed like reflections
of the moon gliding past clouds, free of its dark spot,
cast everywhere on the silver sea alive with rolling waves.[11]

908.
A rutting elephant rolled on the ground, then stretched up to the sky.
It shook off the fragrant dust that covered its own darkness
but only on one side, so the other side stayed white,
then it walked off, half Krishna and half three-eyed Shiva.

909.
Like discerning people who befriend the corrupt
but drop them as soon as they learn of their vices,
swift horses fell down in the dust then instantly got up
to shake it off and stand far apart from each other.

910.
Like the wise on the righteous path sure of this life and the next,
some horses perceived their bondage when they saw open space.
They strained to break that strong three-stranded rope,
succeeded, then went happily where they wanted.[12]

911.
Inside each tent, its sides assailed by wind that swoops in like a fog,
the dark eyes of women playing jacks with molucca beans
were lively fish, glittering as they leap through the waves
where pearls born of roaring conches lie scattered.[13]

912.
The rivers once flooded with clear water have provided for all
and are now dried up, but when dug till water pours,
they are like family, sharing what little they have,
or like a generous lord, giving what he can and never saying no.

913.
Their thick hair blowing in a fragrant wind,
jewels flashing on their chests like lightning mixed with fire,
warriors entered their swaying tents
like murderous lions entering caves.

914.
Massive elephants crowded together wielding their spiked tusks,
hairy foreheads streaked with red, bells jingling with each step.
They plunged into the water and churned it to make waves,
like Madhu and Kaitabha, who tried to churn the primordial sea.[14]

915.
Delirious with rut, elephants like black mountains
gave no heed to the commands of the mahouts who rode them.
They made other elephants panic, as well as their mahouts.
Like lustful men enthralled by love-mounds adorned with girdles,
they refused to get out of the water, caring for nothing else.

916.
Young men joined women who wore sheer cloth around their waists
to bring oudh to the kitchens to use as firewood
The billows of smoke became so thick the camp became a vast sea
surrounded by clouds that never thunder.[15]

917.
Vidyadharas who live in the mountains, dwelling in the cracks,
came to watch and could discern no difference from themselves.
Men and women of stunning beauty stayed there,
and the army seemed as if the world of gods
had fallen from heaven to shine here on the mountain.

918.
Women wandered like a flock of peacocks, glittering like lightning,
with the beauty of sleeplessness from love the night before.
Stubborn in their quarrels now, they outshone the morning sun
and spoke sweetly to cuckoos, voices echoed by the mountains.

919.
Anklets jingled on warriors' feet, bees hummed on their garlands,
swords glittered at their sides, their jewelled armbands sparkled,
as men roamed like splendid lions
gazing at the mountain that soared as tall as their shoulders.

920.
All the seas surrounding the earth seemed to have combined
to circle golden Meru rich with gems and take it for their own.
Kings, queens, young men and women like blooming branches
came together to delight in that charming mountain's virtues.

921.
While bees spread out, humming their song as they swirled in flight,
elephants stretched trunks thick as palm trees to grab tender leaves
from the high branches of trees that shine light into heaven,
then gave them to their mates, sweet as their own lives.

922.
The kino tree is an astrologer for women on kurinji slopes,
their wide eyes like lilies, mouths like coral, speech like music.
Bees had their fill of flowers and soared up to the stars,
mistaking them for gamboge blossoms dripping with nectar.[16]

923.
An elephant with his cows, a silver moon with stars,
drove his two crescent trunks deep into a honeycomb.
The mountain tribe that plants red millet
shifted the channel where honey came splashing down,
and took Ganga water from the sky to plant wild rice instead.

924.
The moon is a mirror that reflects on both sides,
resting at the base of the splendid mountain too tall for it to cross.
On one side, mountain women admired their beauty,
on the other, heavenly women admired theirs.

925.
Though they are not heated by fire that blazes in the smith's forge,
nor greased or dipped in poison on the sharp edge of the blade,
mountain women's* eyes are cruel spears that take men's lives.
When tribal men saw their brows they compared them to the moon.

926.
Happy calves born of elephant cows played with untamed lion cubs
in front of the mountain tribe's huts,
where children played with the crescent moon as it slipped by
curved like the brows of their mothers.

927.
On the ground covered with perfect emeralds,
the mountain revealed the deep footprints of a savage lion
that killed an elephant like a dark mountain, its cheeks wet with rut.
The handsome topknots of the vidyadharas there were marked
with damp footprints of lotus feet dyed with red cotton paste.

928.
Mountain women sang and their music joined the lutes' strings
as they plucked with lotus hands, brows never arching,
mouths never smiling, thick dark hair never falling loose,
and their eyes flashing like fish never reaching back to their ears.[17]

929.
The toddy being poured into countless inlaid cups
was like clear spring water flowing on crystal rocks,
dyed red with kumkum from women who bathe there,
their eyes like marauding swords that stretch to their ears,
their braids dripping wet with the nectar from flowers.[18]

---

*Kuravar.

930.
Apsaras from heaven quarrelled so much they broke their lovers' hearts
and tears streaked with kohl poured down from their red eyes.
They pulled celestial garlands from their hair and threw them away
to lie there shining, never to fade, perfume always drifting.

931.
Mountain women, their bodies glowing like mango buds,
threw their garlands on the arecas' dark spathes
and compared them to their hair.
Apsaras, all perfectly adorned, took off their jewelled bracelets,
slipped them on red glory lilies
and compared them to their hands.

932.
Apsaras who dance like peacocks and sing with the lute
arched their brows like curving bows, took off their necklaces
and threw them aside in their quarrels.
Monkeys roaming their usual trees put them on their mates,
who glanced at the jewellery and capered with delight.

933.
All over the mountain where sandalwood trees thrive,
elephant cows were smeared with ochre, as if wearing crimson tilaks.
When they mixed with the light from heaps of rubies,
the sky glowed with the red of evening in the morning and at night.

934.
Waterfalls spilled down in streams, sifting endless grains of gold,
awash with pearls like jewellery for the earth goddess,
like the Ganga filled with endless shining pearls
that pours from the crown of the matted locks of Shiva,
lord of the daughter of the mountain,
like the golden clothes Vishnu wore when he measured the worlds.[19]

935.
Women with arms wrapped in garlands of mixed flowers,
clove blossoms with gamboge blooms plucked from new boughs,
drank fresh toddy, waving off the joyful bees,
and saw women with horse faces, whose quarrels are calmed
by kinnaras' songs, sweet-sounding as the lute.

936.
They saw the joyful love between male bees delighting in dark hair
and female bees on budding branches that tremble like waists
on red cotton trees filled with flower buds beyond compare
except for breasts that war with men's fine chests strong as elephants.

937.
Women with shining faces like lotuses, wearing garlanded crowns
mistook mountain ponds for smooth crystal rocks and quickly fell in.
When young men with broad anklets and flashing armbands
saw the women's clothes soaked by clear water,
they clapped their hands and laughed among themselves.[20]

938.
They saw many beds made of flowers and necklaces of golden bells,
they saw areca nut from betel chews, red as eager cochineals,
they saw couches of fresh branches, burned by vidhyadhara women
distraught when apart from husbands sweeter than their lives.[21]

939.
They saw eyes dark as lilies flash, mouths red as coral smile,
priceless pearl necklaces shake on tempting full breasts
swarms of honeybees spiral, jewels on earrings sway
as celestial women swing on swings, wafting sweet perfume.

940.
They saw gold cups tossed away by women with bright faces,
emptied out by droves of bees who came to lick them dry
after coral mouths with red lips had finished the sweet mead.
The cups were like men cast aside without compassion
by courtesans with gold girdles who sell themselves for cash.

941.
They saw celestial garlands and jewellery lying next to beds
in rooms made of crystal that turns night to day.
They were taken off and tossed aside when they got in the way
of goddesses with brows finer than a bow
making love with gods whose shoulders terrify wrestlers.

942.
Women look at the glory lily they want to bloom like their hands
and cover their eyes keen as spears, afraid a cobra is poised to strike.
They see the reflections of flowers shining on crystal rocks
and beg their husbands, 'Please pick them and give them to me!'[22]

943.
Women like peacocks, their jewels a bright rainbow,
pluck handfuls of ashoka buds, tear them in strips with their nails,
and apply them to their breasts.
They pick flowers full of nectar, then, like geese gathering,
they slip into mountain ponds to bathe.

944.
Tender new buds of the mango tree shine,
deer, elephants and monkeys roam,
gamboge trees and bamboo slim as women's arms grow,
with sheets of gold born of the mountain between them.[23]

945.
The inviting arms of warriors fierce as lions embrace the breasts
of women with wide, red-streaked eyes that look like swords.
Fragrance from oudh and sandalwood drifts from their arms,
and agarwood, sandalwood, crocuses and cotton trees thrive.

946.
Lush banana trees look like the thighs of heavenly dancers
on the ancient mountain, and many women there
play sweet music on the strings of the lute,
to match the rich song of kinnara couples.

947.
The dark mountain boar are covered with vermilion,
and they rub it off on mango and sandalwood trees.
Women who speak sweetly, shining like goddesses,
make the mountainside look like the heavenly world.

948.
Huge cobras slither along as they hunt,
knocking down stands of bamboo.
Dust flies as the bison run away,
and waterfalls full of pearls roar as they fall.

949.
Rut that flows from huge elephants pours down,
and the bison grow fretful, unable to flee.
Mango trees shake, bamboo stands shake,
and chousinghas and other beasts run up to quench their thirst.

950.
In all the places that tigers frequent,
the dark tribal women who live on the mountain
play drums and other instruments loudly
so they can then dig for tasty root vegetables.[24]

951.
Strong elephants plunge into ponds with their calves,
lotuses and banyan fruit ripen and fall,
and bees swirl and frolic in heavenly dancers' hair
on the mountain's forest slopes where lions prowl.

952.
Dark clouds roll in waves across the mountain heights
while below, garlands from heaven lie scattered.
Vishnu appears to stand right there,
and Lakshmi who lives on his chest shines beneath him.[25]

953.
Men and women gathered everywhere
like bees that feast on nectar dripping from the flowers.
They rested together all over the soaring mountain
and delighted in each other, as if they would never part.

954.
Like virtuous people set on the path to heaven,
they gave no thought to leaving the mountain
and would never forget its treasures and charms.
Descent would mean suffering, like birth in this world.

955.
Veiled in clouds, the mountain seemed like an elephant
and the sun with its hot rays came at it like a lion.
The sky glowed red, like a wash of scarlet blood,
when the lion leaped on the elephant and took it as its prey.

956.
The gentle light of the glowing red sky
made all the trees look like new leaf buds were growing.
It swept over every slope on Chandrashaila
and the mountain seemed like a tower of rubies.

957.
The glowing vistas that dazzle the eye
and the countless glittering peaks
made the mountain seem like Vishnu when he displayed the infinite
wearing rich sandalwood paste on his chest.[26]

958.
Like the deer and the doe, the elephant bull and cow,
and the proud lioness and her mate,
couples bound together like body and spirit
walked down from the mountain as bees hummed around them.

959.
The sun in his one-wheeled chariot is a lion with sharp claws,
his cruel eyes set things ablaze, and each hair is a ray
that burns so bright it can torch a flying arrow.
As it crept behind the western mountain,
dark night spread like an elephant herd running off to hide.

960.
In the army of the king of kings who wears a famous garland
perfumed with the fragrance of celestial flowers' anthers,
lamps flickered and glowed throughout the camp
like lotuses blossoming on the roaring ocean.[27]

961.
The silver moon left the spray of waves in the cool ocean
and rose in the sky, surrounded by glittering stars,
like a radiant conch giving birth to pearls as it glides
through sand that shines like a lovely moonlit night.

962.
When the sea gives birth to the silver moon,
Dasharatha's sea of an army will not stand for it.
Ten million faultless moons appeared,
the faces of wonderfully pleasing women, shining like goddesses.

963.
Everywhere that dancers danced, the sound of women singing,
the sweet sound of the drumhead smeared with paste,
the sound of musicians playing the lutes, and cymbals keeping time
rose up with the sound of the bamboo flute, amazing the gods above.

964.
Women took off their jewellery and their pearl necklaces,
they took off their garlands made of morning jasmine,
and, as oudh smoke dried the creams traced on their breasts,
they put on garlands of malabar jasmine, fresh with new scent.[28]

965.
The sound of trainers singing commands to a newly caught elephant,
the sound of men drinking toddy and chatting with women,
the sound of girdles jingling over courtesans' love-mounds,
mingled with the sound of rutting elephants trumpeting in frenzy.

966.
As the night passed, men pleased their wives, the rarest of women
who savoured the varied joys of love as if it were ambrosia.
People enjoyed songs matched perfectly to their ragas
and admired dances in which hands show true emotion.

Picking Flowers

967.
Furious at the night that is the asura Hiranya,
where the constellations appear as his teeth,
the sun extended a thousand arms, his burning, close-set rays,
and burst forth like Narasimha from a golden pillar
when it rose from Udayagiri, its eastern mountain home.[1]

968.
After his morning rituals, Dasharatha mounted his chariot
and started off while kings saluted him, the army right behind him.
They reached the river Son, where the lowlands were full of gardens,
the hollows filled with red lilies, and the riverbanks full of lotuses.

969.
They rested there until the sun reached its peak,
then kings and princes set off with groups of women
to go to cool, fragrant gardens where bees search for nectar
among clear pools, where they bathed and plucked flowers.

970.
As brows become war bows and red-streaked eyes the arrows,
peacocks seem ready to flee, afraid the women will wound them.
When women speak sweetly while their anklets jingle
parrots fly off because of their shame,
and when the women walk, the geese try to follow.[2]

971.
As men with fragrant garlands watch women dance and play,
and rolled golden earrings and divine earrings shine
as bees hum around them, they stand there bewildered
unable to tell the women from the vines on flowering boughs.[3]

972.
When women gather there, their words sweet as music,
waists covered with jewellery made of gems and gold,
and hair spilling nectar from fresh blossoms,
the cuckoos hear the noise.
They feel no fear but are ashamed to call out:
who could speak before women with such voices?

973.
The women's desire turns poison to ambrosia in their cruel eyes,
and when they grasp soaring branches with their lotus hands
flowers spill on their feet as if falling down in worship.
Who would fail to lie before those women with waists like vines?

974.
Men wearing flower chaplets would make a lion tremble,
but their hard shoulders soften when touched by flowers:
the hands of women lovely as Lakshmi in her lotus.
Is there a point in saying that blossoming branches also bend?[4]

975.
Flowering vines have brows like the crescent moon,
and lotuses in rivers and ponds blossom with the lilies.
When humming bees see this, they swarm to them, amazed,
and when driven off, they are sure to return.
When those seeking freshness find something new,
when will they ever let it alone?[5]

976.
For men wearing garlands strung with fresh flowers,
with handsome, lustrous bodies and shoulders hard as diamond,
some branches bend to their touch, like loving women,
while others refuse to bend, like stubborn women in quarrels.

977.
Charming women see slim branches stripped of flowers, and worry,
'They have lost their beauty. How will they look to our men?'
They take off their necklaces, pearls, golden chains and earrings
and adorn the branches until they bend, then admire their work.

978.
The bees that wander the large flower buds and drink their nectar,
trampling them as they cause them to bloom,
do not want what they once wanted, but swarm to women's hair
free of garlands and cool, scattered petals.
People enjoy every pleasure a place has to offer.[6]

979.
One woman so lovely her body was like Lakshmi's jewel
looks at a shining crystal and sees her own spellbinding image.
'She could be in a portrait, she would captivate my man,' she thinks,
and tears fall from her eyes as flowers fall from her hands.

980.
A young woman like a flowering branch,
her face a full moon hidden by clouds,
sees her man put on a garland for another charming woman.
Tears pour down like rain from eyes as sharp as swords
over breasts pressed close together by a tightly knotted band.[7]

981.
A lover hides in that flawless garden in a shelter of thatched liana
to learn what his woman was thinking as she tried to find him.
She is used to being with him, they have never been apart,
so she stops, trembling with worry, her heart as unsteady
as a languishing body searching for its life.

982.
A man sees tender coconuts in the crown of a tall palm tree
and mentions that they look like women's breasts.
His naive woman says, 'Whose breasts do you mean?'
What anger! Eyes crying, face sweating, she gasps for breath.

983.
One woman quarrels with her man who holds a greased spear
and her dark eyes traced with kohl turn red.
She stands before him, sees a flower out of reach,
and appeals to a cuckoo there, 'Pick that flower and give it to me!'[8]

984.
A woman with hair like a raincloud and a voice sweet as a cuckoo's
comes up behind her man as he wanders picking flowers,
a Kama with arms that rise high as mountains for war.
He says, 'Who is that?' and shocks her, making her gasp like fire.[9]

985.
Two wives reach out their hands, red lotuses not born in mud,
to ask for a new flower dripping nectar from the king who picked it.
He does not give it to either of them, nor does he refuse,
but stands with his hand between them, a truly greedy man.

986.
A woman with eyes deadly as spears stands before her lover,
he is like her life itself, but he calls her by another name.
When she hears it, her pride rears and she seethes,
and when this woman with eyes streaked with kohl smells a flower,
she burns it to ashes as she breathes out.

987.
All the shining eyes of noble queens, their faces like lotuses,
roam around to see what they crave.
The king with strong arms wanders like an elephant in musth
as bees swarm around it, hungry for rut.[10]

988.
A man with a fine body shares flowers with his two wives,
half for the woman with a brow like the crescent moon at twilight
and half for the woman noble people revere.
Their eyes burn red, they toss the flowers away,
and off they go, proud as peacocks with fanned tails.

989.
Some women, unaware their scented hair is loose,
blind to their broken necklaces spilling pearls all around them,
search for new flowers with no time to fix their dresses.
Are their hearts the flowers, or are they something else?

990.
When a triumphant king wants to beg forgiveness,
one golden Lakshmi, her voice sweet as a lute, does not relent.
Later, after she calms down, she feels forlorn
and concocts a clever scheme deep in her mind:
send her parrot to her lover, then pretend to follow.[11]

991.
One man struck in the chest a million times by Kama's five arrows
has no idea what to do, he feels so overwhelmed.
Confused, he asks a woman with sandalwood on her breasts,
'Madhavi creeper, will you give me a mandara flower?'[12]

992.
One woman sulks and makes sure her lover knows it,
but her desire is also clear. She will not calm down,
but finds some fault, then visits each place her lover might have gone.
She picks flowers everywhere then makes a fragrant garland,
but as she adjusts it in the mirror, her heart begins to wilt.[13]

993.
One woman says, 'If my lover whose radiant spear feeds Yama
will not make love to me when I look like this,
there is no point to going further with this body in this life,
and what good does all this splendid jewellery do me?'
She took it all off, as if offering it to a singer.[14]

994.
A young woman sees a goose, and noting its delicate walk,
she tries to treat it like family, calling out to it, 'Friend!
Those who see you are gossips, so unfair. Take this dress to wear,'
and she approaches to give it some clothes.[15]

995.
One woman with a voice sweet as syrup sees a peacock coming
and hides behind a blossoming branch, afraid it will mistake
her love-mound in a sheer dress for a cobra poised to strike.
She trembles with fear, covering her eyes with palms like bouquets.[16]

996.
One woman suffers because of the pain in her waist,
which cannot hold her breasts that press against their band.
Another picks up a golden bowl in her gentle fingers
and murmurs tenderly to a parrot hidden in a flowering branch.

997.
A man no one else can equal calls out to his love,
'Catch me, my earth goddess, rare as gold, sweet as nectar!'
She challenges him, saying, 'First you have to catch me!'
and then laughs, covering her eyes dark as lilies.[17]

998.
One superb man picks a perfect lotus with his strong right hand
well used to drawing the bowstring past his left arm's leather bracer.
As he sees lotus faces blossoming on women with hair dark as night,
he wanders like the sun sending forth its crimson rays.[18]

999.
As evening comes, bees in the garden are the flute that softly hums,
the herdsman is Kama with his flower arrows,
and because he finds his mark, herding them together,
young men are like roaming proud bulls
and women with dark lily eyes surround them like cows.[19]

1000.
Some men who would shame even Kama if they were given
a bow of sugarcane cut from the fields, its juice like ambrosia,
want to hear the naive women who fill them with lust
for they take their prattle as the chanted Vedas.

1001.
Sages who have restrained their senses with their mind
have but one motto for Kama's bow: protection.
Not so when a woman like a vine is picking flowers:
the slight arch of her brow is more than enough.[20]

1002.
A man climbs a laurel tree to pluck flowers, and in his heart
a woman with scented hair and a charming brow climbs with him.
Men may become great, their wisdom grows,
but will they ever conquer women with full, proud breasts?

1003.
One man also climbs in a tree's branches,
but he cannot keep his thoughts or eyes off his love
whose body puts any goddess to shame,
so he plucks only buds and gives them to her.[21]

1004.
A man with arms large as clubs looks at his lover's face
as bees swarm around the blossoms in her hair.
He sees a quiver on her lip like a ripe ivy gourd
and hesitates, sensing the anger inside her.

1005.
All the groups of men and women together in that pristine garden
wanted to play in the river that lapped at its banks,
so they broke off from plucking flowers,
and went to swim in the river's bright waves.

Playing in the Water

1006.
They left the blooming gardens, men so perfect and women so divine
that in the pure heaven where karma ends
they would shame the gods themselves.
They came to tanks of water covered with flowers
like wild elephants coming to drink with their cows
as the bees fly up with a raucous buzz.

1007.
Seeing all the women dive together in fresh water
was to be there long ago when Durvasas erupted in fury,
a sage mighty as Shiva with the Ganga streaming from his hair,
and cursed all King Indra's wealth and his women
to plunge deep within the milk ocean's swelling waves.[1]

1008.
All the dark water lilies are women's eyes in bloom,
and the eyes of those beauties are blooming water lilies.
All the red lotuses are women's mouths in bloom
and the mouths of all those women shine as the red lotus.

1009.
The women grab musk, scented oils and fragrant powders
a feast for the bees, to throw at one another
while others pick up garlands to hurl as well.
Some spray their husbands with mouths red as ivy gourd
and others splash water with white lotus hands.[2]

1010.
Women like Lakshmi on her lotus cling to their men's chests,
others are conquering Vijayalakshmi sitting on men's shoulders.
Some toss water that burst out like areca palm flowers,
others hold their husbands tight, scared by twisting cutlassfish.

1011.
Women with waists thin as lightning, women with eyes like poison
sweep back the hair that falls from piled curls to hide their faces.
Some call out to the geese, 'Come over here to play with me!'
Others are hurt when flowers float past their gold-streaked breasts.[3]

1012.
Women sweet as sugarcane with waists too thin to see,
lily eyes, coral mouths that make music, ivy gourd and a lotus
see the carp that swim below and turn to ask their husbands,
'Do these tanks with swirling waters really all have eyes?'[4]

1013.
A woman like a goddess, fragrant flowers in her hair,
saw her own shapely figure appear on the water's surface.
'When I laugh, she laughs too!' she cried, her heart alive with joy,
'This girl with the beautiful brow, she must be my best friend!'
She took her pearls off her breasts and tossed them at herself.

1014.
Women whose hair is swarmed by bees climb up to the water's edge
yearning to hold their husband's arms, staves hard as diamond.
Earrings flash with rainbow light, necklaces shimmer with gems,
like flocks of gentle peacocks on a mountain touching heaven.

1015.
Who knows what he did, but one woman feels slighted by her man
and storms away, her eyes turning so red they look like shining fish.
She hides among red lotuses, and her husband goes to find her,
but doubt overcomes him for he cannot tell the lotuses from her face.

1016.
Conch bracelets, gold bracelets and others ring and chime
as women's hands splash the water and plunge back in for more.
When girdles made of flowers on their swelling love-mounds
fall off and wrap around their feet, they cry,
'A snake is coiled around my legs!' and faint from the shock.[5]

1017.
Women playing in the water join to form a circle
surrounding a man on every side while his broad armbands shine.
He stands there among them, a true king with a garland,
standing tall as Mandara surrounded by heavenly women
who rose up with the ambrosia the day the ocean was churned.

1018.
Within a group of women with bangles on their red lotus hands,
waists shaking like creepers, coral red mouths with fine white smiles,
a lordly man stands like a mad elephant as all his cows draw near
when he bathes in a mountain stream edged by fragrant lotuses.

1019.
Among a group of women with long hair dark as rainclouds
and a beauty so stirring it shames all peacocks in the forest,
a man stands like the bright moon as it draws near the Milky Way
ringed by all the constellations that rise to shine across the sky.

1020.
Among a beautiful group of women, there is one who shines,
and her perfect long eyes, besides being so attractive,
shoot Kama's five arrows from his sugarcane bow.
She stands, a single lotus in a pond
where water flowers everywhere are bursting into bloom.

1021.
A beauty stands with women like peacocks, and on her glowing face
her eyes glitter, fierce as cruel spears, shimmering like swords.
She is a divine creeper in golden blossom that rose from the milk sea
surrounded by flowering vines.

1022.
Love-mound like a chariot dais and breasts like tender coconuts,
one woman has beauty beyond reason, no matter where she goes.
When she dives, her breasts fall out of her tightly wrapped top,
and her face reflects a moon without flaw, shining in the water.

1023.
Men's arms that triumph over mountains,
women's broad love-mounds that surpass their dresses,
and breasts like waterpots all rush together,
pressing so close that the ponds flood their banks.

1024.
Crimson lips turn white and eyes grow red in turn,
fine creams applied to bodies wash away,
and dresses on girls with round breasts come loose
as bathing turns ponds into passionate husbands.

1025.
When ordinary people spend time with true sages
they too become filled with wisdom.
Even the fish here are scented with honey, musk
and oudh incense, what more could anyone ask for?

1026.
The sweet water is covered with young women's kumkum
mixed with sandalwood paste that washed off
when rubbed from the bodies of mighty lords:
a red sky spreads over dark clouds below.

1027.
Since all their oudh cream is gone,
rinsed off together with fragrant sandalwood paste,
women who speak words sweet as sugar
glow like polished gemstones.

1028.
The patterns traced in wet sandalwood paste
on the arms of a man like a pouncing lion
are washed off when he swims in the water,
and a gentle girl's dark, streaked eyes burn with anger.

1029.
One woman with a wide love-mound and beautiful jewels
burns with lust, and given all this searing heat,
the cool, rippling water is full of her scented powder,
fresh sandalwood paste, flower perfume and dusted pollen.

1030.
As a royal elephant pours sweet water from its trunk
to bathe Lakshmi as she sits on her red lotus,
a man with a garland on his broad shoulders
splashes water on a woman's civet-streaked hair.

1031.
Little goslings at rest on lotuses grow vexed
when a woman walks more gently than they ever could,
so they treat those flowers as her own shining feet
and trample them down in a show of fury.

1032.
As the sandalwood smeared on them washes away,
bare breasts look like golden pots crisscrossed with thread
wrapped by fingernails sharpened with care.
Shall I count the young men now seething with rage?[6]

1033.
A king who turns the wheel of command gives a sign
with a broad lotus hand that hangs down to his knees,
and a gentle girl with a mouth like ripe cadaba fruit
gives the answer to her friend with the corner of her eye.[7]

1034.
The water grows choppy as waves rise and fall
and lotuses bend, then sink in the water
as if they were hiding with shame in their hearts,
no match for the faces of girls with doe eyes.

1035.
The young men with thick anklets and the young women
who were playing in the water in these sorts of ways
climbed up the banks and left the ponds empty
to put on their jewels and their fine scented clothes.[8]

1036.
The swimmers left the broad pools of water
empty now, as if all their lotuses had gone,
like a sky where the stars have gone out
and the cool moon that joined them has stolen away.

1037.
The fiery sun had been watching these games
as men played in the water along with doe-eyed girls.
As if he, too, wanted to come and join them,
he slipped down and joined the fish deep in the western sea.

1038.
Like a king who still comes back to face his rivals
even after being routed because his force was weak,
once challenged on all sides by women's faces
the moon again appeared, to rally from his loss.

Drinking and Playing

1039.
Like a leaping flood of pure white toddy,
music given form and spreading everywhere,
or desire filling hearts, poured to overflowing,
the moon's cool light swept over the world.

1040.
To become the liquor that gives lovers pleasure,
a poison to scald the exhausted lives of couples kept apart,
a messenger newly made, to help women feigning quarrels,
the moonlight grows full, just as Kama the mind-churner wants it.[1]

1041.
All of the rivers become the white Ganga,
and the seas are the fabled milk ocean.
Every mountain is Kailasa, immortal Shiva's home:
what more need I say about the creamy thickness of the moon?

1042.
Since everyone, everything and every unsullied place
turns beautiful under the vivid white moonlight,
the whole sea-girt world seems to celebrate the birthday
of Kama with a sword hard as diamond and sea-monster banner.[2]

1043.
Women hid, screened from view,
in glowing bowers and flower groves set in crystal crags,
deep in groves where rolling clouds gather,
and shady awnings edged with pearls like rows of glittering stars.

1044.
As battle played out on beds strewn with flowers,
women with the scent of blossoms drifting from their hair
decided to enjoy themselves fully and drank fresh toddy
from golden cups, revelling in ambrosia made real.

1045.
Heavenly women from the starry sky, voluptuous women,
women from the magical world, women with doe eyes,
and women with perfect bodies took sips of toddy
as if pouring nectar back into flowers.

1046.
When one girl drinks, the rosy colour of her hand
makes her cup and its milky liquor turn red,
yet the toddy looks like white ambrosia as she sips it
and as it flows through her body, her kohl-streaked eyes turn red.[3]

1047.
Women, their hair scented with oudh smoke,
adorned with flower garlands and streaked civet musk,
drink the clear liquor, and lust bursts into flame
as when ghee is poured on the sacrificial fire.

1048.
One woman with a shining brow sees her own reflection
in a golden cup full of cool, sweet toddy and exclaims,
'Let's drink, my dear friend, and celebrate together!'
Is there anything more foolish than a woman,
sweet words like ambrosia, long eyes like poison?

1049.
A woman like a goddess, her waist so thin it seems ready to break,
hair piled high, a red mouth and dark eyes like poison-tipped spears
sees her face in her liquor. 'You're mad, what are you doing?
All this toddy, and you'll drink what I don't finish?
What a waste!' she laughs, and her teeth glow like jasmine buds.

1050.
Her eyes like spears set on murder or another sort of cruelty,
one woman thinks her crystal cup, opaque with light, is full.
She feels deep shame when she puts it empty to her lips
and everyone around her laughs.

1051.
One woman with a mouth like a red palash blossom
murmuring sweetly like lutes or gentle flutes
sees the reflection of her bladed eyes in her cup of cool toddy
and tries to shoo them off, sure those dark lilies are really bees.[4]

1052.
A woman with gold earrings and friendly eyes that glow with drink
gazes at the silvery moon reflected in her jar of toddy and calls,
'You're frightened of the serpent Rahu as he glides across the sky
and must have come down here to hide!
Don't be afraid,' she assures him, 'I will keep you safe.'

1053.
One woman sees her laughing face reflected in her cup
and thinks the moon has fallen from the sky in its thirst for liquor.
'I will give you this toddy if your heat subsides,
and you become cool when I quarrel with my carefree man!'

1054.
The flower hands of a woman with a nose as fine as a sesame flower
tremble as she splashes toddy all over her seat.
Too drunk to understand, she thinks it has returned to her cup
so she raises it to her ruby lips and turns it upside down.

1055.
One woman is scared to open her lotus mouth and drink,
so she sucks toddy from the jar with the hollow stem of a lily.
A swarm of bees, making constant circles in the sky,
buzz like beggars around a miser, clamouring for his riches.[5]

1056.
One woman as fine as a dancing peacock, her soft hair full of flowers,
has piercing eyes like swords pulled from leather sheathes
that could make brawling carp flee in lotus ponds where birds play.
Her husband is not drinking, and since her mind is fixed on him,
she never gives a moment to the thought of drinking toddy.

1057.
A woman with a navel like a whirlpool,
whether due to drunken thoughts or her own innocence,
thinks the rich moonlight is toddy as it pours through an awning
and raises her cup to catch some as it streams through the thatch.

1058.
A woman with a waist that shimmers like lightning
stumbles over words sweet as the gods' clear ambrosia.
She removes the girdle on her love-mound,
wraps her waist with garlands,
then takes off her golden necklace and puts it in her hair.

1059.
One woman could be an actor staging fury.
Her red eyes burn like Death, her arched brow rises high,
she grinds her lustrous teeth, and her perfect hands,
which put flower buds to shame, wave wildly about her.

1060.
A woman bites her quivering lip, an ivy gourd for her shining teeth
which put the white moon to shame.
Her eyes stare like vicious, bloodied spears,
and the sweat on her body looks like beads of splashed toddy.

1061.
The redness of one woman's lips, plump as an ivy gourd,
has left to enter her eyes, and on her perfect lotus face
her eyebrows are a war bow bent fully back.
Her brow, the crescent moon, glistens with cool dew
as she thinks one thing but speaks of another.

1062.
Lips red as cotton tree flowers lose their colour,
liquid honey flows over teeth to spill from open mouths,
knots come undone on dresses and breast bands,
tussled hair falls loose, and bodies are languorous:
how is toddy any different from a good lover?

1063.
'Go to my husband, dear friend, and tell him I have been undone
by Kama, whose war anklets jingle,' said one jewelled woman.
'But when you find him, will you be like my heart
and stay right there, or will you come back?'

1064.
One young woman with a doe's gentle gaze
sent all her dear friends, one after another
to go and find her husband. After they left,
she set out alone to find him.

1065.
A woman with a shining brow cooled by the scented breeze
held her pet parrot close to her breast and raged at it, crying,
'You refuse to leave now and bring back my man, he is my life!
What use are you to me? You're nothing but a krauncha bird!'[6]

1066.
One woman who lisps baby words sweet as honey
lay on a bed of flowers, a raft on the infinite sea of desire.
She joyfully held her parrot close
as it called out her husband's many names.

1067.
A woman gorgeous as a peacock, bangles stacked on her hands,
forced a smile when her husband cried his younger wife's name.
Her teeth are jasmine buds but tears pooled in her eyes,
spilling from those liquid fish in pattering drops.

1068.
One woman with golden bracelets, faking anger,
struggled to be free of her man who grabbed her girdle in lust.
Before the pearls fell from the girdle's torn thread,
tears from her eyes trickled down her cheeks.

1069.
A woman with flower petals scattered in her hair could not decide.
'Should I start quarrelling with my husband? Or make love,
and end the brutal lust that is burning up my life?
Or should I play the lute and praise his virtues in song?'

1070.
One woman was quarrelling with her husband
but did not tell her maids, choosing instead to play her carved lute.
Her hands turned red, like lotus blossoms spreading their petals
as she sang of the truth that lay within her heart.

1071.
A woman like a blossoming vine traced circles in the sand,
but each one she drew went astray and did not join.
Maimed by Desire's lethal arrows,
her sighs gave the only proof she still lived.[7]

1072.
A woman holding a ball her fingers made graceful
was unbearably lonely, and sent her maid to see her man.
He came to her, but she shut the door and would not let him in.
We may not know her thoughts, but we know her eyes burned red.[8]

1073.
Lying on a bed of flowers her friends had made
one woman decided to end her quarrel, but her lover did not know.
She shook off her feigned languor, giving signs for him to see,
stretched out her arms and legs and asked,
'How long have I been like this?'

1074.
Anger got the best of one woman,
and she kicked her man with her soft, red foot.
His pleasure was water on his body, a tended dry field,
and the seeds of a delicate passion once sown
became sprouts breaking earth, the hair thrilling on his skin.[9]

1075.
One handsome man, when he approached his love,
saw the tender buds on her couch of flowers
scattered as if Kama's own flower arrows had rained down,
and rejoiced when he saw they were all scorched black.

1076.
One man who had reaped enemy kings with his sword
saw how the breasts of his love were wasting away
and he felt a joy too great to contain,
his arms flexing wide, his face shining bright.

1077.
To one young man, a master of swordplay
so heated with lust the sandalwood smeared on his body burned up,
the breasts of his lover were golden pots filled with the holy water
his noble elders pour in blessing as they cry, 'Go, protect our land!'[10]

1078.
One woman decided to go to her man, as sweet as her own life.
She removed her jingling anklets and the girdle from her waist,
took off her jewellery and diamonds,
but looked up with fury at the villainous moon.[11]

1079.
The hands of one man were hard as diamond,
but he was like sugarcane crushed in the press.
The woman he loves, her voice sweet as a cuckoo in the garden
bound them tight with a flower garland
and he could not break it. Imagine its strength!

1080.
One woman with flowing hair glanced at a portrait of Kama
for she could not stand being apart from her man.
She looked at her friend, who at once saw her plight
and hurried off to see the lover with fine garlands.[12]

1081.
One woman graceful as a peacock, wearing golden earrings,
quickly ran to her man who carries a furious spear.
Her friend, who had been a go-between, called after her,
'Does toddy cloud your mind? Is it the setting sun?
Is it bodiless Kama himself? What makes you act this way?'[13]

1082.
One woman with a brow like the crescent moon
grew furious at the clear signs of her consuming desire,
and tears poured down from her dark, liquid eyes.
'What has happened to you?' asked her lover with a smile,
and she smiled back, leaving shyness behind.

1083.
One woman with a waist that suffers, so thin it disappears,
pushed away her lover's hands when he tried to hold her.
She knew what he wanted, but to him this shocking turn
was a sword driven straight through his chest.

1084.
One gentle woman took her maid's hands, revealing her desire,
and allowed herself to tell her, 'Go to him as my messenger...'
But she said no more, for shyness overwhelmed her,
and so she suffered throughout the endless night.

1085.
One woman very much in love with her man
turned to her friend with a garland in her hair,
but was too ashamed to say what her lover had done.
He is devoted to her wholly, he is her very life!
She could only stammer, making no sense with words.[14]

1086.
Two lives that seem separate became one,
their desires for each other the same.
A man and a woman joined their bodies together
and held each other close, knowing all this to be true.[15]

1087.
The heart of one woman with arms slim as new bamboo
flowed out to her husband when she happened to see him.
She quickly raised her pressed hands to revere him,
but he froze with fear: why so formal?[16]

1088.
One woman with an arched brow was apart from her husband
and, like the beauty of her body, she was wasting away.
Her maid returning alone and the sight of her mother
were like the scented southern breeze and the dark of night.[17]

1089.
One woman overwhelmed with desire
urged her mind to follow the messenger she had sent.
When evening came she seemed possessed by a god,
standing there staring, unable to form words.

1090.
One woman like a blossoming bough kept thinking of her husband
and waited, but her mind kept turning, like birth and death.
Like lightning in a raincloud, appearing and then vanishing,
she set off to find him, only to turn back.

1091.
One woman placed her hands stacked with bangles
on breasts that cannot be equalled in painting,
and felt the grievous wounds Kama's arrows cause.
She cried, she laughed, she could not express her pain,
but needing her maid as a messenger, she raised her pressed hands.[18]

1092.
'Is this useless or not?' one woman agonized.
Would anyone aware of her tortured heart, her misery,
need words to learn of her ruin?
She lay down, soaked with sweat, and looked over at her maid.

1093.
Kama rejoices far and wide, exulting thrice more
than the young women with full breasts.
A thief, he entered deep within their hearts,
wanting to drink up the clarity of their liquor.

1094.
Young men wearing garlands that swing from their topknots
joined women now ready for the ways of erotic texts.
The women took off their dresses and unfastened the fine chains
that ring with small bells on their broad, swelling love-mounds,
then cast them aside, like drums proclaiming the news.
Now were they ready for those rare, secret deeds?[19]

1095.
Who cares that a woman with a charming brow
removed her dress and the jewellery underneath!
She cast away the modesty that lives deep within her.
Like a man of great strength, intent on ascetic power,
the way to discard ego lies in passion, does it not?

1096.
Take a man equal to Kama, no other likeness does justice,
and a woman like Lakshmi seated on her lotus throne:
neither loses to the other in the battle on their bed.
Both share one consciousness, one breath of life,
so how could one of them win?

1097.
One woman had eyes like swords seeking to pillage in battle,
and her love, fine as Murugan, shielded his chest with lotus hands.
She saw this and cried, 'You cover yourself because of your lies!'
She was sure he deserved a kick for wrongdoing,
and then she grew angrier still.[20]

1098.
A gentle woman with eyes that slice like spears,
full breasts, soft arms of equal beauty,
and a mouth red as coral that holds sweet milk,
made a man with hands generous as rainclouds feel total desire,
passion deep as the sea for the woman he knows is a goddess.

1099.
One woman, delightful as a peacock on the wooded slopes
was incensed by thoughts of her husband's lies,
but when the battle on their bed began,
the lust in her heart conquered her resolve.

1100.
One woman with eyes so cruel they are murder given form
and a love-mound that swells, visible beneath her dress,
held her husband so tightly she checked to see
if her breasts pierced his chest stronger than a mountain.

1101.
When young men enjoy new pleasures with young women,
braided hair fell loose, kumkum tracings crumbled,
dresses slipped off, stacked conch bracelets jingled
and anklets roared like thunder.

1102.
One sulking woman wearing jewels, gorgeous as a peacock,
feigned sleep, but her heart kept throbbing,
for passion bests a wounding quarrel as the blazing sun melts frost.
She held her husband close, as if acting on a dream.

1103.
When a young man joined his lover,
a woman like a peacock with a round, lustrous face,
they held each other close, never to let go.
Bodies became one for they could not imagine two,
and they did not see the newly breaking dawn.

1104.
A man strong as an elephant in musth
joined a woman with dark hair in the battle of love.
Like a waist that cannot bear full breasts pressed tight,
nighttime weakened and faded away.

1105.
The moon disappeared, like a fortune gained only in part
by those blind to its full worth,
and like the king of jewels on the supreme lord's chest
the sun arose from the dark stormy ocean.[21]

The Welcoming Party

1106.
King Dasharatha, master of the arts who never turns to cruelty
and who never wavers from the laws of the precious Vedas,
master of the white parasol and the righteous sceptre,
rode his elephant, a clothed mountain, in the ocean of his army
where rivers of rut flow like rushing mountain streams
and he approached the River Ganga.

1107.
The army, a sea of men, drank so much water from the Ganga
it dried up to reveal its sands, then the underworld appeared,
the realm of the nagas with forked tongues.
The salty ocean thirsted too, craving the Ganga's fresh water.

1108.
The lord of the vast earth travelled on, to reach
the city of Mithila, its rice fields soaked with water.
Let us turn to a man named Janaka, with solid arms like iron pillars,
a lord who grants vital favour, whose cavalry horses race and leap.

1109.
Surrounded by elephants that break their hitching posts,
chariots, and the bridled horses of his cavalry, Janaka was overjoyed.
The moon, it seemed, was joining the sun
approaching to welcome a lord richer than Indra.[1]

1110.
The troops of Dasharatha, master of the land where the Ganga flows,
were like the oceans joined together with all their conches blowing.
The welcoming army of King Janaka, father of young Sita,
was like the milk ocean that brought forth Lakshmi on her lotus.[2]

1111.
Since Janaka's armed troops came as the seventh sea,
all the oceans filled with sea monsters, full to overflowing,
can only be compared to the earth gathered in one place,
all infantry, horses, chariots and elephants united.

1112.
White parasols decked with garlands, peacock-feather parasols
and other regalia joined together, hiding the sky on all sides
so that daylight faded and the night appeared
over a vast bed of lotuses, red mixed with white.[3]

1113.
Lakshmi cannot decide about this flawless, eloquent king.
Is she at home on his chest, or on his crown?
Is she on his victory banner, on his supreme parasol,
in the ocean of his marshalled army, or part of his noble lineage?

1114.
The charming sound of bees that merrily hum
on the dark hair of women whose breasts strain their breast bands
is the sound of music in all seven tones,
the rumble of chariots, the roar of clear waves,
the trumpeting of bull elephants, the boom of the rainclouds.

1115.
It is easy to describe how the dust arose
joining the seven isles of the earth together,
how it turned the vast sea around this new earth into a sandy knoll.
It flew up to soar through the hole made long ago
by Vishnu's own foot when he traversed the three worlds.*

---

*See vv. 429–50.

1116.
The dazzling gems set in heavy golden jewellery
flashed like lightning, shone like rainbows,
glowed like the moon and blazed like the sun,
but the wide parasols crowded together to hide the sky,
and the cool shade they offered let darkness survive.

1117.
When the faultless lord Dasharatha arrived,
mighty Janaka, holding a bow used to arrows,
had made the dust along the way ready for welcome.
Now it was fresh scented powder, fine gold dust
and a fine mist of nectar from flowers.[4]

1118.
Blended with civet musk, delicate saffron,
oudh powder, the scented nectar of flowers,
droplets of deer musk, fragrant salves, and pure sandalwood cream,
mud mixed with torrents of elephant rut to make a lavish paste.

1119.
The even shadow from huge flags and vast canopies
and the shadows under white victory parasols
flashed with light from the jewels on palace women
but still offered shade to all.

1120.
Janaka looked at the troops of the perfect, dominant king
and when the army of this joyful lord approached
the sound was as noisy as a river rushing
into a thundering, shimmering ocean in storm.

1121.
With a marvellous dignity prompted by love,
Janaka, commander of elephants that strain at their tethers,
approached on his chariot with the swiftness of thought
to face worthy Dasharatha, the father of all on earth.[5]

1122.
Janaka rode up, his troops ranked behind him,
then stepped down from his chariot and walked towards the king.
Dasharatha's joyful face shone, and he beckoned Janaka to join him,
so the lord climbed up, and the king held him tight to his chest.

1123.
Like a lion standing before a tiger, greater than all others
Dasharatha, still keeping Janaka in his embrace,
asked after the health of the king's family and retinue,
then gladly declared, 'Let us enter the city.'

1124.
The two kings went on, and Rama, in every way their equal,
the young man who had reached out his hand
and broken the immense golden bow of the god red as fire,
looked forward to his welcome in the vast, thriving city.

1125.
Rama, whom gods, humankind, and nagas should worship,
was surrounded by Janaka's army, along with his younger brother.
With Janaka's soldiers and horses from Mithila around them,
they ascended a golden, gem-studded chariot and rode into the city.

1126.
As the two noble youths approached their righteous father,
the army surrounded them with Janaka at the fore.
Who could gauge its enormous size, impossible to reckon,
with so many horses, chariots and elephant bulls and cows?

1127.
The young man whose feet are worshipped by gods,
so impossibly beautiful that any portrait of him painted
in hues of lotus, lily, and the vivid kaya flower* looks drab,
neared the presence of the king, and it seemed a shining life
earlier split apart was made whole again.

---

*The kaya tree blooms with striking purple flowers.

1128.
The army came and bowed at Rama's feet, then drew back,
and Rama touched the king's golden anklets and arose.
Dasharatha embraced him, and Rama's own massive arms,
which once turned a true mountain of a bow into a plaything,
disappeared in the chest of a king truly known as Manu.*

1129.
Young Lakshmana approached the lord greater than all others,
famed in heaven and on earth for ending their harsh distress.
He touched his feet, then arose, and Dasharatha held him
tight against his chest adorned with a thick flower garland.[6]

1130.
Lordly Rama, who reached out with his broad, conquering hands
to break the mighty bow of the god with a crown of matted locks
bowed to revere his three mothers in turn.
When he stood before them,
could anyone describe the joy that filled their hearts?

1131.
Tears poured from Bharata's lustrous eyes in waves
streaming down as if his great love simply had to overflow.
He touched Rama's feet and arose,
then Rama hugged him to his golden chest
with the same love his father had shown
and two lives joined as one.

1132.
Noble Lakshmana and Shatrughna whom all the world praises
as younger brothers exalted by their perfect love of dark Rama,
touched their crowned heads with hair dressed and scented
to Bharata's feet, and then Rama's in turn.

---

*The royal primogenitor of humankind, archetype of the perfect ruler.

1133.
The four brothers, princes who uphold the four perfect Vedas,
shone with honour just like their worthy father
who in the shade of his parasol and the justice of his sceptre
was truly a man of remarkable wealth.

1134.
The king with a straight sceptre, a clear emblem of his rule,
a lord with such compassion he is the mother of his subjects,
looked over all the riches assembled in his presence,
knew Rama to be the finest, and told him, 'Lead the way!'[7]

1135.
We cannot fathom the love felt by the soldiers strong as elephants,
their happiness was pure. Was it fleeting? It was total!
When Rama, wearing a crown decked with garlands
advanced to lead them, his own father's joy echoed in their hearts.[8]

1136.
His brothers surrounded him, love constant in their hearts
and mounted strong horses to honour him as they followed.
Then, as the conches roared and kettle drums pounded,
Rama mounted a splendid chariot and quickly set off.

1137.
Groups of women in tall mansions cloaked in soft clouds
raced to the doorways, their soft feet stained with lac.
Their stares fell upon him, ruthless as poison,
when Rama entered Mithila as flowers rained down
and he passed through its thick walls to reach the royal street.

1138.
Stacked bangles jingled, garlands fell loose in women's hair,
round breasts had nipples harder than rutting elephants' tusks
and anklets on lotus feet stamped out the rhythms set by Bharata.*
Are the courtyards of fine mansions not stages for dance?

1139.
When the king of gods, the foremost lord, came down the street
women raced to join him as Desire rained arrows down.
Dark-haired women, from children to older women, came running,
and now I shall tell you what happened to them there.[9]

---

*The Natyashastra of Bharata, a foundational prescriptive text on dramatic and artistic performance.

The Procession

1140.
Approaching like a group of does, roving like a peacock flock,
glittering like a set of stars, gathering like lightning bolts,
swarming bees hummed and anklets shimmered everywhere
as women rushed into a crowd, braids damp with fresh blossoms.

1141.
No care for braids that had fallen loose, no eye for girdles missing,
no hold on fine dresses falling down, no break for punished waists:
crowded in, they crowded more, 'Give me room, I need some room,'
women fine as gems pressed close, bees swarming to drink nectar.

1142.
Flower feet danced, anklets jingled, and slim waists suffered
as women with beautiful eyes ran like fresh water into a valley,
blue lotuses blossoming in a vast flood,
rushing forth as if Rama dragged them in,
knowing their hearts had been caught.

1143.
They saw nothing but lust in each others' eyes, and said,
'Now we obtain the reward that a good woman can expect!'
They seemed like herds of does in summer's heat
when the earth dries out and no rain falls down from the skies
seeing good water and racing to drink.

1144.
Like flies buzzing on honey, women swept into the street
to see the feet that redeemed Ahalya, so red she could have drunk blood,
and the arms broad as a mountain, so strong they broke the bow
to win the girl with dark, sweet hair.

1145.
He came on a chariot yoked to quick horses
past the eyes of the women who stared, never blinking,
as though he were walking right down in the street.
Everyone saw the truth of the name good men chose to praise him,
'He has come, a Krishna for everyone!'[1]

1146.
'His chariot is racing past,' cried women to each other,
'It's here right now but moving too fast, how can this be?'
As they wailed, crazed in their anguish,
one beauty trapped this man who once passed
beyond the earth, beyond the sky where gods dwell,
keeping him so he could not pass the confines of her eyes.

1147.
One woman stood there raining everything down
her bangles and her rustling dress, her culture and her virtues,
the glow of her skin, her reason, mind, and blooming beauty,
her diamond jewellery, modesty and childlike ways:
everything but her life.

1148.
One woman stood raining tears like a cloud
from glittering eyes that swept back to her earrings.
Her firm breasts, so full a thread could not fit between them,
were pierced by arrows fired by Desire from his sugarcane bow,
and she trembled, barely able to stand, her waist like
a bolt of lightning free of clouds.

1149.
We'll never be able to say how it happened,
did those long, forceful eyes of these women with red fingers
suffuse the darkness in the body of the lord,
or did the sapphire hue of his thundercloud body
darken the women's kohl-streaked eyes?

1150.
A woman with a bright brow and a body the hue of the mango leaf
watched Kama wage battle, firing his flower arrows.
'Doesn't he see the king's army, or the full strength of Rama's bow?
What kind of man shoots arrows at women with elegant jewels?'

1151.
A woman like a peacock stood, heart melting, skin blanching,
with sweat on her arched brow as she lit up her surroundings.
Fierce as Death, her eyes were like triumphant, killing spears,
which saw nothing else but him. She asked, 'Is the lord alone?'

1152.
One woman stood as if an artist who had never known pleasure
painted the truth of a supreme passion into one perfect form.
She kept the honour of her virtue, but all her jewels fell off,
her body collapsed, and she held up only her dress.

1153.
One woman with hair black as ink, a red mouth and bright brow
felt her heart giving way and called out to her friend,
'This rogue has made his way to my heart! I've trapped him there,
closed the door to my eyes, and now I feel ready for bed.'

1154.
One woman like a perfect sculpture
never saw Desire's arrows pierce her young body,
never felt her dress and knotted girdle come apart.
She watched every woman gaze at his perfect figure
and fire burned in her eyes.

1155.
A woman with eyes like spears, so long they touch her hair,
joyful and deep, concealing her guile and showing it too,
plunging in to pierce the heart, so white, so black, so red,
came to watch with joy in her heart
then took refuge in her home.[2]

1156.
Tresses of hair, full breasts bound tight, and girdled waists
were packed so close nothing else could be seen.
One suffering woman with wide, full eyes
burned with desire to see Rama's beauty
but finding no room, saw the compassionate lord
through the space between waists.

1157.
Bodiless Kama, his sword at the ready,
rained arrows deep in women's hearts,
and the falling girdles, heaps of jewels, pearls, bangles,
sandalwood washed off by the sweat on their breasts,
and flowers falling from flowing hair
left no trace of bare street to be seen.

1158.
Those who looked at his arms could see nothing but arms,
those who looked at his lotus feet could see nothing but feet,
those who looked at his broad hands, just those and no more.
Of those women with eyes like swords, who saw his body in full?
They were like those who looked at his infinite form* long ago.

1159.
So one woman with flowing hair and a tiny waist
could truly live when he shrank to rest inside her heart.
Who could be greater than this lord
who held the whole world in his stomach?

1160.
One woman with long wavy hair and well-chosen jewels
drew close to him, walking like a perfect flowering vine
her anklets and girdle jingling,
but was carried back in the arms of her crestfallen maids.

---

*The vishwarupa, see v. 957.

1161.
One woman with fine jewels and full breasts cried,
'For the sake of one poor girl, you took a bow
and crushed it into dust, righteous man.
Protect me, even if you have an iron heart!
Break the sugarcane bow, take me for your own.'

1162.
'This man who has prevailed over trials stops his chariot,'
called a woman with a bright brow and dark eyes traced with kohl,
'then he comes and stands right before me!
Is this all illusion? All a dream?'

1163.
One woman with no messenger to send, beside herself,
felt her sweet life slipping away and cried,
'This Sita, with gold earrings, red-streaked eyes like flowers,
and breasts adorned with gold and jewels,
what penance did she do?'

1164.
One perfectly sculpted woman gasped, cried,
and started to faint, panting with hot breaths.
She called out to a loving friend,
'Was it Kama, then, who drew this vision of a man?'

1165.
'When you think about his qualities,'
said a woman with bright mouth and radiant brow,
'is there any man who comes close?
I tell you he is Krishna! Just look, you will see.'

1166.
'This faultless man has come to our city,'
said a woman with a radiant brow, pitifully frail in her lust,
as her gold anklets fell off, her bangles too.
'The reward for every good deed done for Janaka's sake is here!'

1167.
'Maybe he will come alone,'
called a woman wearing a golden girdle
suffering terribly, ruining her looks as her tears rained down,
'away from sages and noble kings who crowd in,
if only in my dreams?'

1168.
One woman with gold bangles,
like a peacock enjoying the clouds on high fields,
thought she could conceal the lust kept close within her heart,
but the bodiless god has seen it all before.
Can a face conceal a private truth as easily as the heart?

1169.
One woman with long eyes, wearing splendid jewels
lay down on her flower-strewn bed.
Shining with health, her full, tightly bound breasts
burned as she panicked, and her breath came in gasps
like a snake who feels thunder coming.[3]

1170.
These women with red lips, like lilies wet with nectar
trembled as their spirits reeled within.
They tasted none of the pleasure Sita felt,
her slender waist trembling weary,
but somehow or other they lived.

1171.
'This godly man,' one woman called,
'sees none of these women sobbing in pain,
bodies sweating, spirits ebbing,
not with his fine eyes, nor in his thoughts,
is there love in him at all?'

1172.
The women obsessed with his chariot were endless,
and there was no end to the noble lord's beauty.
Shooting with his golden bow, what else could Kama do?
His arrows spent, he gripped the hilt of his sword.

1173.
As well as the women with long, fragrant braids
we may speak of the war that Desire, god of summer, waged above
on the women who live in the heavenly land
as his darts flew to plunge in their breasts.

1174.
'He goes,' said one woman, 'and just keeps on going,
a man who spurns women left stunned by their fantasies!
What is he, a man with no hint of compassion?
Some perfect mystic? Some brutal killer?'

1175.
One woman with a waist on the verge of collapse
since her hot breasts traced with painted lines are so heavy
sensed nothing of her body, nothing of her hands,
and even as they said, 'She'll live, she'll live,'
she fell down and lay quite still.

1176.
Like people who swing on planks tied to areca palms,
a sweet woman went after the warrior's chariot
coming and going, coming and going
until her flower feet grew rough.
Now what a way to do things!

1177.
Among the women driven crazy by their lust,
one saw another standing there and thought,
'Did she see where my mind just went?'
Doesn't shyness always follow after tasting desire?

1178.
One Lakshmi said, 'His forefather gave up his life
so the subjects he loved could live!
But he will not give us sweet lives of our own,
how did he become so cruel?'[4]

1179.
'When you wonder why he broke that protecting bow,'
said a woman overwhelmed by the sound of his name,
'it was just to show his expertise, it wasn't because he loved Sita,
that sweet-sounding peacock with a long scented braid.'

1180.
Her necklace falling, dress falling, all her jewellery falling
as her sweet life fell away, a woman with long hair fallen free
said, 'He's murdering me in front of this man with a dreadful bow!
Who is stronger than Desire, the god of death?'

1181.
As women fell apart like this, the caring lord moved on
and surrounded by a crowd of kings, approached the marriage hall
where Vasishtha and all-knowing Kaushika, master of the Vedas,
stood ready to perform the wedding.

1182.
Like a vast cloud that sweeps over the ground,
Lakshmi's lord lay down at their feet, his necklace twisting
like a bolt of lightning as its pristine gems swayed,
and he revered them as tradition ordains.

1183.
He worshipped, and at the word of those two great sages,
the man born in Ayodhya to keep dharma safe in the world
ascended to the throne strewn with flowers,
and so close to his famed brothers they seemed like shadows
he glowed, he truly glowed.

1184.
Then Dasharatha, leader of vast armies,
reached the jewelled marriage hall with his retinue
like the moon surrounded by the gathered stars
that came to illuminate the sky.

1185.
He entered, bent low to touch the sages' feet,
then he ascended the throne
as a rain of fresh flowers poured down from above
and Indra turned his face in shame.

1186.
There were Gangas, the Kongus, Kalingas and Telugus,
the rulers of the Sinhalas, the Cheras, the Pandyas,
the kings of Anga, Kulinga, and Avanti,
the Vanga kings, the Malava kings, the Cholas, the Marathas,[5]

1187.
The mighty kings of Magadha, the Maccha kings, foreign kings,
and still more, the heroic Lata kings, the kings of Vidarbha,
the Chinese kings, the Seguna kings, the Sindhi kings, the Panchala kings,
the Sonaka lords, the Muslim kings, the Kuru kings.[6]

1188.
Joined by armed Yadavas, the kings of Chedi*
and the seven valiant Konkani kings,
the finest of men all crowded close,
kings with shining crowns beaming light into the sky.

1189.
Held by women who speak words sweeter than sugarcane,
chowries glittered at Dasharatha's sides
as brilliant as the light of a noble fame
laid out in an anthology.

---

*Southern Madyha Pradesh.

1190.
Women, their hair dark as black sand
swarmed by black bees, honeybees, drones and dragonflies,
sang out in praise, joining flutes and gentle lutes
until music filled the air.

1191.
That supreme white parasol of the king
as strong as an elephant with fiery eyes,
the moon watched Sita's wedding as the father of her line,*
rising high, overflowing with favour,
showing how much his family had thrived.

1192.
Packed in so tight no one could move,
the army stood as one, a vast, mighty sea.
The land of King Janaka, lord of horses and elephants,
looked like one immense city.

1193.
The father of that girl with a fine brow followed his heart
and handed over all his worldly wealth,
rejoicing in his guests' celebration.
He felt pure love for Rama and the lowly alike:
what more is left to say?

*Sita is of the lunar lineage.

Creating Beauty

1194.
As Dasharatha sat with his queens in a royal hall so marvellous
the paintings in Indra's own chambers might have come to life,
Vasishtha smiled at Janaka holding his sceptre, white parasol aloft,
and called for Sita, a lovely Lakshmi, to be summoned before them.[1]

1195.
Janaka raised his pressed hands to accept the sage's request,
then turned to his palace women who wore precious jewels
and ordered them to bring Sita, queen of women, before them.
Driven by immense love, the women with voices like honey
hastened to give the king's order to Sita's ladies in waiting.

1196.
Sita's maids knew her dazzling jewellery would not veil her beauty.
Are the eyes not more pleasing because eyelids hide them?
They adorned her, placing beauty on her beauty
as if trying to infuse a flavour more exquisite than ambrosia
unknown to this world bound by the wave-tossed sea.

1197.
Sita's thoughts never strayed from the hue of Krishna's* body,
they rose in her heart like vines creeping over the earth.
Her maids adorned her black hair, upswept in a bun
with a garland of flowers, like the moon next to a cloud.

1198.
On her brow they placed a brilliant jewel strung on a golden chain
as if the stars that dictate fate had caught the crescent moon.
They adorned the front of her hair with jewellery
that made it seem like a black raincloud,
sticking out its tongue at the moon, trying to make it laugh.[2]

---

*On Rama as Krishna, see v. 1145.

1199.
They adorned her with gleaming earrings that swayed
like Sita's heart as she doubted herself, her weary life reeling
wondering whether the hero who broke the fearsome bow of Shiva,
the god who holds the flooding Ganga in his matted locks,
was the same man who had enthralled her female perfection.

1200.
They hung the best of her splendid jewels around her neck
as if Lord Vishnu's splendid conch had come to join her.
When Sita is the gem for every woman who wears a wedding cord,
what other ornament could be right for her?[3]

1201.
Was the strand of pearls on her breasts bright with jewellery
the constellations in the sky, matched in size and strung together?
Or was it the glowing crescent moon split and made into a circle?
Was it the cool moonlight that appeared in Sita's modest smile?
I say a refreshing light swept over her, what else is there to tell?

1202.
Sita's divine body shone like ambrosia,
she turned lotuses red when her tiny feet touched them
and her white pearls glowed red on her charming breasts.
People do shine when they befriend the righteous!

1203.
Sita's breasts were like vermilion jewel boxes,
and her waist quivered beneath them,
but just one thing compared to her arms bright with jewellery:
young bamboo holding pearls and crimson rubies
flashing so brightly they forced eyes to close.[4]

1204.
Sita's hair was decked with a garland of flowers,
and her hands were red lotuses that had done penance

to take Rama's red hands as the Vedas command.
They do not close at night, and seem to glow with moonlight
so her maids placed bangles on her hands for their own protection.[5]

1205.
They used deer musk mixed with sandalwood
to trace Kama's bow and divine creepers on Sita's round, full breasts,
gold water pots each inlaid with an emerald,
and her hair was combed in a wedding style.
The designs hurt her waist invisible to everyone,
like the supreme being studied by all the different creeds.[6]

1206.
They adorned young Sita's hips,
covered by the pleats of her fine silken dress,
with a girdle and the pearl ornament called 'carrying the stars'.
The rainbow of gems she wore accented her red body
so the bright eyes of everyone around her dimmed.

1207.
On Sita whose waist is like a dancing cobra's hood,
around her lotus feet red without lac, they wrapped anklets,
more exquisite than flowers that fade when they are smelled
to ring loudly on her delicate feet, those wondrous delicate feet.

1208.
Sita's eyes, streaked with red, paired ambrosia with poison,
they went out to her ears then came back, unable to go on.
They blossomed wide, fresh as a raincloud, without deceit or guile,
should we say they were black from kohl or Rama's dark body?

1209.
As if placing a star in the centre of a perfect crescent moon
rising on a lotus blossom where two flourishing lilies bloom,
they placed a tilak on Sita, herself like a tilak even finer
than women on earth, in heaven, and in the serpent world.[7]

1210.
Loose flowers, fragile flowers in her hair,
flowers atop her head and fresh flowers placed over her ears
all shone like flowers budding in heaven
as rock bees, hive bees, honey bees, and black bees swarmed,
and they covered her with a powder golden as laurel pollen.

1211.
They waved the burning ghee lamp before her,
scattered flowers and fresh water, worshipped the family god,
made a gift of pure gold to the masters of the Vedas,
placed tiny white mustard seeds and harialli grass on her head,
waved red rice mixed with water in front of her,
then walked around Sita, the peacock who thrives under their care
and placed water on her forehead.[8]

1212.
Her maids stood there overwhelmed,
stammering, their femininity in doubt,
as they drank in the beauty of Sita
who teaches sweet words to the parrots,
which are like bees drinking the lotus nectar that brings them joy.
What differs between men and women in ways the heart can feel?

1213.
These gorgeous women, their glossy hair dark as a raincloud,
stood there enchanted, looking at Sita,
whose breasts gave jewellery beauty, as if she were the full moon.
Every part of women's bodies provokes desire.
If it were all to be there at one time, in one place,
who could possibly stand it?

1214.
Because she wears conch bangles and she dwells in a lotus
as he wields the Panchajanya conch and has lotuses for eyes,
and her exquisite beauty spreads everywhere like he does

pervading everything as if inscribed in all hearts,
Sita, her virtue as pure as Arundhati's, is like Lord Rama.
How can I compare her to anything else?

1215.
As Sita's girdle on her broad hips, the bees at her hair,
her foot rings, ankle chains, and anklets shaped like a serpent
all rang, chimed and hummed,
countless women who prattle sweet childish words went with her,
like heavenly dancers around Indrani, Indra's queen.

1216.
Dwarves, little people, hunchbacks and maids crowded together,
surrounding Sita to worship her feet.
Shaded by an awning covered with jewels,
she walked like a glowing lamp towards the wedding canopy,
like the new moon coming with the gathered constellations.

1217.
The light from the gems on Sita's jewellery swept over the land
as if the earth goddess who gave birth to this blooming vine
feared the ground might cause her delicate feet some pain,
and lay down a blanket of flowers and tender budding branches.

1218.
Happy geese could not match her dainty stride and began to fly off
but then settled back on the ground, feeling miserable.
The fly-whisks swept back and forth, delicate as tender sprouts
as Sita walked like a peacock displaying its train.[9]

1219.
She walked shaded by a shining canopy,
as if the sun, the first of noble Rama's line,
had swept down from heaven to see the gorgeous maiden Sita
whom every woman in every world beginning with the earth
is right to praise as the sparkle in their own eyes.

1220.
As her jewellery and waist ornament of sixteen gold strands
sparkled like a war bow and gleamed like a sword,
Sita walked on her small, red feet, her tiny waist trembled,
and her body and jewellery blazed like lightning.

1221.
The lustre of gold, the scent of flowers, the beauty of sandalwood
and the sheen of lightning all merged with Sita's divine body,
putting geese, celestial dancers and precious ambrosia to shame
as she entered the wedding canopy that held the gathered kings.[10]

1222.
Every man and every woman with arms like bamboo stared at Sita,
perfect as a painting, weighed down by her round breasts,
herself a Veda, for no one created her,
and they could not blink their eyes, nor draw a single breath.

1223.
Rama, dark as the deep blue sea, stared at that heavenly girl,
unsure if she was the same woman he had seen before.
He struggled when he recognized her, striving to stay solemn,
as joyful as Indra when the ambrosia rose from the milk sea.

1224.
'She has a voice like a cuckoo and lovely lips like coral,'
Rama thought, 'and was brought before me on her terrace
like the fruits of good karma and ambrosia aged to perfection.
Besides dwelling in my heart, here she is outside as well!'

1225.
Vasishtha was elated, and thought, 'He is Vishnu, the supreme being,
come as Rama because of the ascetic deeds those like me have done,
lord of all worlds with lovely eyes who wields the conch and discus,
so this Sita is truly Lakshmi who rules from her lotus throne.'

1226.
Dasharatha, who turns the single wheel of command over the earth
with a righteous sceptre that treats everyone equally,
saw the beauty of Sita with thick, curly hair and thought,
'Even if I rule the seven worlds forever,
I have gained all its wealth today.'

1227.
As soon as Sita entered, her voice sweet as the naivalam mode,
everyone but the great ascetics and Rama, delight of the world,
raised their pressed hands in reverence.
Their senses told them she was a goddess:
does the mind not govern the body?[11]

1228.
In place of her lotus throne, she entered the king's golden palace
then raised her hands to revere the mighty ascetics there.
She kneeled to touch the emperor's feet, then went to her father
and sat at his side as tears of joy poured from his eyes.

1229.
The brahman Kaushika, who perceived the divine light in her,
thought that if Rama, his body like a fresh gamboge leaf,
knew he would gain Lakshmi, her eyes like leaf-bladed spears,
sitting in state on her lotus throne,
he would have broken seven mountains more
than the one he already broke.[12]

1230.
Sita had heard that a man bent Shiva's bow and broke it,
and when she saw the truth of this standing before her,
her earlier doubts fell away.
Rama's form was in her heart, and now he stood before her,
so she shifted the bangles on her arm to give him a sidelong glance.

1231.
When the river of sidelong glances from her wide, dark eyes
swept into the vast sea of dark Rama,
she drew healing breaths, her life grew steady,
and Sita, whose finest jewel was her chastity,
felt her body swell like a god who drinks the rare ambrosia.

1232.
Sita, round earrings on her ears,
realized that this prince, the thief who stole her heart,
had broken Shiva's bow, and she forgot every sorrow.
She realized God within her,
and the ignorance that causes suffering in life fell away,
as if she had gained the joy of liberation
through the ripened fruit of perceived truth.

1233.
Dasharatha, king of kings, master of murderous elephants,
turned to Kaushika, sage of endless learning, and said,
'Please tell us, great one. When is the day of countless blessings,
the wedding day for my daughter whose waist is as thin as a vine?'

1234.
'Lord of Kosala, that fertile land where scabbard fish leap,
carp bite the heads and backs of buffalo resting in the water,
and powerful murrel fish leap high, splitting the palm spathes open,
tomorrow is the proper day for the wedding,' the great ascetic said.

1235.
Once Kaushika had spoken, the emperor rose from his throne,
and as the gathered kings revered him with pressed hands,
the massive conches blared, and his crown shone like the dawn,
he bid goodbye to the ascetics and entered his palace.

1236.
Walking gently as a goose,
Sita turned from the place she never wanted to leave,
and Rama left too, entering a palace with a soaring golden terrace.
The kings adorned with jewels left with the great ascetics
as the blazing sun came down to set behind Mount Meru.

A Splendid Wedding

1237.
Famed Janaka refreshed his guests so thoroughly,
great kings with rutting elephants, grand ministers beneath them,
and lowly servants with powerful bodies and strength to spare
felt like they had gone to heaven while in their living bodies.

1238.
When people are sick with thirst
and wander in search of fresh, clean water,
then see a nearby pond but have no way to get there,
their strength ebbs and they feel faint, can they think clearly?
Sita, her voice like a cuckoo, suffered this awful plight.

1239.
'Where would you find liars who tie a thread around their wrists
and vow to destroy the lives of women who are helpless?
Nighttime, you are ruthless!
You still won't leave, for when the sun rises,
the lord who has taken me as his slave will come for me.[1]

1240.
'My heart, you went to the feet of my lord who is a black sun
and you will be near him the day he comes back for me.
You have been with me forever, never letting me be for a moment:
will you ever lose patience and finally let me be?

1241.
'Krauncha bird on your palmyra tree, you never fly alone.
If nighttime, vast as the seven loud seas, never breaks into dawn
because I have done wrong and my bad karma hurts me,
you will have no honour, and I will blame you for my ruin!*

---

*See v. 1065.

1242.
'Your rays, moon, are like sharp spears that flow with fire,
and you blaze with a burning heat. Tell me,
is there anyone else who enjoys capturing the lives
of people like me, innocent even as you grind our bodies down?

1243.
'Sweet southern wind with your charming perfumes, you are a tiger!
At home in the giant caves of Mount Malaya,
you prowl after me, roaring, as your mouth blasts fire
baring teeth that are glowing moonbeams.

1244.
'A hero as beautiful as a black cloud came down this street,
and he follows me day and night without ever leaving.
How does he do it? Are there kings of noble birth
who can come right up to unmarried women?[2]

1245.
'The hero who acts with blind cruelty does not hold me close,
but my desire? It drives me to a man who shows me no favour!
This night, is it a vast black ocean? I cannot see the shore,
and time keeps dragging over the aeons.

1246.
'All the music will never stop, the daytime never comes,
my thoughts can never be avoided, nighttime never ends.
Pain in life never leaves, my breathing never stops,
and my eyes never close in sleep,
is this the price I have to pay?[3]

1247.
'Are you a virgin like me, ocean?
The conches spill from you, rising up then falling down,
your body is listless, but you do not sleep the entire day.
Do you fear Kama's lethal arrows? Tell me!'[4]

1248.
Sita thought these things as she suffered so much,
exhausted in her heart and mind, obsessing over her pain.
Now I will tell you what perfect Rama thought and said
in a mansion under the moonlight of an endless night.

1249.
'I saw her once before, and in my endless passion
I used my eyes as brushes to paint her in my heart.
Seeing her again, I saw no end to the sea of her perfect beauty.
When people see lightning strike, do they know how to put it to use?

1250.
'When I think about you, moon, and the seed of a growing passion,
you are its soil, its green sprout and ripe fruit.
You are like the round face of that young woman like Lakshmi,
why are you doing this?
You should not look like that to a man who is alone.

1251.
'The spreading night has come like that gorgeous woman's eyes
which take my life though I do not die, and it does not leave.
It keeps growing, like the shame of a general who has run off in fear
when his king has been killed in the brutality of war.

1252.
'My heart, you pursue that girl, a deer wandering the forest.
You do not think of me in any way at all.
Is it a long way to return to me?
Will you tell me about the woman who does not know you at all?
You are like her, you have forgotten me completely.

1253.
'People take it as an ancient truth that lethal poison is found
in the teeth of vicious cobras that spit fire from their eyes.
For me, though, it is in the tender glance of that queen of women
who is always in my eyes, always in my heart.

1254.
'Even though there are mansions built by a master hand
and vast flower gardens where she can enjoy herself,
this beautiful girl with soft hair and a heart like stone
has taken my own heart as the place to spend her time!'

1255.
As Rama, lord of gods, suffered like this deep in his heart,
Janaka ordered the news to be spread by drums held by elephants:
'Tomorrow, Sita with bee-swarmed hair is to be wed.
You will beautify the city with flowers,
with shining jewels, and with your fine clothes.'

1256.
When the drums sounded to announce the wedding,
old people, youths and women with fragrant hair all gathered
and hastened to decorate the city, talking merrily about the news.
They saw an end to the night that had seemed to have no end.

1257.
When he learned that dark Rama and Sita who dwells in the lotus
were to be wed with perfect ceremony on the following day,
The sun ripped apart the drapes of night with his hands, red rays,
and rose in his chariot to see the splendid rites for his heir.

1258.
Men drove in posts for gateways and dug holes for columns,
they made the city beautiful with water pots and fancy cloth,
using gems to decorate mansions so tall they soar into the clouds,
and cooked for brahmans who embrace the Vedas' branching truths.

1259.
Young men like bulls and women who walk like geese
planted banana trees and areca palms in this city of endless virtues.
They selected the largest pearls to string on priceless strands,
adorned themselves with gold and covered themselves with gems.

1260.
People sprinkled the streets with oudh and sandalwood,
covering them with a blanket of newly bloomed flowers,
and hung strands of priceless pearls on mansions' upper stories
set with jewels that even a rainbow would covet.

1261.
All over the city, gems sparkled on tiered balconies,
and on high porches that shone with the moonlight glow of crystal
and golden eaves bright as the sun,
people laid down rows of lamps that spread rays of light
and an array of fine clay pots full of fresh green sprouts.[5]

1262.
In front of mansions as tall as Mount Mandara, they erected awnings
to drive off the sun's constant heat and offer sweet shade.
The thick strands of pearls on them glittered with light
like the stars coming out to twinkle in the night sky above.

1263.
Servant women placed lamps that shone with perfect light
on stages set with diamonds and emeralds that flash like lightning.
They put flags with golden borders
on walls so tall they brushed the moon,
and burned chunks of agarwood that yields perfumed smoke.

1264.
They brought cartloads of fragrant flowers, banana leaves,
betel leaves and all sorts of fruit from the gardens.
Women danced the kuruvai dance, arm in arm as their earrings flashed,
and painted the foreheads of elephants that feast on balls of rice.

1265.
They smeared themselves with sandalwood paste,
put on their finest clothing and put flowers in their hair,
then looked in the mirror to apply the tilak to their brows.
They styled their hair, and painted their lips as red as clove flowers.

1266.
Women graceful as peacocks adorned themselves
but one fight with their lovers and they threw everything off.
Jewels, chains of golden coins, conch bangles, flower pollen,
and fragrant powder red as coral: they tossed it all aside like trash.

1267.
Kings arrived, the city filled with brahmans,
people drank in the honey of sweet songs and lute music,
bards wandered and singing dancers gathered together,
and pundits used the hourglass to fix the wedding's appointed hour.

1268.
Courtesans gathered and displayed their skill in many arts
and lordly kings, calling, 'Please command us into service!'
crowded the palace gates, their crowns pressed so close
gems and gold scraped off to spill in a heap tall as a mountain.[6]

1269.
Young men wandered the streets proud as elephants hardened by war,
their shields shining like the sun, swords glowing like the moon.
Women danced with such grace they delighted the crowds
and captured young men's hearts with the joy in their smiles.

1270.
So much light poured from gems on both sides of the street
anything catching the eye could not be clearly seen.
Young men and women with fresh flowers in their hair
could not tell one walled mansion from another
as they made their way back home.

1271.
People rode in on chariots, they rode in on palanquins,
rode in on their mounts, rode on elephant cows,
rode on elephant bulls like rainclouds with rows of gems on their brows,
they came in on foot, they came in bullock carts.

1272.
Women adorned themselves with pearls, put on many gems,
and delighted in dressing themselves in gold ornaments.
They pinned the finest garlands in the curls of their hair
and put on silk dresses made from coloured thread.

1273.
Women with eyes like poison spoke with voices sweet as ambrosia,
their lips red as sholapith, their smiles shining bright.
Their breasts were full, waists incredibly thin,
they walked gently as geese and swayed like elephant cows.

1274.
If it was hard to take in the glories of that city,
how easy can they be to describe?
The wedding day was as magnificent
as the day Indra was crowned in the blessed heavens.

1275.
Dasharatha, king of kings, paraded towards the canopy
where Sita, her arms stacked with bangles, was going to be wed.
It was adorned with gems and covered with gold foil,
tall as a mountain, so immense no one could see its edge.

1276.
The white shading parasols spread the glow of moonlight
and gems on the crowns shading kings' eyes shone like the dawn.
Swarms of bees that shade the flowers were humming
and dust from horses shaded the sky when Dasharatha rode in.

1277.
The ritual drums roared out like thunderclouds
as the conches blared, and the horns and kettle drums sounded.
The tones of the four Vedas chanted by brahmans
seemed like an ocean roaring in the middle of the night.

1278.
Large chariots, elephants and prancing horses
arrived in vast numbers, advancing row by row.
Powerful kings who always honour Dasharatha, lord of armies,
surrounded him like gods around Indra, sacker of cities.

1279.
The emperor entered the wedding canopy
and sat in state on a throne made of gold and gems.
Court ministers, sages and kings sat in their proper place,
then Janaka, surrounded by his relatives, sat on his own throne.

1280.
The kings, sages and other men there,
and women like Lakshmi who walk gently as geese
were so crowded together, it seemed like Mount Meru
was surrounded by a shining sphere of planets and stars.

1281.
Under that canopy adorned with the nine gems,
built perfectly in ancient times by Maya the divine craftsman,
there were clouds, bolts of lightning, shining stars,
many gems and the sun and moon.
It seemed like the universe Brahma created.[7]

1282.
Sages who practise awesome deeds, every king,
the gods, and all the rest were crowded so closely together
the wedding canopy seemed like the emerald belly
of Vishnu who swallowed earth and heaven.[8]

1283.
Every soul in this world and all others rushed in,
crowding together to gather under the canopy.
Who would need to describe it?
I will speak of the acts of Rama,
the lord who left his serpent couch to come and dwell in Ayodhya.

1284.
Rama bathed, as is proper, in a holy bath poured with scented water
brought from the holy bathing sites known from the perfect Vedas:
water brought from the Ganga and many other rivers
and water brought from the seven seas where hosts of conches creep.

1285.
He gave virgin women with eyes that reach back to their ears
to celibate students who recite the Vedas as those perfect texts order,
then he worshipped Ranganatha,* the primordial boundless Light
whom his ancestors had worshipped over the generations.[9]

1286.
As if infinite compassion had come to incarnate in a body
to restore ascetic deeds and dharma that were being destroyed,
he made himself beautiful, worthy of a painting,
smearing sandalwood like a dark cloud stroked by moonlight.

1287.
He was crowned with a circlet made of sholapith
a topknot ornament, and flowers and gold on his brow,
so his hair looked like a dark ocean surging with waves
with the full moon risen above it.[10]

1288.
His two perfect earrings seemed like the sun and moon
well aware of Sita's love each day and every night,
who then went to him as messengers
to pour her secrets in his ear.

1289.
Shiva who carries a battle axe and has a throat black with poison
wears the crescent moon on his crown of long matted locks.
On Rama's brow, a golden plate and its central gem flashed
as though he wore every divine light forged into a circle.

---

*The family deity (kuladevata) of Rama's royal line; see vv. 713, 880.

1290.
Strands of white pearls on his neck shone
as though Vishnu's conch lay next to his discus.
It seemed like the smile of Sita with thick, dark hair
had overflowed Rama's heart and emerged into view.[11]

1291.
Set with rows of diamonds that shone like a snake's stripes
and lustrous rubies that blazed like fire,
the armbands wrapped around his beautiful arms
seemed like the serpent roped around Mount Mandara long ago.[12]

1292.
The three thick strands of perfectly matched pearls
that glittered on his large hands that grant protection
seemed like a sure and noble sign:
he is master of the three worlds.

1293.
Bangles flashed on his broad hands that everyone loves to see
as if a wishing tree created them, worked in gems and gold,
and hung them on its branches which grow to offer gifts
for all who wish for things when they stand before it.[13]

1294.
Amid the pearl necklaces on Rama's chest, embraced
by Lakshmi who lives in a lotus dripping nectar,
the necklace made of nine gems shone like a rainbow
on a cloud alive with the light of stars above.[14]

1295.
His upper garment, which glowed like the pure knowledge
of the masters of reality who take the path so difficult to reach,
shone on the holy chest of Rama, his compassion without end,
as bright as the pearl necklaces that adorned his holy chest.

1296.
The sacred thread on his chest glowed with the three lights,
sun, moon and fire, impossible to approach,
braided so everyone can see what gods and sages do not know:
the three foremost gods are Rama standing there before them.[15]

1297.
His stomach band dazzled with the light of flawless gold
and the single immense gem on its front shone bright,
it seemed like a vast golden lotus was blooming
for Brahma to arise and create a different universe.

1298.
The pure white silk cloth that shone on his waist
was like the cool milk sea with its crashing waves
embracing a dark ocean with a luminous glow
filled with shining gems washed by its waters.

1299.
His handsome golden sash shone with different colours,
its emeralds set against the light of lustrous pearls.
The dagger tied at his side made him look like golden Meru
as the sun circled it correctly, keeping the mountain on his right.

1300.
A strand of lustrous pearls as large as jasmine buds
made the glow of his belt surround him with a shining light.
Strands of rubies hung from it like the glowing dawn
of the sun that is the shining dagger at his waist.

1301.
On the front of his thigh ornaments made by a master hand,
a sea monster with open jaws displayed its dazzling colours.
Its shining eyes were jewels, its teeth had the glow of moonlight,
each one casting its light out to the edge of the world.

1302.
Anklets and thick legbands crafted with exquisite care
were wrapped around his holy feet, lotuses that will never fade.
They seemed to halt his feet, one after the other, saying,
'They measured the worlds, but where are his feet now?'[16]

1303.
Each one of these jewels and ornaments shone, and Rama,
who awoke from dreams on his serpent couch that glows with lamps,
gems that are the fruits of divine deeds,
stood there looking absolutely perfect, equal to himself alone.

1304.
How can I describe the magnificence of the jewellery worn by Rama,
the ultimate source of every world, equal only to himself,
father of all beings, like the ambrosia that rose up from the milk sea,
the ecstasy the wise pursue as they strive to remove
the burdens that are the fetters in this world.

1305.
As gifts, he gave tens of thousands of cows, pure gold,
land beyond measure, and the nine gems* to deserving people.
Then he came out and mounted his chariot
as brahmans whose wealth is the Vedas offered him their praise.

1306.
It shone like the one-wheeled chariot of the sun
with a dais made of diamond,
rolling on silver wheels set on an axle forged from gold,
and it glittered with the nine gems inlaid on every side.

1307.
The horses yoked to his chariot had obvious power,
and displayed the marks of good fortune listed in equestrian texts.
They were like the four goals of humankind starting with dharma
each one equal to the other, all truly splendid.

---

*See vv. 713; 880; 1295.

1308.
Bharata, his lotus eyes swimming with tears of joy, was the charioteer
driving the horses with his whip as if he were Aruna* himself.
As Rama drove, Lakshmana and Shatrughna, holding curved bows,
fanned him with fine white chowries set in handles of gold.

1309.
Perhaps it was due to Rama's unique beauty, his perfect, holy body,
or drawing close to him by meditating with a patient mind.
We cannot know which, let that be as it may,
but everyone there seemed like a god whose eyes never blink.

1310.
The gods gathered together, joined by crowds of heavenly women
and danced with joy, sure that the time had now arrived
for the destruction of the rakshasas, who seemed so safe, invincible,
and who tormented the worlds with no end in sight.

1311.
The women in that thriving city showered Rama with flowers
and sprinkled fragrant powder everywhere.
We cannot know why, they threw down clothes, gold and gems,
desiring him so much they seemed to take his beauty in and drink it.

1312.
All the women staring at Rama were like the finest nobles
giving away their jewellery and everything they had, saying,
'Anyone who wants should take it, for it is more than we need.'
They stood there as the jewellery on their bodies fell off.

1313.
The host of kings who bear weapons on the faultless earth
surrounded him like a herd of elephants
as Rama rode in, a master of the bow, vicious towards his enemies,
and he entered the jewelled canopy like the rising sun
when it rises at the side of grand Mount Meru.

---

*'Dawn', the sun's charioteer.

1314.
Rama descended from his chariot in front of the canopy,
then Bharata and Lakshmana took him by the hands and he entered.
He offered reverence to the glorious ascetics,*
touched the feet of his father whose lawful vow is truth,
then sat down at his side.

1315.
A blossoming branch made of rose gold bearing the full moon
with two fish, two bows above, and jasmine buds in blossom,
Sita, once born on the milk ocean, now born on the earth,
seemed to rise in her chariot, and she entered the wedding canopy
as if rising once more next to Mount Meru.[17]

1316.
Gazing at Lord Rama sitting in state, the gods were filled with thanks
and said, 'Today is even finer than that day long ago
when Lakshmi with scented hair was churned from the milk ocean,
and placed the wedding garland around her husband's neck.'[18]

1317.
If Sita's beauty shone beyond the earth bounded by the roaring sea,
the world of the gods, and the world of the serpents,
what can I say for certain about the splendour of her wedding
when I know so little about it?

1318.
Indra arrived in the sky with his wife Indrani,
Shiva wearing the crescent moon came with his wife Uma,
and Brahma came on his lotus with Saraswati on his tongue
all wanting to see the glorious wedding and everyone there.

---

*Vasishtha, Kaushika, Shatananda and the other ascetics present for the wedding ceremony.

1319.
Surrounded by countless brahmans wearing sacred threads,
masters of the Vedas full as an ocean no one can swim across,
Vasishtha entered joyously, ready to perform the wedding
and all its varied services as laid down by ancient law.

1320.
He traced a square of white sand, put darbha grass at each edge,
then made a circle in it for the fire, as law and tradition hold.
He set down white blossoms, lit the fire and stoked its flames,
then began the homa ritual, chanting ancient Vedic mantras.

1321.
Sita entered like a goose, the perfect mate for a sweet life,
with enormous love for Rama, her own noble champion.
She went to her seat so they sat close together, as if to show
the path of yogic love and the passion they had for each other.

1322.
Janaka stepped before the prince and declared,
'May you live as one with my beloved daughter Sita
like the supreme being Vishnu and Lakshmi in her lotus,'
then he poured the holy water over Rama's lotus hands.

1323.
The good conches roared out like the brahmans' blessings,
the prayers for long life sung by married women,
the devotion of kings wearing garlanded crowns
and the calls of love from great ascetics.

1324.
A rain of heavenly flowers showered down by the gods,
golden flowers lavished by kings and flowers thrown by all others
fell with pearls and flowers that blossomed on their own,
making the broad earth shine like the night sky filled with stars.

1325.
Rama pondered all the oblations poured,
lit with ghee in the grand sacrificial fire.
He chanted all the perfect Vedic mantras,
then clasped Sita's hand as if holding a flower bud.

1326.
Sita, her heart as innocent as a woman's should be,
began her own role in the essential wedding rites.
She walked with Rama around the sacred fire
as a body in a different birth becomes one with its new life.[19]

1327.
They walked around the sacred fire and worshipped it,
fed the flames with parched grain and completed the fire rites,
then Sita placed her foot on the sparkling grindstone
and they looked at Arundhati, the woman of perfect chastity.[20]

1328.
Overjoyed, they finished the wedding rite,
then kneeled to touch their heads to the feet of each ascetic in turn.
After bowing to grasp the emperor Dasharatha's feet,
Rama took Sita's bangled hand and they entered his elegant palace.

1329.
The drums of fortune pounded, conches blared,
the gods shouted with delight, the noise of varied arts was heard,
the chants of the four Vedas resounded, swarms of bees hummed,
prayers for long life soared, and the universe clamoured with joy.

1330.
Rama bent low to revere Sita's shining feet
with a love even deeper than the love he had for his mother.
He then placed his head at his loving mother's feet
and worshipped the feet of righteous Sumitra.

1331.
Graceful as a goose, Sita came before the three queens
and placed her head at their shining lotus feet.
The queens exclaimed, 'She looks gorgeous, like faithful Arundhati,
she is the jewel of honour for our virtuous son Rama.'[21]

1332.
They embraced Sita, her voice sweet as a cuckoo, and asked,
'Of all the women who could have married our son charming son,
who could be better than her?'
Their eyes danced with delight, and their hearts shone with joy.

1333.
'Sita, this goddess among women, must receive gifts,' they cried.
'Untold millions of golden coins, exquisite jewels and clothing,
endless millions of rare ornaments in every colour,
companies of maidservants and a vast amount of land.'

1334.
As the wise, a sea of shastras, dictate for the wedding rites,
Rama, sea of compassion, went with Sita, her heart a sea of love,
and joined her on his royal bed, white as the ancient milk sea
which became a sea the wind has blown into a forceful storm.[22]

1335.
On a day of the Uttara Phalguni asterism
after finishing the wedding rites for Rama,
Vasishtha, the lion with a thousand names in the Vedas,
performed the last ritual of fire to complete the wedding.[23]

1336.
Janaka, lord of unfailing victory, said to Rama's three brothers,
'My younger brother Kushadhvaja and I have three daughters,
each one like Lakshmi who rules on her mud-born lotus.
You shall take them as your wives,' and his relatives agreed.[24]

1337.
The daughters of Janaka, king with a garland of fresh flowers,
and Kushadhvaja, master of the well-greased spear, came forward,
and Rama's brothers took these three women as their brides,
their eyes streaked with kohl and beauty true to heaven.

1338.
After the couples had married, each of them filled with longing,
King Janaka gave away an enormous amount of wealth.
He gave gifts to all who wanted them, indeed more than they sought,
keeping only the vast fame he had gained throughout the years.

1339.
After the gifts were handed out, Dasharatha stayed in the city
filled with a tremendous joy that nothing could equal
as he passed gentle days with Janaka and deeply learned ascetics.
Now I shall recount the events that were to happen next.

Parashu Rama

1340.
For days, the one who could be none but himself
enjoyed many pleasures with Janaka's sweet daughter.
The ascetic Kaushika, who taught Rama the Vedas' righteous ways,
then travelled on towards the golden Himalaya mountains.

1341.
After Kaushika left, the emperor Dasharatha
decided to marshal his army and attendants
and return to his charming city, so he set off in his grand chariot
as kings strong as elephants rushed to worship at his feet.

1342.
As his sons and their wives touched his feet and followed him,
and princes and many other lords crowded around them,
families living in Mithila felt their hearts break,
and they plunged into a stormy sea of pain
as if the breath of life were leaving them.

1343.
The emperor rode first, as is right, taking the city's hearts with him.
Mighty Rama rode surrounded by his three noble brothers
along with Sita, her waist a slim bolt of lightning
flashing among the dark clouds.[1]

1344.
Peacocks crossed their path clockwise as they travelled,
but crows and other dark omens turned before them on their left.
The emperor, unyielding as a mountain, always true to justice,
recognized something might obstruct them on their way
so he soon stopped his chariot so tall it swept the clouds.[2]

1345.
He stood there and called for a man learned in the ways of omens
and said, 'Tell me honestly, does fortune favour us or not?'
The master of bird omens said to the king with arms like mountains,
'An obstacle lies before us, but all will end well.'

1346.
As the soothsayer spoke and night veiled the heavens,
a man with coppery knotted locks appeared carrying an axe.
His wild eyes spit fire, his words roared like thunder,
he was golden Meru standing before them, driving off the night.

1347.
He thrummed the string on his bow made of gold
and the world was rocked like a ship in a tempest,
the elephants who hold the earth were shaken off their feet,
the gods fled in horror, the boiling seas shifted,
then he pulled out his iron-tipped arrows.

1348.
Like blood pouring out when a wound is ripped open,
an inferno of fury poured from his eyes, and everyone wondered,
'Is the earth strained for the heavens, or are the heavens falling?
Will every living thing in the worlds fall into Yama's mouth?'

1349.
The head of his axe smouldered as he lifted it for battle,
forcing the sun to veer in his chariot as he circled Mount Meru.
Blazing wrath poured from him, as if the submarine mare's fire
had swept over the earth and launched into the sky.

1350.
His mighty arms stretched to the ends of the earth
and his coiled, matted locks scraped the heavens,
catching the moon on one side.
Here stood a match for Uma's husband dancing on doomsday,
destroying seas of water, blazing fire, wind, earth and space.[3]

1351.
He had once hurled his axe at Kartavirya Arjuna,
and its razor edge severed each of the king's thousand arms
diamonds branching off a living tree.
He killed that master of armies, who alone overran
the vast earth all the way to the sea and its fine sands.[4]

1352.
He alone had bathed in so much blood,
diving into its torrents that crashed like the sea.
He swung his axe clean through all kings' lives on earth,
killing twenty-one times over to end each generation.
He shamed them all as he ripped royalty out by its roots.

1353.
He was a man apart, two natures intertwined:
stunning austerities that are patience embodied
and a fury that burned like seething fire.
When the soaring geese faltered, stopped by a mountain
he was irate, and chose a perfect arrow
to pierce its craggy heights so they could fly through it.[5]

1354.
King Dasharatha saw this warrior advance with his axe,
a man who had humbled the peak that pierced the clouds
and who forced the sea to obey his command
though its waves could crash through a mountain.
Dasharatha who, incredibly, once gave life to the lord himself
was sick with dread, for he did not know why this man had come.[6]

1355.
Parashu Rama raced towards the prince in a towering chariot
that flew as fast as lightning, scaring the army itself.
His stern brow arched, his savage eyes shot sparks,
and Rama wondered, 'Who on earth can this be?'

1356.
The king approached and greeted him with reverence,
falling at his feet and touching the earth with his perfumed crown.
His challenger was unswayed, and, spitting fire like doomsday,
spoke with a voice like a thundering drum.

1357.
'I know the worth of that bow you broke,' said the champion,
'and I want to test the strength of your arms!
My powerful arms have killed before and now they itch for battle,
so I face you here, seeking nothing else.'

1358.
King Dasharatha agonized when he heard these words, and said,
'You are great, for you conquered the earth and gave it to a sage.
No one has equalled such deeds, not Brahma, Vishnu, or Shiva.
How could a trifling king like me be important to you?
This boy here is my life, and I implore you, give us refuge.

1359.
'You rage like a fractious man, carrying an axe that spews fire,
but isn't that the way of a man set on evil?
Rama is not haughty, he has not slighted you at all.
What comes of besting the weak when there is no cause to fight?

1360.
'You must accept this, great ascetic. Is your present outrage just?
You once gave the seven worlds as a gift,
you are a unique master!
Calm your fury as you once showed mercy to the rulers of men
when you relinquished the earth surrounded by frosty seas.

1361.
'Spurn justice, mighty hero, and all will revile you.
What good would your power be then?
How would dharma be served if you now display your might?

True courage is shown by standing fast with dharma,
the straight path to lasting fame.
Please heed my words, for you are now bent on crime!

1362.
'Your lasting fame covers the earth and the sweeping heavens,
and your arms could best stone columns.
My young son has no grudge against you, and if you take his life
I will lose my own and the lives of my forebears.
I am your slave, and I beg you:
do not kill him and end my royal line!'

1363.
But Parashu Rama paid no heed to the man at his feet
and the fire danced in his eyes.
He turned instead to face Rama, who was holding his golden bow,
and Dasharatha despaired, being tortured
like a gleaming snake who dreads the coming lightning*
for he was now sure his son could not be saved.

1364.
Parashu Rama cared nothing for the ruined heart
of the crowned king who wore his chest jewel as his honour,
he could not evade the karma that would drive his glory to ruin.
'That bow, once owned by the husband of Uma who carries a drum
has a flaw,' he said. 'Now attend to its true story.[7]

1365.
'There were once two bows, mind-wrought creations
of the craftsman whose work never has the slightest flaw.
They shone like the sun as he rides his one-wheeled chariot,
solid with eternal strength, like northern Meru swept by clouds,
not a bow in the world was their equal.[8]

---

*See v. 1169.

1366.
'The husband of Uma admired one and took it, and mighty Vishnu
who wields the discus and once measured out the worlds
took the other as was his right.
When the gods learned this, clever Brahma asked them
which bow would prove the finer. That very day,[9]

1367.
'Brahma, seated in his fragrant lotus,
thought favourably of the gods' debate about this,
and he used those strong, cruel bows for his clever scheme
to judge which of the two gods was superior.
He drove Vishnu and Shiva, who had assumed different forms
to commit themselves to fierce battle.

1368.
'The two gods strung the bows they had chosen
and the roaring fires of their rage flared higher and higher.
As they fought each other, never relenting,
the seven worlds trembled, the cardinal points shifted,
and Shiva's bow snapped, only making his fury grow fiercer.

1369.
'When battle started again, the gods stepped in to stop it.
Three-eyed Shiva handed his bow to Indra, king of gods
while dark Vishnu, revelling in his victory
went over and handed his bow to Ricika
a sage whose austerities had filled him with power.[10]

1370.
'Ricika gave this sturdy bow to his son, my own father,*
and my father in turn gave it to me.
Now take it, prince, and see if you can bend it.
If it proves easy, you will be greater than all others
and I will refrain from the fight I have promised you.
Now heed me, for I have more to say.

---

*Jamadagni.

1371.
'I respect the strength you showed when you broke that bow,
but that was nothing special, young prince of Manu's line.
Listen further. My father was a man without flaw,
he was kind to all life, and had rid himself of anger.
He was killed by a savage king long ago,
and from that day on I have known only anger.[11]

1372.
'I killed every king on earth, twenty-one times over
as my raging axe ripped them out by the roots.
I dove in the blood that streamed from their flesh
using it to pour the ancestral rites for my father,
and then I held back, keeping my anger contained.

1373.
'I offered the whole earth to the sage*
and made my home on a secluded mountain
where I kept my anger within, performing brutal austerities.
I was there when I heard the crack of the bow you broke,
and I came here, for that sound rekindled my anger.
If you have true power, you will bend my bow,
then you and I will do battle.'

1374.
Rama listened to him with a slight smile on his tranquil face
and said, 'Give me the bow that Narayana took as its master.'
The ascetic handed it to the young hero
who took it, quite calm, and making Parashu Rama cringe,
bent it back with his massive arms.
Rama then spoke,

---

*Kashyapa; see vv. 1354; 1358.

1375.
'You are the son of Jamadagni, perfect master of the Vedas,
and you are also great, well practised in ascetic vows
even though you killed every king on earth.
It would not be just to kill you, then, but tell me,
this arrow will not miss its mark, so what should its target be?'[12]

1376.
'I now understand your true nature, the cause of all on earth,
do not turn your anger on me, for you are virtue itself.
Source of the Vedas, master of the discus come to earth as man,
apart from breaking the bow that Shiva himself once held
what could reveal your true power?' asked Parashu Rama

1377.
'Since it is clear you are the lord who wields the discus,
garbed in yellow, your feet adorned with finely wrought anklets,
what sorrows will the earth now bear?
I gave you a bow that was already yours,
no match for your own strength.

1378.
'Now let that arrow fly true and take
all my ascetic power as its own.'
Rama loosed the arrow from his hand,
and away it flew, collecting pure ascetic strength
before it returned to its owner.

1379.
'You are the substance of every thought,
the colour of sparkling sapphire, wearing a garland of basil,
the embodiment of merit that all the world holds dear.
Go, fulfil your aims, I bid you farewell.'
Parashu Rama bowed to him, then departed.

1380.
After Parashu Rama left, his fury expended,
the immaculate lord felt vast love for his father
who stood robbed of his senses, his life at the precipice
as his heart flowed out to his son.
Rama touched his feet, and ferried him
across the sea of pain that had engulfed him.

1381.
Dasharatha's senses returned as his agony left him,
and the commander of rutting elephants felt his mind bloom.
He reached the far bank of the sea of misery that had trapped him
and plunged into a different sea, the boundless ocean of joy.

1382.
He hugged his son whose mind had stayed serene
when he took the sturdy bow to loose blame on Parashu Rama.
He smelled his son's hair and bathed him with two water pots,
his eyes filled with tears that poured down like a waterfall.[13]

1383.
'Could anyone in all three worlds do the manly deeds
that Rama has done in childhood, free from any guile?
Since this is true,' Dasharatha exclaimed,
'this young man is the creator, here to ripen karma
for every virtuous being, in this life and the next!'[14]

1384.
As the gods rained down flowers from the sky
Rama turned to Varuna, said, 'Protect this glorious, lethal bow,'
and handed it to him as the armies roared with delight.
He then entered the glorious city Ayodhya
which is guarded by forbidding waters.

1385.
On the day they reached Ayodhya, Dasharatha, best of men,
the mighty commander of armies whose shining weapons
are roused by booming drums coated with resonant paste
gave Bharata news almost beyond belief.

1386.
'My noble son, jewellery shining on your chest,
your grandfather, the ruling king of Kekaya,
said he wanted to see you, so go to the land of the Kekayas,
where conches blare in the ponds,' he said.[15]

1387.
When he heard his father's command, Bharata bowed before him
then went to Rama, and crowned himself with Rama's lotus feet,
for there was nothing but Rama for him, the source of his own life.
He left as though only his body was leaving,
parting from that source of life that cannot be divided.

1388.
Bharata mounted a chariot pulled by horses with flowing manes,
and in seven days reached Kekaya, and its cool waters,
with his uncle Yudhajit, commander of armies whose conches blare,
who had accompanied him along with his brother Shatrughna.

1389.
Once Bharata left, Dasharatha, lord of kings,
governed his vast realm perfectly.
I will recount the events that were to come
caused by the gods' powerful deeds long ago.[16]

Glossary

Adishesha: (primal Shesha) the thousand-headed serpent who holds up the earth, and bears Vishnu on the primordial ocean during cosmic dissolution

Aditi: (boundless) a wife of Kashyapa, mother of the gods

Agastya: a Vedic seer, introduced Tamil to humankind as author of the first Tamil grammar

Agni: (fire) god of fire, the conveyor of sacrifice to the gods

Airavata: (son of Iravati) a white elephant that serves as Indra's vehicle

Alaka: divine capital of Kubera, lord of yakshas

Amaravati: (belonging to the gods) Indra's divine capital, abode of the gods

Ananga: (bodiless) epithet of Kama, who lives invisibly in beings after Shiva burned him to ashes

Ananta: (endless) see Adishesha

Apsaras: a class of gorgeous celestial women who inhabit the sky and are superb dancers, often sent to earth to tempt a sage's celibacy

Aruna: (red) the dawn, personified as the sun's charioteer

Arundhati: wife of the sage Vasishtha, celebrated for her marital constancy and devotion

Asura: anti-god, a class of divine beings opposed to the gods

Cataiyan: (possessing matted locks, a name of Shiva) Kampan's patron, lord of the town Venneynallur

Cakravala: (circle) a ring of mountains said to encircle the earth as a boundary wall, beyond which lies the sea

Diti: (splitting) a wife of Kashyapa, mother of the Daityas and the Maruts

Durga: (indomitable) a fierce manifestation of Shiva's wife, who slayed the buffalo demon Mahishasura

Durvasas: (possessing tattered clothing) a sage noted for his furious temper, who by cursing Indra to lose his kingdom and riches indirectly prompts the churning of the ocean

Garuda: the lord of birds, a son of Kashyapa and elder brother of Aruna who serves as Vishnu's eagle mount

Gautama: one of the seven great seers, husband of Ahalya

Hara: (ravisher) epithet of Shiva

Hari: (tawny) epithet of Vishnu

Himalaya: (snowy abode) the Himalaya mountains personified as Uma's father

Isha: (ruler) epithet of Shiva

Jambavan: a mortal emanation of Brahma as the king of bears, immensely strong and long-lived

Kakutstha: (descendant of Kakutstha) patronymic epithet of Rama

Kali: (black) a fierce manifestation of Shiva's wife

Kama: (desire, eros) the god of love

Kapila: (reddish) a sage, destroyer of the sons of Sagara
Kashyapa: (tortoise) one of the seven great seers, husband of Diti and Aditi
Kaushika: (descendent of Kusha) patronymic epithet of Vishwamitra, the preceptor of Rama and Lakshmana
Kinnara: celestial musicians and paradigmatic lovers, half-human and half-horse
Krauncha: a bird said to be inseparable from its mate; its cry causes lovers great pain
Krishna: (black) Vishnu's eighth avatar
Kumbhakarna: (pot-ears) Ravana's enormous elder brother, who sleeps for six months at a time
Lakshmi: (possessed of fortune) wife of Vishnu, the goddess of prosperity, beauty, and success
Madana: (intoxicating) epithet of Kama
Mal: (great one) a Tamil name of Vishnu
Mandara: mountain used by the gods and asuras to churn the primordial ocean
Manmatha: (mind-churner) epithet of Kama
Marut: (wind) storm gods born of Diti after being split in the womb by Indra
Maya: the divine architect of the asuras
Meghanada: (thunderous) epithet of Indrajit, son of Ravana
Meru: a fabulous golden mountain that is the axis mundi of Indian cosmology
Murugan: (youth) Tamil name of Shiva's son Skanda
Naga: a shape-changing serpent being with a human face, said to inhabit the underworld
Nala: monkey son of the divine architect Vishwakarman
Narayana: epithet of Vishnu, the supreme being
Panchajanya: (relating to the demon Panchajana) Vishnu's divine conch
Purandara: (sacker of cities) epithet of Indra
Rakshasa: a class of earthly demons that roam during the night and eat human beings
Raghava: (descendant of Raghu) patronymic epithet of Rama
Rahu: the severed head of an asura, which swallows the sun during an eclipse
Ranganatha: (lord of the riverine island) the image of Vishnu worshiped at Shrirangam
Rati: (passion) wife of Kama
Ricika: a sage, husband to Vishwamitra's elder sister Satyavati (Kaushiki) and Parashu Rama's paternal grandfather
Rishyashringa: (possessing an antelope horn) a sage with a horn on his forehead who was brought up by his father in isolation from women and was therefore perfectly chaste. When brought to Anga, he relieved a terrible drought there, and subsequently directed Dasharatha's sacrifice for sons
Rudra: (the howler) epithet of Shiva
Samsara: the flow of earthly existence in which living beings live, die, and are reborn in accordance with their karma
Shambara: an asura who seized Indra's capital Amaravati and was killed by Dasharatha

Shambhu: (source of joy) epithet of Shiva
Shanta: (peaceful) daughter of King Romapada, wife of Rishyashringa
Shatananda: (manifold bliss) Janaka's family priest, the son of Gautama and Ahalya
Shibi: mythic king of Rama's solar line (claimed as an ancestor by the Cholas)
Shukra: (shining) the guru of the asuras, planet Venus embodied
Shri: (auspicious) epithet of Lakshmi
Skanda: (spill) Shiva's son
Surabhi: (fragrant) the cow of plenty or wishing cow, which miraculously produces whatever its owner asks of it
Udayagiri: (ascension mountain) the eastern mountain behind which the sun is said to rise
Uma: Shiva's wife
Vaikuntha: (relating to Vikuntha, i.e. Vishnu) Vishnu's heaven
Vamana: (dwarf) Vishnu's fifth avatar, a dwarf who in three steps claims the universe from Mahabali
Varaha: (boar) Vishnu's third avatar, a boar who raises the earth from the ocean with its tusks
Varuna: (encompasser) god of the waters and lord of the western cardinal point
Vasava: (relating to the Vasus) epithet of Indra
Vasishtha: (most excellent) one of the seven great seers, owner of Surabhi the wishing cow
Vasuki: lord of the nagas, used as the rope during the churning of the primordial ocean
Vayu: (wind) god of the wind
Vidyadhara: (wise ones) semi-divine beings associated with air and sky, possessed of magical powers
Vishwakarman: (all-maker) divine architect of the gods
Yaksha: a class of semi-divine nature spirits associated with trees and mountains
Yama: (the seizer) Death, lord of the southern cardinal point

Notes

Kampan's Ramayana: An Introduction

1 Aiyar 1950: 4; Arunachalam 1974: 114–15; Blackburn 1991: 380; Hart 1988: 1; Jesudasan 1961: 168; Karuttiruman xxvii–xix, 1; Meenakshisundaram 1961 48; 1965: 102; Nagaswamy: 410; Nilakanta Sastri 1975: 377; Purnalingam Pillai 1985: 216; Shulman 1978: 135; 2016: 166; Srinivasan 1997: 1; Subramanian 1993: 158; Vaiyapuri Pillai 1938: 1; 1962: 18, 79; Zvelebil: 1995.

2 On the critical and still underappreciated significance of the South Asian literary tradition and its theorizations, see Pollock 2003: 1–38 esp. pp. 2–16.

3 Ramanujan 1991; Lugendorf 1990.

4 I v. 11 appears to name the text directly, and the great Tamil scholar U. Ve. Caminataiyar determined from a manuscript copy and a verse in the 15th c. anthology *Pruratttirattu* that the text historically circulated under the name *Iramavataram*. (Caminataiyar 1997: 647; Vaiyapuri Pillai 1962: 12) Rama is understood as an incarnation of Vishnu in *Harivamsha* (*ca*. 2nd–4th c. CE), and the conception of an avatar (Skt. avatara) as one of a series of ten earthly incarnations of Vishnu appears to have matured towards the middle of the first millennium. (Hardy 1983: 24)

5 *Kamparamayanam* comprises anywhere from 10,500 to roughly 12,000 verses, depending on how many are judged to be authentic. The text is said to have been substantially augmented by one Velli Tampiran, an ascetic from the Dharmapuram Mutt also said to have made interpolations in other major works such as the *Periyapuranam*.

6 Kampan is popularly held to have composed two other works, *Erezhupatu* and *Cadakopar Antati*. In style and substance, neither poem approaches the calibre of *Kamparamayanam* and should not be assigned to the same author.

7 Irakavaiyankar 1938: 20.

8 Pollock 1984: 519.

9 Aiyar 1950 and Narayan 2006 (English) and Karuttiruman 1963, Kopalakirusnak Kon 1922, and Namaccivaya Mutaliyar 1914 (Tamil) provide synopses of Kampan's text and useful character studies.

10 He is, as Kampan asserts, the 'best of the three greatest beings' (mupparam porulinum mutalvan), e.g. the triumvirate of Brahma, Shiva, and Vishnu (I v. 1305; II v. 39; IV v. 209; V vv. 1117, 1122).

11 On the moral complexities that surround Rama's killing of Valin, see the seminal article by Shulman (1979).

12 The number of Ramayana tellings and their artistic variety are unparalleled, from some twenty-five versions in Sanskrit to tellings in seemingly every Indian vernacular and many in Southeast Asia, to countless dramatic performances and representations in the plastic arts. (Ramanujan 1991: 22–24)

13 By the 12th century, Shrivaishnavas increasingly viewed the epic as a highly saturated allegory that guides a believer's path to God through self-surrender (prapatti, prapannam), a judgement developed in a series of authoritative commentaries composed from the 13th century onwards. See Jagannathan 2015: 121–22.

14 Pollock 2006: 286; on the intentionality of these acts of composition see p. 441. Kampan lists three sources for his text (I v. 10), but beyond Valmiki leaves them unnamed. Tradition identifies the other authors as Vyasa (*Ramakatha* in *Mahabharata*) and Vasishtha (*Yogavasishtha*), while U. Ve. Caminataiyar speculates that Kampan may have been influenced by the Ramayana of Bodhayana (extant in minimal fragments). The likeliest candidates, in my view, are *Ramayanacampu* of King Bhoja of Dhara (*fl.* 1011–55), which quickly enjoyed great prestige in the Sanskrit literary canon, and *Bhattikavya* (early 7th c.), which given its cultural authority in Southeast Asia, particularly Java, must have been well known on the Tamil coast, from which such maritime patterns of textual transmission originated.

15 The archer is Rama; the curse a reference to the creation of poetry, when the 'noble ascetic' Valmiki began to declaim in shloka meter when he cursed a hunter for killing one of a pair of mating krauncha (sarus crane) birds.

16 Goldman 1984: 14–15.

17 On the principal differences between the Ramayanas of Kampan and Valmiki, see Irakavaiyankar 1938: 20–21.

18 *Kamparamayanam* thereby falls within the category of Tamil religious works held to be partial recoveries of an earlier flawless whole. (Shulman 2001: 111)

19 When U. Ve. Caminataiyar taught the text at the Government Arts College in Kumbakonam, his Tamil students found it confusing, as Caminataiyar himself did when attempting to spontaneously gloss a verse for an older relative deeply familiar with the text. (Caminataiyar 1997: 344–45; 501–02)

20 To narrow its scope still further and class it as a Vaishnava text (as its portrayal of Vishnu-Rama might suggest) does not account for the text's popularity across religious groups: see, for instance, the diverse claims of Cupparettiyar 1996; Jesudasan 1961: 165–66; Purnalingam Pillai 1985: 223.

21 Kampan's *Sundarakanda* appears to constitute something of an exception, though the premodern history of its religious allegoresis remains enigmatic (I thank Vishruth Venkataraman for discussion of this point). This role may result from a long-held parallel understanding of the *Sundarakanda* of Valmiki as a highly condensed expression of Shrivaishnava theology. (Rao 2014: 78)

22 Narayanan 2000: 280.

23 Viruttam, while an organic Tamil form, is also informed by Sanskrit poetics; see the engaged discussion in Peterson 1991: 64–65.

24 As Hart and Heifetz have argued, 'It would be nearly impossible to stress

too strongly the importance of rhythm in Kampan. His poetry works in passages of stanzas bound together by the same meter and subject matter or narrative episode. He shows enormous sensitivity in the fitting of meter to emotional tone and content; there are usually very clear reasons for rhythmic choices, and the points at which rhythms change serve important dramatic and mood-shifting purposes.' (Hart and Heifetz 1988: 11)

25 On the debate between early historians on whether or not to compose speeches for their characters in the vernacular, see Grafton 2007: 34–40.

26 Kanapatiraman 1970: 12.

27 Myths and proper nouns, moreover, are often presented telegraphically through participial nouns. These descriptive condensations have a powerful effect: when Rama is 'the stringer of the bow', this tells what he *is* as well as what he did. The grammar effects continuous circumstance, drawing actions out of historical time and into the shared experience of the present.

28 See for example I v. 29, which names the tinai directly.

29 Irakavaiyankar 1938: 37–39.

30 Arunachalam 1974: 122.

31 Shulman 1978: 145.

32 Shulman 1978.

33 Shulman 1978: 155.

34 This is a complex question in *Valmiki Ramayana,* in which the deification of Rama may not be attributable to the work as a whole. Goldman argues, 'The Ramayana, then, although it has come to be regarded as an essentially devotional text has become one only as a result of accretions. The devotional element never permeated the Sanskrit epic and has left the bulk of it untouched.' (1984: 43) *Cf.* Pollock, who contends that 'the divinity of the hero of the Ramayana cannot be eliminated by the facile excision of any portions of the text. It is constitutive of the whole'. (1984: 508)

35 David Shulman has argued that this flowing, unitary life-force, uyir, constitutes an implicit metapsychology, and understanding of breath that at the individual level journeys beyond the body in movement and at the cosmic level describes life-rhythm. (1978, 1979, 1991, 2012, 2016)

36 Shulman 2012: 179.

37 Discussed in Shulman 1991: 97.

38 Hart and Heifetz, echoing Meenakshisundaram 1965: 109, argue that the contest between Rama and Ravana is effectively the triumph of dharma, with its brahmanic connotations, over the Tamil ethos of maram: battle valour and strength, and royal glorification (28–29). While this view has probing explanatory value, I do not believe that it is the paramount interpretive key without which the text cannot be read well. Ravana exhibits vaunted qualities of dharma, and Rama epitomizes heroic maram. Rather, like the concepts of uyir, beauty, fate (viti, Skt. vidhi), blame (pizhai), etc., dharma and maram condition the possibilities of the lives Kampan charts in his Ramayana, the continuing circumstances that draw the poet's life as author

and devotee into alignment with his text, and invites his audience to do the same.

39 Erndl 1991: 73.

40 Consider also Lakshmana's subsequent mutilation of the rakshasi Ayomukhi, who like Surpanakha is overwhelmed with desire. (III.9)

41 Sita's guileless nature is critical here, for the animals, particularly snakes, are able to see through Ravana's pretence and recognize his true intent.

42 Shulman 1991: 109–10.

43 Those favouring a 12th-century date include Celvak Kecavaraya Mutaliyar 1974: 17–19; Hart 1988: 1–2; Jesudasan 1961: 184; Karuttiruman̲ 1963: *xxi*; Ramanujan 1991: 32; Shulman 2016: 166–67; Subramanian 1993: 159; Vaiyapuri Pillai 1962; Zvelebil 1973: 208. Meenakshisundaram 1961: 48 favours a 10th-century date, while Arunachalam 1974: 116, 123–24 and Nagasamy 1980: 410 argue for a 9th-century date. The Shrivaishnava acharya (spiritual master) Periyavaccan Piḷḷai (b. 1228), who cites a Kampan verse in his commentary on Tirumankai Alvar's *Periya Tirumozhi* (*Nalayira Divyaprabandham* v. 957), provides a sure *terminus ante quem*.

44 Zvelebil 1973: 208 and Celvak Kecavaraya Mutaliyar 1974: 13–19 offer useful expositions of the range of evidence cited for dating the text. For a more involved discussion, see Vaiyapuri Pillai 1959: 111–33. One such stanza, which marks the public inauguration of the text at the great temple complex of Srirangam, can be read to date either to 885 or 1185. If accepted as valid, the earlier date places the text under the rule of Aditya Chola (*fl.* 870–907) in the early years of Chola rule over the Tamil south. The later date aligns it with the rule of Kulottunga Chola III (*fl.* 1178–1218), when the Chola empire, while still exercising dominant political power, was beginning to fragment under the growing power of local lords. If the earlier date is accepted, Kampan stands at the beginning of a period of intense vernacularization, when new literary theorizations coincided with a remarkable efflorescence of textual production and the systematization of ancient poetry and religious hymns into canonical anthologies; in the latter case he can be read as their consummation.

45 Vaiyapuri Pillai 1962: 15–16; he notes, moreover, that all manuscripts contain the Tyagamahavinoda verse.

46 *Kulottunga Colan Ula* vv. 156–57.

47 See, for instance, Goldman's caution not to mistake philological and hermeneutic skill for the sure ability to read a premodern text correctly. (1993: 375)

48 The theorization of poetry, unlike any other variety of shastra, dictates a precise moment when its subject began: Valmiki's 'first poem'. Thereafter poets placed themselves in lineages of forebears who reach back to Valmiki as their wellspring. See McCrea 2011: 231*ff.*

49 Pollock 2003b: 86–87.

50 The notion that Kampan refers to Cataiyappan in every thousandth verse is a canard; references to him are inconstant.

51 This does not make him a 'Chola court poet', or even, as Zvelebil has termed him, 'the imperial poet'. (1973: 206–17) Kampan devotes his text entirely to Vishnu-Rama and his devotees. (Shulman 2016: 166)

52 Consider in this regard the kings who commissioned or composed Ramayanas in the millennium preceding Kampan: Pravarasena (*Setubandha*); Yashovarman (*Ramabhyudaya*); Bhimata (*Svapnadashanama*); and Bhoja (*Campuramayana*). See Pollock 1993: 262.

53 On the literarization of Indian regional vernaculars and the parallel concretization of territorial governance, see the magisterial publications of Pollock 1998, 2003, 2006

54 A fragmentarily preserved Tamil adaptation of *Mahabharata* by Peruntevanar, *Paratavenpa,* dates to the Pallava court of Nandivarman III (9th c.), which if it indeed was once complete would make it the first vernacular rendition of the *Mahabharata* in South Asia. In the deep southern capital of Madurai, a Pandya copper plate charter (the Larger Cinnamanur Plates, 10th c.) declares royal mastery of the language, establishment of a Tamil sangha (literary academy), and the commissioning of a translation of the *Mahabharata* into Tamil. The plates also declare that the Pandya king's royal ancestor had 'investigated the brilliant Tamil language along with Sanskrit, making him foremost among the learned'. (*SII* vol. 3, pt. 4, no. 206) See further Krishnaswami Aiyangar 1933: 71; Shulman 2016: 25–29; 84–88; Zvelebil 1992: 66. In the mid-10th century, the poet Pampa ('The Teacher of the Natu') composed an interpretation of *Mahabharata* immersed in the courtly world of Arikesari, a Rashtrakuta and Eastern Chalukya feudatory. Entitled *Vikramarjunavijayam* ('The Triumph of Conquering Arjuna'), his Kannada poem aligns the *Mahabharata* with his political environment, comparing Arikesari to the Pandava hero Arjuna. A couple of generations later, the Kannada poet Ranna authored *Sahasabhimavijayam* ('Bhima's Brutal Victory'), a similar synthesis of the *Mahabharata* with his political world, in this case the Kalyana Chalukya court. In Telugu, Nannaya, family preceptor of the Eastern Chalukya king Rajarajanarendra (*fl.* 1018–61), plays a similarly decisive role, authoring the first books of a Telugu *Mahabharata.*

55 Pollock 2003a: 27; 2003b: 105.

56 *Pahrodai* Ramayana (7th c.), so named after its meter; on the Jain Ramayana see Irakavaiyankar 1938: 17; Monius 2001: 120. *Shripuranam*'s date is highly uncertain; perhaps 10th–14th c.

57 In *Kamparamayanam,* Rama's perfect kingdom of Ayodhya is metaphorically centred in the fertile Kaveri delta, the home of the Chola rulers around which the courtly practices of lordship and brahmanic land settlement had long revolved. Kampan is steeped in this land; his poem explicitly references the Kaveri as a standard of comparison (*e.g.* I vv. 501, 565). Kampan's description of the River Son, in particular, evokes cherished Tamil portrayals of the Kaveri (I vv. 15–17).

58 See, for instance, Nilakanta Sastri 2000, 1955: 375*ff.*

59 Veluthat 1993: 21.

60 Shulman 2016: 185. The Cholas still patronized Sanskrit, to be sure, but these two languages, which had been interwoven in mutually imbricated ways throughout their shared history in south India, also started to impact each other in new ways, as Sanskritic modes of poesis influenced new Tamil theorizations, while southern Sanskrit textuality went on to assume characteristically Tamil hues.

61 Pollock 2006: 384. Shulman's caveat that understanding the influence of Sanskrit rhetorical theory on Tamil poetics as 'Sanskritization' implies both idealized purity and mutual exclusivity is well taken: the two languages have mutually inflected each other throughout their shared history in the south. (Shulman 2016: 183) This caveat, I believe, can be made of any languages that share a geographic expanse, and linguistic boundaries between Tamil and Sanskrit were asserted, even though the reality was invariably complicated.

62 Freeman 2013: 200.

63 Works on prosody: *Yapparunkalam* and *Yapparunkalakkarikai* (10th c.), *Viracholiyam* (11th c.), *Tandiyalankaram* (12th c.); on genre: *Panniru Pattiyal* (12th c.); the commentaries on *Tolkappiyam* and *Tirukkural* by Ilampuranar (11th c.). See Monius 2001: 120; Nilakanta Sastri 1975: 380; Irakavaiyankar 1938: 17.

64 Said to have been lost to time and then miraculously recovered through recitation by the greatest of the Alvars, Nammalvar, to his amanuensis Nathamuni (d. 920), they were then patronized for temple performance by the reigning Chola king. The hagiographic tradition surrounding the Alvars and the compilation of their hymns into the *Divyaprabandham* was crystallizing into textual form in the *Divyasuricarita* of Garudavahana, a text roughly contemporary to Kampan himself. Shortly after Kampan's time, the term '*Dravida Veda*' ('Tamil Veda,' that is, divinely revealed scripture) was standard, and the hymns of *Divyaprabandham*—particularly those of of Nammalvar—were gaining authoritative commentaries. See Cutler 1987: 8; the commentaries of Tirukkurukaippiran Pillan (11th c.) and Nanchiyar (b. 1113); Rao 2014: 7.

65 It appears that in the case of Tevaram, at least, the trope of partial recovery is accurate, as a hymn of Campantar's unknown to Tevaram is engraved on a wall of the Tiruvilaiyadal temple in the Kaveri heartland.

66 By the time that Shrivaishnavism had been magisterially formulated by Ramanuja in the 11th century, the Alvars had come to be seen as amshas (mortal emanations) of Vishnu. (Venkatesan 2014: 84) *Kamparamayanam* plays no part in these religious trends. It garners no promodern commentary, and is not significant to the Shrivaishnava esoteric religious literature that began to emerge in the 11th century (Rao 2014: 7). Indeed, given the Shaiva aversion to written commentary on scripture, for those committed to viewing Kampan's work solely as a religious text, its lack of old commentaries

may hint that his Ramayana was understood to have Shaiva leanings. In later centuries, Kampan comes to be associated with the Shrivaishnava community, holding the poet to have inaugurated *Kamparamayanam* at Srirangam, a disciple of Nammalvar's who also authored a poem in praise of his master entitled *Cadakopar Antati*.

67 Early expressions of Ramayana themes are found in Undavalli, Andhra Pradesh (4th-5th c.?) and in Karnataka within the Virupaksa and Papanatha temples at Pattadakallu near Aihole (7th-8th c.), which offer systematic narrative panels identified by Prakrit inscriptions. (Pollock 1993: 265) In the Tamil country, royal Pallava temples, Kailasanatha and Vaikuntha Perumal in Kanchi, and Olakkanneshvara in Mamallapuram (7th–8th c.), bear the earliest Ramayana panels. (*SII* 1, no. 18, v. 3; see also Pollock 1993: 265; Nagaswamy 1980: 413–14) In the Adivaraha cave at Mamallapuram, an 8th-century inscription notes the ten incarnations of Vishnu. (*SII* 12, no. 116; Nagaswamy 1980: 413) These are all, crucially, imperially patronized temples, and they emphasize the glorification of Ravana, who shakes Shiva's mountain home of Kailasa and receives the god's boon of unassailable power.

68 Sanford 1974: 74–108, 134–48; for a close study of the iconography of Tirucennampunti see Schmid 2014. The 12th-century Hoysala Halebidu temple is also notable for its depiction of Ravana flying in his sky chariot as he carries off Sita in her forest hut: the fact that he has not therefore touched her, preserving her chaste purity, is a well-known 'innovation' of Kampan's Ramayana, but this scene indicates that this narrative detail was already present in oral currents in south India.

69 The crown prince Rajaditya also bore the title Kodanda Rama, but after his death at the battle of Takkolam (949–50) facing the invading forces of the Rashtrakuta king Krishna III, which threw Chola rule into dire uncertainty for the next quarter century, the title appears to have taken on inauspicious connotations, and was not assumed by subsequent Chola kings. (*SII* 11, no 105; Jagadisa Ayyar 1982: 56; Desikachari 1991: 66)

70 Irakavaiyankar 1938: 29; Meenakshisundaram 1965; Vaiyapuri Pillai 1962; Zvelebil 1974: 131.

71 Irakavaiyankar 1938: 49.

72 Hardy 1983, see further Shulman 1985: 41.

73 Narayanan 2000: 266. A repeated narrative element, for example, treats Vishnu taking the form of a baby on Brahma's lap when Ravana approaches to ask the latter for endless life (Poykai Alvar *Tiruvantati* 1.45; Pey Alvar *Tiruvantati* 3.77; Tirumazhicai Alvar *Nanmukam Tiruvantati* v. 44); see further Irakavaiyankar 1938: 44–46.

74 Venkatesan 2014: 11.

75 Venkatesan 2010: 106–07.

76 Zvelebil 1974: 146. See Periyalvar's depiction of Hanuman's speech when he finds Sita and wants to prove he has indeed been sent by Rama

(*Periyalvar Tirumozhi: Anuman Citaikkuk kuriya adaiyalam* 1–10; *cf.* further the latter portion of his *Tirupallandu*); Tirumankai Alvar's (*ca.* 9th c.) repeated reference to Rama in his *Periyatirumozhi,* most provocatively in dance songs that assume the voice of the rakshasas in Lanka who seek refuge in Rama after their defeat (10.2–3), as well his praise of the Vishnu temple in Terazhundur, traditionally held to be Kampan's hometown.

77 His advisors resolve the matter by reciting the verse in which Sita embraces Rama after his triumph, thereby healing the wounds he sustained in battle; see Jagannathan 2015: 53.

78 Hardy 1983: 430. The hymns are addressed to particular temple sites: chapter eight is addressed to Vishnu at Tirukannapuram, while the tenth chapter offering the synopsis of the Ramayana is sung in praise of Vishnu in Chidambaram, which Kulacekara associates with Rama's forest residence at Chitrakoot. See Nagaswamy 1980: 415.

79 Cutler 1987: 40–41; Venkatesan 2014: 81; Nilakanta Sastri 1975: 372.

80 On Nammalvar's transformed aesthetics of cankam landscapes, see Cutler 1987; Shulman 2016: 108.

81 Venkatesan 2014: 4.

82 As is true for *Valmiki Ramayana,* the Shrivaishnava commentators will, in the period roughly contemporaneous to Kampan and in subsequent centuries, take *Tiruviruttam* as a densely allegorical text; see Venkatesan 2014: 102.

83 *E.g.* the tale of Vamana, Vishnu's dwarf avatar, who claims three strides of land from the asura Mahabali (I.7), *cf. Bhagavata Purana* 9; Vibhishana's appeal to the tale of Hiranyakashipu when he counsels Ravana to avoid fighting Rama, *cf. Bhagavata Purana* 7.

84 Purnalingam Pillai 1985: 21; *Tevaram* 4.34.10; the Ramayana reliefs of the Kailasanatha temple in Kanchipuram offer a notable counterpart.

85 Appar refers to Ravana at the end of virtually every decad; Campantar references him in the eighth verse of his decads; Cuntarar's references are not as regular, but are present in abundance (7.2.10, 7.3.8, 7.4.8, 7.16.7, 7.18.9, 7.20.8, 7.22.7; 7.23.8, 7.38.9, 7.40.11, 7.46.7, 7.47.9, 7.53.7, 7.55.9, 7.62.9, 7.67.9, 7.68.9, 7.70.5, 7.73.8, 7.78.9, 7.82.10, 7.87.9, 7.90.7, 7.91.9, 7.93.4, 7.97.8, 7.98.10).

86 Manikkavacakar's *Tiruvacakam* (*ca.* 9th c.) describes Ravana's queen Mandodari receiving Shiva's blessing as well (18.2, *Tiruvarttai* 43.5); see Irakavaiyankar 1938: 50–51.

87 In the famed description of his personal discovery of *Civakacintamani* in the late 19th century, for example, U. Ve. Caminataiyar describes how his newfound mentor Ramacami Mutaliyar tells Caminataiyar that he will loan him his own rare palm-leaf copy of the text, for it served as a model for all the poetic beauty and excellence of Kampan's Ramayana (Caminataiyar 1997: 534). See further Jesudasan 1961: 147–48; Nilakanta Sastri 1975: 375–76; Shulman 2016: 176.

88 Shulman 2016: 176.

89 Such varied scenes are enjoined by *Tandiyalankaram*, the poetic treatise roughly contemporaneous with *Kamparamayanam*, but as *Civakacintamani*'s encyclopaedic nature precedes this Tamil reworking of *Kavyadarsha* (7th c.), it is probable that Kampan followed the pattern established by Tiruttakkatevar rather than fulfilling the stipulations of a text he might not have known. See Monious 2000: 2, 4–5*ff*; Subramanian 1993: 168.

90 Another 10th-century Jain text, *Perunkatai* of Konkuvelir (late 6th c.) invokes some of these topical elements, such as a water festival quite similar to the later versions found in *Civakacintamani* and *Kamparamayanam*, and references Rama and Lakshmana directly (3.24.90–94).

91 On representative parallels between *Kalingattup Parani* and *Kamparamayanam*, see Arunachlam 2005 vol. 5 pp. 52–54. *Kalingattup Parani* itself draws the Chola battle into parallel with the Ramayana war (11.161), and its royal hero, Kulottunka I, is described as a mortal emanation of Vishnu who destroyed Lanka.

92 On the stages of desire, see Wilden 2013: 99–101.

93 Prior to Cayankontar, Chola genealogies were traced in Sanskrit in epigraphy, most prominently in copper-plate charters (*e.g.* Anbil plates of Sundara Chola [*fl. 957–70*]; Leiden plates of Rajaraja I [*fl.* 985–1014]; the Esalam and Tiruvalangadu plates of Rajendra [*fl.* 1012–44]; and the Kanyakumari temple inscription of Virarajendra [*fl.* 1063–70]). Cayankontar and Ottakkuttar transposed such genealogies into circulated Tamil literary texts, the former in his *Kalingattup Parani*, the latter in his three *ulas*.

94 *E.g.* Mandhatr, famed for a reign so peaceful that a deer and a tiger could drink from the same stream (1.716); Mucukunda, who ruled heaven in Indra's absence (1.717); Shibi, so just he offered up his own flesh to protect a dove who came to him for refuge (1.718); and Bhagiratha (1.720), whose awesome austerities brought the Ganges down from heaven.

95 Comparison of the relevant genealogies reveals a detail that may offer some precision in dating Kampan. The first of Ottakkuttar's *ulas* makes no mention of Rama or his family; they do not appear to be central figures in Chola ancestry. In his latter two *ulas*, composed in praise of Kulottunga II (*fl.*1133–50) and Rajaraja II (*fl.* 1146–73), Ottakkuttar emphasizes the fact that the Cholas are direct heirs to Rama's perfect rule. Tentatively, we might ascribe Rama's emergence here to *Kamparamayanam*'s influence on Ottakkuttar, which would situate the text in the reign of Kulottunga II.

96 Kampan was not a Chola court poet, to be sure, but given his textual influences and his mastery of the elite Tamil idiom, he was linked to the courtly sphere. Some have taken Kampan's apparent distance from the Chola court itself as a result of his Vaishnavism (Vaiyapuri Pillai 1962: 162; Cuppurettiyar 1996), and indeed, Kulottunga II appears to have been assertively sectarian: Ottakkuttar's ulas describe him removing an image of Vishnu—'the galling nuisance, the minor god on his animal mount'—and throwing this 'alien nuisance' in the sea (Wentworth 2011: 197–98).

97 Emmrich 2011: 602.

98 *E.g.* Mu. Arunachalam; M.S. Purnalingam Pillai, who wrote, 'He was evidently a Shaiva and took up the story of Ramayana to please his patron. All his invocations are to the primal Divinity, and the expressions found in the body of the work are more in favour of Shiva.' (1929: 223)

99 The royal sage Vishwamitra is closely associated with Shiva's antinomianism (Shulman 1979: 656), and Valin is a devotee of Shiva in Kampan's telling, though he ultimately seeks refuge in Rama.

100 *E.g.* the Thai, Javanese, and Malay renditions (Raghavan 1973: 69, 161).

101 Blackburn 1991a: 170; 1991b: 50.

102 Meenakshisundaram 1965: 106.

103 Goldman 1984: 28; see further 26–28; Irakavaiyankar 1938: 1–4, 7–13.

104 *SII* 2.3, no. 73, v. 22; Pollock 1993: 271. See further the Bahur plates of Nandivarman's son Nrpatunga (c. 877), which praise him as 'renowned not only on the earth, (but) even in the other (world), like Rama'. (*EI* 18, no. 2, v. 17), and the Udayendiram plates of Prithivipati II, a feudatory of Parantaka I, in which Parantaka (*fl.*907–50) is given the title samagramaraghava ('Rama in battle'), and is said to cause Vibhishana terror by Parantaka's proximity during his military triumph in Maturai.

105 *SII* 3.3, no. 205, v. 80.

106 *EI* 18.21*ff*, 37.139*ff*; see further Pollock 1993: 271.

107 Chola incursions ended in the final decades of the 11th century, when the Sinhala king Vijayabahu retook the island.

108 Valmiki, by contrast, makes no mention of the Tamil kingdoms.

109 *Valmiki Ramayana* 6.131.88; see also Rao 2014: 39–40.

110 Narayanan 1994; Rao 2014: 107. See also the temporal transposition in Vedanta Desika's description of Srirangam in *Hamsasandesha* 1.45, in which Ranganatha is still in Ayodhya and has yet to make his home in the southern temple; see Bronner and Shulman 2009: *xxxvi*.

111 Even his name, which does not appear to be a personal name, has no unambiguous significance. Some take Kampan as a name for Shiva, as in the Ekamparanatha Temple in Kanchipuram (Zvelebil 1974: 146); others, following folk tradition, understand it to mean 'post' or 'pillar' (on the name's uncertain meaning, see Emeneau 1985)

112 Jesudasan 1961: 185; Nilakanta Sastri 1975: 378; Zvelebil 1974: 146; see further Caminataiyar 1997: 716–18, in which he describes hearing about Kampan's birthplace from a Shrivaishnava from that town who was visiting him in Tiruvavaduthurai, and making a visit there, seeing 'Kampar Medu' (Kampan's Hill), where his house was said to be located, as well as icons of Kampan and his wife in the local Perumal temple.

113 *E.g.* I vv. 195, 205, 308, 312, 475, 1103, 1169; these professions of faith appear to have a narrative arc, beginning with Garuda, the vehicle upon whom Vishnu appears when the gods seek his aid, then Vishnu in his cosmic form, then numerous mentions of Rama himself.

114 *E.g.* I v. 495.
115 See Shulman's typology of Tamil poets (2001): 'one often finds in the *bhakti* traditions an aversion to claims of technical mastery and learning—such as the *kavya* poets must have—an aversion, indeed, to anything that smacks of premeditated, "artistic" effort... the whole subsequent tradition insists, as a matter of principle, that the major canonical poems, at least, were *improvised*, usually during a pilgrimage to a shrine. The poems are felt to represent a spontaneous outpouring of divinely inspired emotion.' (104–05)
116 See, for example, the verses collected in Puliyur Kecikan 2001; Narayana Rao and Shulman 1998: 99–100; Shulman 2001a: 239–44.
117 Shulman 2001b: 86–88.
118 These tales coalesce in two 19th-century texts that synthesize late medieval biographic currents about Tamil poets, *Tamil Navalar Caritai* and *Vinotaracamancari* (*Vinodarasamanjari*). Namaccivaya Mutaliyar 1914 and Kopalakirusnak Kon 1922 offer useful synopses of these tales.
119 On Kampan's associations with courtesans, see Caminataiyar 1997: 717–18; Narayana Rao and Shulman 1998: 152–54.
120 On the feud between Kampan and Ottakkuttar, see Blackburn 1996: 49, 105–07; Shulman 2016: 159–60; Wentworth 172–76.
121 *Cf.* a traditional account that Kampan composed 700 vv. a day; see Zvelebil 1995: 268.
122 *Cf.* the tale of Kampan attempting to protect his son Ampikapati, who has fallen in love with a Chola princess and betrayed his feelings by praising her beauty in verse before the king. Kampan transforms the verse into a description of a kataiciyar woman selling food outside, and when the king looks out the window to see her, Saraswati transforms into the woman; Narayana Rao and Shulman 1998: 162–63.
123 The *Uttarakanda,* which has never been ascribed to Kampan, is almost certainly not Ottakkuttar's: he worked in the poetic genres such as parani and ula, and his style contrasts patently with *Uttarakanda*'s own.
124 See Shulman 2001b: 113–20 for an exposition of this larger tale, and the corresponding movement of *Kamparamayanam* from Kampan's authorial voice to the communities who accept it as speaking of and for them.
125 The text did not garner authoritative commentaries. In his own commentary, Caminataiyar makes sporadic mention of an unnamed 'old commentary' (pazhaiya urai) and 'old annotation' (pazhaiya kurippu) but provides no further information, and I have been unable to locate them.
126 *EC* rev. vol. 8, Hassan no. 89; see also Pollock 2006: 559*fn*; Vaiyapuri Pillai 13, 66, 68.
127 Narayanan 2000: 267–73; Shulman 2016: 265–66. Umaruppulavar's patron was the eminent Muslim community leader Citakkati (Shaikh 'Abd al-Qadir, d. 1715), said to have sent the young poet to study in Arabia.
128 Narayanan 2000: 268.
129 *E.g.* Caminataiyar 1933–34: vol. 1, 35, 60, 62, 88, 292, 301; vol. 2, 24; 1997: 74, 106, 144, 190, 344–45.

130 Caminataiyar 1997: 89–90; 115–16.

131 On Minatchicuntaram Pillai's mastery of Kampan, see Ebeling 2010: 45–46; Cutler 2003: 273–87. Caminataiyar, who positions himself at the nexus of traditional manuscript circulation and print culture, describes spending his entire salary to purchase a full edition of Kampan, and speaks of a humorous moment when an elderly teacher is bemused to learn that the text has been printed in book form. (Caminataiyar 1997: 387–88; 1933–344, vol. 2, p. 218.) Towards the end of his life, when Minatchicuntaram Pillai had fallen ill, Caminataiyar and a few other students appeal to him to teach *Kamparamayanam*. He agrees, and Caminataiyar describes how the text had a healing effect on his teacher, who delights in its beauty so much it brings him to tears, and proclaims it a spontaneous work of inspired genius. (Caminataiyar 1997: 381–84)

132 The munsif, who is more interested in Caminataiyar's knowledge of earlier texts, remains unimpressed. The exchange demonstrates the extent to which Kampan moved in the sociotextual currents of Shaiva religious practice, whereas the text the munsif later gives Caminataiyar, *Civakacintamani*, is unknown to him even though, as the munsif says, it provides the model for *Kamparamayanam* itself. (Caminataiyar 1997: 531–32)

133 On the inexpensive digests of religious texts at this time, see Venkatachalapathy 2012: 139.

134 Aiyar held *Kamparamayanam* in such regard that he took a complete edition with him when escaping out the window on an arrest warrant, and wrote the study while serving a nine-month prison sentence for sedition.

135 Venkatachalapathy 2012: 240–41, quoting the poet Bharatidasan: 'they would congregate "like the inhabitants of Kishkinda". In one such reading session, there was a lectern shaped like an "x". Nachiaramma would place a heavy tome of *Kambaramayana* in paraphrase, with the other women seated around her. She would sing at the top of her voice, and, as she recited, the women would start shedding tears. Nachiaramma would wipe away her tears and continue to recite the paraphrase in a choked voice. All the while [they would] wipe their eyes and blow their noses.'

136 Purnalingam Pillai 1928: 50–66 *et passim*.

137 Purnalingam Pillai 1985: 229.

138 See, for instance, Pulavur Kulantai's *Iravana Kavyam*, another Dravidianist classic that makes Ravana the hero of the Ramayana (Venkatachalapathy 2012: 163); T. Ponemballam Pillai's 'The Morality of the Ramayana' (Irschick 1964: 284); 'Obscenities in the Ramayana' by E.M. Subramania Pillai (under the pseudonym Chandrasekara Pavalar) (*Kuti Aracu* 8/26/1928).

139 Sivathamby 1971: 214.

140 See the rich discussion of Periyar's publications condemning the Ramayana in Richman 1991.

141 Blackburn 1996: 29.

142 Blackburn 1996 offers a careful, rewarding study of these performances,

emphasizing the transposition of the text into a local register as the puppeteers explicate its verses on the stage.

143 Narayanan discusses the numerous Muslim scholars of the text, focusing particularly on former Madras High Court chief justice M.M. Ismail, who has given hundreds of talks and has authored numerous books on the text.

Note on Text and Translation

1 There are two other major editions of the text, the Vai. Mu. Kopalakirusnamacaryar edition and the Annamalai University edition. Kopalakirusnamacaryar draws heavily from Caminataiyar's commentary.

2 In *Balakandam*, paronomasia is employed in vv. 18, 22, 23, 101, 104, 124, 471, 891, 959, 1214.

Prologue

1 The 'three ordered natures' are the three constituent strands of the material universe, ordered hierarchically: sattva, rajas and tamas. Sattva is quiescent, peaceful and all-knowing; rajas is swift, active and mercurial; and tamas is slothful, inert, and ignorant. Notably these are material: Kampan here refers to Vishnu's presence in the physical world, and notes that a full understanding of his auspicious qualities lies beyond the limits of human comprehension.

2 'Noble ascetic': Valmiki, author of the original Ramayana, the first work of Sanskrit poetry. The 'curse once launched' refers to the famous origin of Sanskrit poetry, when Valmiki sees a hunter kill a male krauncha bird while it is mating with its partner, and his grief provokes him to cry out in verse, cursing the hunter to a life without peace.

3 Acunam: a mythical creature so susceptible to the influence of music that it is enraptured by the lute, but the single beat of a drum is powerful enough to kill it. See *Narrinai* v. 304; *Perunkatai* 1.47.241–43; *Civakacintamani* 1402.

4 The three fields of Tamil are literature, music and drama, said to have been first propounded in the (non-extant) grammar of the sage Agastya. No premodern instances of Tamil drama are known to exist.

5 A carpenter snaps chalk lines to ensure that cuts are made properly according to a building's design.

6 The 'finest among them' is Valmiki; Kampan offers no guidance as to the identity of the other two authors. U. Ve. Caminataiyar (henceforth U. Ve. Ca.) suggests the other two might be Vasishtha (*Yogavasishtharamayana*) and Bodhayana (*Bodhayana Ramayana*, non-extant). Other likely sources, given their prominence in south India, are Bhatti (*Bhattikavya*, 7th c.) and King Bhoja of Malva (*Ramayanacampu*, 11th c.).

7 Repeatedly honoured in Kampan's Ramayana, Cataiyan of Venneynallur is the poet's patron. If per, 'great', is taken instead to mean 'named',

Iramavataram, 'The Descent of Rama' (lit. 'The *Avatar Rama*') is the name of Kampan's text.

The River

1 The river is the Sarayu, which flows from Uttarakhand into Uttar Pradesh. Here Kampan implies that the men of Kosala are fully in control of their senses, and the women do not look at men other than their husbands.

2 The unnamed 'old commentary' that U. Ve. Ca. quotes in his own exegesis of the text identifies this king as Rama's father Dasharatha. He might alternatively be identified as Rama himself.

3 At the direction of Nala—the monkey son of the divine architect Vishwakarman—Rama's monkey army builds a bridge of stones between the Indian mainland and Ravana's island kingdom of Lanka in order to invade it.

4 Rama is a king descended from the solar line that begins with the deified sun.

5 'Flooding river' may also be read as 'a hail of arrows', enhancing the simile.

6 'Serpent': Kaliya, held to have lived in the Yamuna River as it terrorized the herding folk of Vrindavana. Kaliya tried to crush Krishna when he entered the river, but Krishna swelled in size until Kaliya released him, then he danced upon the serpent's head until Kaliya was at the brink of death. When his serpent wives came to Krishna and prayed for his release and Kaliya pledged to cease his evil deeds, Krishna spared his life.

7 Bees are said to swarm at the rut fluid that flows from the temporal glands of a bull elephant in musth.

8 The four landscapes that the flooding river passes through, mixing their respective environments (tinai mayakkam), are familiar topoi from the body of classical Tamil literature known as cankam poetry (tentatively dated to the early centuries CE). They are: kurinji (mountainside); mullai (forested pastures); marutam (agricultural fields); and neytal (seashore). The four paths of rebirth determined by good and bad karma are gods; humankind; animals; and insentient matter.

9 'Fields' (turai) also means 'harbours', enhancing the simile.

10 A tank is a reservoir—either constructed, or developed by harvesting a natural water source such as a spring through digging or embankment—used for irrigation, drinking water, or bathing.

The Land

1 'The land': Kosala (eastern Uttar Pradesh).

2 Eyes: blue lilies; hands, feet and faces: lotuses; mouths: red lily. All of these plants would be considered weeds in a rice paddy under cultivation.

3 Sandalwood (talam) may also be read as 'camphor'.

4 Women's eyes are regularly compared to fish because of their similar shape, sparkle, liquidity and quick movement.

5 The pastoral mode is a primary melody-type emblematic of the landscape of forested pastures (mullai).

6 If taken as anchu ura rather than manchu ura, the phrase in line 3 reads 'terrifying [those who hear them]' instead of 'till their voices reach the clouds'.

7 'Wondrous conch' (chalanchalam): an immense conch surrounded by a thousand auspicious right-turning conches.

8 Kampan regularly employs the conceit that a woman's waist is so thin that it wears away day after day.

9 The crushed areca nuts will have flowed down from the agricultural fields, making this verse an instance of the poetic technique of mixing landscapes (tinai mayakkam); in this case, the seashore (neytal) and land under watered cultivation (marutam).

10 These songs, vallaippattu, are auspicious songs dedicated to male heroes sung by women while they husk grain.

11 'Tortoises feast on low-hanging mangoes' may also be read as 'low-hanging mangoes drip with sweet-tasting nectar'. In another instance of tinai mayakkam (compare v. 61), this verse blends three landscapes: the mountainside (kurinji); land under watered cultivation (marutam); and seashore (neytal).

12 The cassia fruit is tubular, 30–60 cm long and roughly 2 cm in diameter. It is emblematic of the landscape of forested pastures (mullai). This verse blends four landscapes. In the agricultural fields (marutam), women sing songs of the rice paddies, which frighten calves in front of cowherds' homes located in forested pastures (mullai). Fisherfolk women by the seashore (neytal) sing songs that distract women in the mountains (kurinji) from their duty of protecting fields of dry-cultivated crops from birds. Women who plant rice: kataiciyar, lit. 'women at the bottom'.

13 The landscapes blended here are the mountainside (kurinji) and land under watered cultivation (marutam).

14 This verse is an instance of the rhetorical device of ozhippani (Skt. apahnuti) dependent upon shlesa (compare v. 18 *et passim*), a figure of speech in which paronomasia allows the verse to deny an object one of its own attributes and ascribe another foreign to it.

15 The young women are said to bear the fragrance of champak blossoms, lending the sandalwood grove where they play a semblance of a champak garden. When young men (and Skanda) practise the arts of war in garden spaces, the fragrance of jasmine that drifts from their garlands makes the gardens seem like jasmine forests.

16 This instance of blending landscapes is achieved by naming their emblematic goods: honey from the mountain slopes (kurinji); rock candy and sweet syrup from the agricultural fields (marutam); curds from the forested pastures (mullai); and toddy from the seashore (neytal).

17 In Kampan's time, young children were adorned with a gold pendant (aimpadai taali) shaped like the five emblematic weapons of Vishnu (conch, discus, bow, sword and mace) in order to protect them from childhood illnesses believed to be due to the malign influence of planetary alignment.

The City

1 The kaustubha, said to have emerged from the churning of the primordial ocean, is Vishnu's emblematic chest jewel.

2 U. Ve. Ca. comments, 'Vaikuntha is exponentially more difficult to reach than heaven. If Ayodhya, where Rama has come as an avatar to rule, is itself Vaikuntha, who is capable of detailing all of its merits (happiness, etc.)? Therefore under Rama's rule, Ayodhya is superior to heaven itself. Since the karmic result of deeds does not occur in a different place than the deeds themselves, moreover, Ayodhya has the distinction of being a place where the karmic world and the world of experience merge together as one.'

3 Mal, 'the great one', is a common Tamil name of Vishnu (its pronunciation rhymes with 'all').

4 The goddess Durga is held to protect cities; usually represented as seated on a lion, she may also take an antelope stag as her vehicle. 'Because they restrain the driving senses' (tinpori yadakkiya ceyalal) may also be read as 'because they contain war engines'. 'Because they hold the trident' (cuzhattal) may also be read as 'because they bear lightning rods'. City walls appear to have been topped at regular intervals by lightning rods, see *Civakacintamani* v. 2527. U. Ve. Ca. comments, just as God can easily be reached by those devoted to him but remains inaccessible to those who are not, the city walls are a familiar barrier to Ayodhya's residents, who may easily cross in and out, but their massive breadth and subtle design prevent enemies from entering. He cites an unidentified old annotation (pazhaiya kurippurai) to identify this god as Kalagni Rudra.

5 The lotuses are overcome because they have closed after sunset, whereas the women's faces remain full and shining. They will 'regain their former strength', their fully opened blossoms, once the sun rises again.

6 The rutting elephants in this verse are imagined to attack ships plying the ocean, mistaking them for rival beasts, just as crocodiles in the moat would attack wooden siege craft.

7 Vishnu's fifth avatar, the dwarf Vamana, takes three strides traversing heaven, earth and the underworld to claim them from Bali, the ruling antigod (asura). See vv. 429–50, which narrates the myth in detail.

8 U. Ve. Ca. quotes an unidentified old commentary: 'The emerald capitals bear the weight of diamond blocks and crossbeams, then heated gold is used like mortar and driven into the joints. Small rubies are tapped in to serve as the crushed pieces of brick found in mortar, then a cornice of sardonyx is laid down.'

9 The subjects of this paronomastic verse are not explicitly stated. The primary reading describes paintings of women, while the secondary one describes the mansions in which they are found.

10 The ropes of white pearls hanging amid the multicoloured banners are likened to garlands or flowering creeper vines hanging from the wishing trees in Indra's heaven.

11 In Tamil literature, manmade hillocks are a regular site where highborn children play.

12 Since Ayodhya, full of gold and jewels, is a constant source of light, and the sun's rays lengthen as it rises, shorten at noon, and then disappear together—as would the shadow of an object over the passage of a day—the sun appears to be the shadow of the city itself.

13 U. Ve. Ca. notes that while it is in an elephant's nature to dig the earth up with their feet, some readers take this verse to mean that the elephants are so bellicose they kick the earth in order to defeat their own shadows.

14 The southern wind (tenral) and the buzz of bees are both held to increase the anguish of parted lovers.

15 The ivy gourd, *coccinia indica,* bears a scarlet fruit that is roughly the size and shape of a woman's lower lip. It is customary in the Indian poetic tradition for an unfaithful man to fall at the feet of his lover when she is sulking in order to end their quarrel. If the woman remains unswayed, she may kick him in the face, an act held to cause the man pleasure.

16 This verse turns on multiple meanings of the word kali, first translated as 'joy'. Dependant on context, kali can also mean: flower nectar (lotuses); mud (carp); toddy (bees); rut (elephants); and kohl (women's eyes).

17 In the Tamil, all four lines employ the same verb, narutal, its meaning—smell, look, shine, drift out—shifting with semantic context.

18 The singing women are virali, professional singers and dancers familiar from the earliest period of Tamil literature onward.

19 Putting a horse through its paces or racing it on a course (cendadi) may also be taken to mean a ball game played on horseback. See *Periyapuranam, Kazhaitrarivan Puranam* v. 126.

20 The Ganga in heaven is the Milky Way; the flapping banners on top of mansions are likened to tongues jokingly stuck out, then drinking up the Ganga before it reaches earth.

Governance

1 The giving of gifts is accompanied by chanted mantras and the pouring of sanctified water. Since brahmans are the traditional recipients of royal gifts, this passage likely refers specifically to them. Grand royal sacrifices such as the horse sacrifice (ashvamedha), royal consecration (rajasuya), and the drink of strength (vajapeya) are performed by kings desirous of asserting the status of imperial rule over other kings, and thereby becoming an emperor, the 'king of kings'.

2 'Darkness' (irul) has the secondary significance of 'pain, suffering'. The fact that the king's parasol is described as greater than the moon that illuminates the entire earth and affects every life on earth demonstrates Dasharatha's status as emperor, the 'king of kings' who has no rival.

3 Everything, the verse suggests, functions together perfectly, moving in harmony under Dasharatha's rule just as a body is properly governed by its animating spirit (here implicitly identified as Dasharatha himself).

The Holy Avatar

1 Dasharatha refers to his mothers in the plural because his father Aja had multiple wives, and there are five types of mothers in traditional Tamil culture: birth mother; foster mother; wet nurse; governess; and matron.

2 Vasishtha is himself a ruler of the Ikshvaku lineage, making Dasharatha's use of the word 'favour' (arul) particularly apt.

3 Dasharatha's extraordinarily long rule of sixty thousand years is matched by his sixty thousand ministers; see *Ayodhyakandam* v. 13.

4 'Emperor': Kampan stresses that King Dasharatha is a cakravartin, a 'turner of the wheel' of royal command, meaning that as a 'king of kings' (rajaraja), he rules over other kings to control the entirety of India (Bharatavarsha).

5 Brahma had earlier granted Ravana the boon that he cannot be conquered by gods, asuras (anti-gods), nagas (serpent beings of the underworld) and beasts. Dismissive of humans, Ravana does not include them in this boon. Subsequently, Shiva granted Ravana immense strength and the Chandrahasa, a divinely powerful sword.

6 Meghanada is Indrajit, son of Ravana, so named because his cries sounded like a thundercloud when he was born.

7 The 'twin lights of sun and moon' have the secondary significance of Vishnu's emblematic weapons: the conch and the discus. The god himself is said to have eyes, mouth, hands, feet and a navel that are like lotuses, making the twinned lights that cause lotuses to blossom a particularly fine metaphor.

8 'The lord who is a sea of compassion' (arulin azhiyan) may also be read as 'the lord who wields the favour of his discus'.

9 The discus will be born as Bharata; the conch as Shatrughna; the serpent couch (Adishesha) as Lakshmana. The 'doomsday mare' is a fire-breathing mare that lies at the bottom of the ocean; on doomsday it emerges to spread fire over the world.

10 Said to be born from Brahma's mouth, Jambavan is known for his vast lifespan and strength. He helps Rama to find Sita and fight Ravana. In addition, he makes Hanuman aware of his own vast strength, and encourages him to leap across the ocean to search for Sita in Lanka.

11 Valin is the king of the monkey kingdom of Kishkindha. Angada is general of the monkey army under the command of Sugriva; he leads the search

for Sita in the south and plays a leading role in Rama's battle with the rakshasas. Nila is the son of Valin and Tara, king and queen of Kishkindha.

12 In *Valmiki Ramayana*, Shiva does not incarnate as a share of Hanuman.

13 The two gods are Brahma and Shiva, whom the other gods first approached when they sought to be delivered from the rakshasas' oppression.

14 'King with shoulders strong as a mountain' (matirum poruta tin tol manna) may also be read as 'king who has conquered the entire earth'.

15 Adishesha is the world serpent, Vishnu's couch when he lies immersed in yogic sleep on the primordial ocean. As the sage Vasishtha describes, Rishyashringa ('the antlered sage'), is so innocent and has so little experience with the world at large that he thinks of human beings as simply another sort of creature, free of the complexities of human thought, intrigues, failings, and—most importantly—sexual desire.

16 The land ruled by Uttanapada and, after him, Romapada is Anga (eastern Bihar).

17 Rishyashringa's father is Vibhandaka Rishi. As U. Ve. Ca. quotes the old commentary, 'This true ascetic saw the female sages, and did not think of them as animals because he mistook their clothing. Therefore, as respect for ascetics dictates, he offered them ritual water and bid them to stay.' Aatithya, traditional rites of hospitality, are services (upacara) offered to a guest that include giving water for ablutions and drinking, a formal declaration of welcome, offering a seat, the lighting of lamps, the giving of flowers, etc.

18 The women are pleased that their ploy to have Rishyashringa follow them seems to be working so well, but they are also uneasy about the consequences of fooling this purely innocent boy with their ascetic guise and taking him to Romapada's kingdom of Anga.

19 Shanta, in *Valmiki Ramayana*, said to be the biological child of Dasharatha, who gave the child to Romapada to raise as his own adoptive daughter.

20 *Valmiki Ramayana* varies considerably from this narrative (1.8–1.14). Dasharatha himself heads directly to Anga, appeals to Rishyashringa, and completes a horse sacrifice (ashvamedha), at the conclusion of which they perform the putrakaameshti (sacrifice performed out of the desire for sons) rite, causing Dasharatha's four sons to appear.

21 Dasharatha 'returned heaven to the gods' when he defeated the mighty asura Shambara (Timidhvaja), who had seized control of Indra's city Amaravati. When Indra hastened to Dasharatha and appealed for help, Dasharatha took to his chariot and killed the asura and his kin. During battle, Dasharatha's wife Kaikeyi kept the king's chariot functional by inserting her finger into the axle, thus gaining the boon that later results in Rama's banishment. See vv. 244; 323; 960.

22 Shibi is a mythic king of the solar line tested by Indra and Dharma, who take, respectively, the form of a hawk and a dove. Pursued by the hawk, the dove comes to Shibi for protection, but the hawk claims his rightful

need for sustenance under the just king's reign. Shibi offers his own flesh in equal exchange for the dove's weight. When his own chunks of flesh are weighed upon the scales against the dove, however, the dove grows heavier and heavier, so that Shibi is required to keep cutting off portions of his own body. When at last the king places his entire body on the scales, the gods reveal their true identities and glorify his reign of perfect justice.

23 In *Valmiki Ramayana*, since Dasharatha is Shanta's true father, Rishyashringa treats him as a father-in-law, thereby enhancing the appeal for the sage to visit Ayodhya.

24 The use of the past tense indicates the certainty of future events; compare v. 236.

25 Kekaya is a western region of India adjoining Gandhara in what is now northwestern Punjab.

26 Sumitra, having received two portions of the rice ball, gives birth to the twins Lakshmana and Shatrughna. Tamil tradition holds that the left eye and shoulder of men will tremble as an evil omen, whereas their right eye and shoulder will tremble as an auspicious one.

27 Tradition holds that after a grand royal sacrifice such as the one Dasharatha has just held, his feudatories will seek the emperor's presence in his chambers in order to present tribute and gifts, and attend to the king's worship of his family deity.

28 The royal bath (avaprutha snanam) is another requisite act of purification and reentry into the social order after the performance of sacrifice.

29 Verses 278–79 are absent from some manuscripts.

30 'Virtuous Kausalya' (tiran kol Kocalai) may also be read as 'Kausalya, pregnant with the mighty one'. Kausalya's son is Rama, here referenced both in his cosmological aspects ('the Pure Light, the perfect one who has realized the holy Vedas') and his earthly appearance ('the stormcloud and the darkness'), referring to his dark blue hue.

31 Indra 'raged against the mountains' when he clipped the wings of the mountains so they could no longer fly.

32 Sumitra's second son is Shatrughna, Lakshmana's twin brother, held to be an embodiment of Vishnu's conch Panchajanya.

33 Kinnaras: mythological creatures that are half human, half horse, often associated with music and said to be devoted lovers.

34 Ritual impurity after the birth of a child lasts for twelve days, then the child's naming ceremony occurs on the thirteenth day.

35 'Mountain with a trunk': Gajendra, an elephant that Vishnu saves from being devoured by a crocodile when it begs for him to save him. See *Bhagavata Purana* 8, which narrates the myth as follows: Indradyumna is a Pandya king who does not immediately offer the sage Agastya hospitality when he arrives. Agastya, enraged, curses the king to become an elephant. The king appeals to the sage, who says that the king will be saved from the curse by Vishnu's touch. In his next birth, Indradyumna lives as the

elephant Gajendra. One day, he drinks from a lake on Mount Trikuta, where a gandharva named Huhu cursed to be a crocodile (for disturbing the sage Devala) lives. The crocodile tries to drag Gajendra under the water when he drinks, and they fight for a thousand years. When Gajendra is exhausted and is about to be dragged under the water, he appeals to Vishnu, offering lotus flowers with his trunk and chanting the *Vishnu Stuti*. Vishnu appears and redeems Indradyumna from the curse, and the king immediately attains Vishnu's heaven Vaikuntha. See *Civakacintamani* vv. 2481, 2683. As U. Ve. Ca. notes, this verse not only reveals that Rama is the avatar of Vishnu, it focuses on a famous myth that has assumed immense importance in the Vaishnava faith due to its allegorical significance: the crocodile is sin, the elephant gripped by the leg is humankind trapped in karma, and the muddy lake from which the crocodile emerges is samsara.

36 That is, the king gives extraordinarily generously to brahmans.

37 Rama's body is blue like the lilies, while his eyes, hands and feet are red like lotuses.

38 Ceremonial head-shaving is a ritual of purity (*samskara*) that the legal texts dictate should take place, variously, on the baby's first, third, or seventh birthday. Investiture of the sacred thread is a 'second birth' of the child that indicates the beginning of his education under a guru (here Vasishtha). For kshatriyas, the rite is to take place in the child's tenth year in spring or summer (*Baudhayana Grihya Sutra* 2.5.8–9).

39 The various places that Rama and Lakshmana's feet touch become blessed, hence the earth goddess is said here to have gained the rewards of ascetic practice.

40 The imagery depends upon Rama and Lakshmana's skin: Rama is blue like the ocean and the rainclouds, while his eyes, hands and feet are like shining lotuses; Lakshmana is golden like Mount Meru.

41 The passing of a day of Brahma signifies the end of a cosmic age.

Taking in Hand

1 'Newly create all lives, all worlds': this refers to the myth of King Trishanku, whom Kaushika (Vishwamitra) attempted to raise into heaven while the king was still in his living body. Unwilling to accept this, Indra and the other gods send Trishanku down to earth, so that in the end he hangs upside down in the sky, balanced between these two opposing wills. Kaushika then begins to create a new parallel world in the southern sky for Trishanku to rule as its lord, but—persuaded by Indra that his own power should not be usurped—Trishanku remains upside down, now visible as the Southern Cross constellation. His story is told more fully in vv. 662–73.

2 These heavenly locations refer, respectively, to the worlds of Shiva, Vishnu, Brahma and Indra.

3 The king's three drums symbolize charity, fortune and victory.

4 As U. Ve. Ca. notes, anger and desire are the most treacherous of the passions that threaten a sage's equanimity. They are likened, respectively, to Subahu and Maricha, the two rakshasas who are disturbing Kaushika's sacrifice, while their mother Tataka is likened to delusion.

5 Dasharatha remembers that he will die when separated from his son, for he was cursed by the parent of a boy he had killed in the forest when he mistook him for a deer. He realizes that his time has now come.

6 U. Ve. Ca. notes that Vasishtha, an omniscient sage who comprehends events spanning the future, here considers the implicit reasons for Kaushika's wrath, and sees that the latter will transmit many powerful mantras to Rama and perform his marriage to Sita. He therefore allays Kaushika's anger and counsels Dasharatha to accede to the visiting sage's request. On Vasishtha's knowledge of Kaushika's power, see *Valmiki Ramayana* 1.20.9–19.

7 Rama is here likened to the forceful ocean (blue like his body), while his mastery of warfare is the flood, fed by the rains equated with the mantric weapons he will learn from Kaushika. No matter how much water pours in from flooding rivers, the ocean can always hold it; Rama, likewise, masters any amount of knowledge.

8 Rama's quivers are inexhaustible.

9 The sun is said to have a single-wheeled chariot (the solar disc) pulled by seven horses, which are alternatively explained as the days of the week, the seven colours of the rainbow, or the seven Vedic meters. The chariot's single wheel and the unequal number of horses cause the sun's circular orbit.

The Killing of Tataka

1 Ananga, 'bodiless', is another name of Kama ('desire'). This verse refers to the famous myth of Shiva burning Kama to ashes when the latter tries to fire his arrows at the god to provoke his interest in Uma.

2 This series of verses describes another classical Tamil landscape, palai, the wasteland parched by the sun's heat.

3 Snakes are said to subsist on wind, and here the wind is so hot their mouths cannot bear it.

4 'Pity', pacai, also means 'moisture'. The 'three relentless foes' are lust, anger and mental delusion. Both good and bad karma must be eradicated if the proliferating effects of deeds are to be brought to an end.

5 When Indra slays the serpent Vritra, many asuras flee and hide within the ocean. Agastya drinks it away so that Indra can finish them off.

6 Sumali is Ravana's maternal grandfather, who lived in Lanka with his brothers Mali and Malyavan, who committed great evil until they were routed by Vishnu in a battle that left Mali dead. Fearing for his life, Sumali fled to the underworld, where he remained.

7 Mountains: breasts; poison: gaze of the eyes; roar like thunder: voice; fire: hair; crescent moons: fangs.
8 Kakutstha, here referring to Rama, is a patronymic for kings of the solar line.
9 Rama is the blue stormcloud, the rainbow is his war bow.

The Sacrifice

1 Teaching the use of a divine weapon consists of the weapon's specific power, its god, mantra, means of launch and return.
2 Compare *Valmiki Ramayana* 1.31.1–5, where the sons are named Kushambha, Kushanabha, Adhurtarajasa and Vasu, and their father, in order for them to fulfil their kshatriya duty, orders them to found the kingdoms named in this verse (absent from some manuscripts).
3 Varaha is Vishnu's third avatar, the boar, who rescues the earth from sinking into the primordial waters, lifting it up with his powerful tusks.
4 To the gods, Mahabali (Bali) is evil and his sacrifice foul because it will grant him complete control over heaven and earth, usurping their own position, and because he will give the earth and its contents entirely away, leaving no role for the gods themselves.
5 The sacred thread, reed waistcord, and ring of darbha grass are all marks of celibate studenthood (brahmacharya).
6 Shukra, identified with Venus, is the asuras' guru and Mahabali's brahman counsellor (purohit).
7 Bali here argues that if the dwarf were actually the supreme lord Vishnu, the fact that he came to the asura as a supplicant and placed his hands below Bali's own, thereby signifying a relationship of patron and beneficiary, means that Bali's conferral of the gift would make him superior to Vishnu himself.
8 Bali here tells Shukra that it would be contrary to dharma to deny Vamana a gift because he is a god, and therefore a natural foe of the asuras. U. Ve. Ca. notes, moreover, that Bali is thinking of Vishnu through the lens of bhakti (sharing in a lord's beneficence through devotion), and the god is therefore giving him an immense boon by appearing directly before him. Apart from his promise to the gods that he will deliver them from the threat posed by Bali's control of heaven and earth, he has no desire to harm the asura.
9 'Without thinking' (velli) is also an insulting pun on Shukra's Tamil name Velli: 'You have spoken as Velli'.
10 This dictum is almost identical to *Tirukkural* 166: 'Someone envious of a gift will perish without food and clothes'.
11 The promise of a gift is formalized by offering mantras while the donor pours consecrated water over the recipient's hands.
12 By placing his foot on Bali's head, Vishnu effects the posture of a master

granting refuge to a devotee. All the damaging consequences the gods have endured because of Bali's grand sacrifice and control over heaven are thereby eliminated, and Bali himself is blessed as a great devotee.

13 Valmiki names the location (1.28) as Siddhashrama, where Kashyapa and his wife Aditi practised asceticism and received Vishnu's boon that they would have him as a child (Vamana).

14 The 'lethal poison' is the halahala poison, which rose from the primordial ocean when the gods and the asuras churned it, and which Shiva trapped in his neck in order to keep it from killing the gods.

15 Verses 462–63 are absent from some manuscripts.

16 Headless bodies (kabandhakas) dancing in circles, ghouls who feast on the flesh of the dead, and the arrival of carrion birds are characteristic Tamil descriptions of a battlefield where many enemies have been slaughtered.

17 In this key verse, Vishwamitra reveals to Rama who he really is: an avatar of the god who created the worlds, and protected them from cosmic dissolution by swallowing them entire before lying down to dream on a banyan leaf floating on the primordial sea.

Ahalya

1 Kashyapa's second wife Diti loses her sons, the asuras, in their war with the gods.

2 Rambha, Menaka, Tilottama and Urvashi are all apsaras, heavenly courtesans from Indra's world. 'Songs full of longing', literally 'songs filled with vilari' (the sixth note of the scale), are representative of the seaside, the cankam landscape of longing.

3 Surabhi is the divine wishing cow (kamadhenu) created during the churning of the primordial ocean, who can produce any desired object from her milk. Kannan is another name for Cataiyan, Kampan's patron.

4 Vishnu takes the female form of Mohini in order to entice the asuras away from the ambrosia that rose from the churning of the primordial ocean.

5 Brahma emerged from the primal lotus that grows from Vishnu's navel as he slept on the ocean upon his serpent couch, and with his four faces blew the world into creation.

6 The Kaveri, the river central to the Chola kingdom's agricultural world and ideology of fertile productivity.

7 'Princess from Vidarbha': Keshini. Vidarbha is located in eastern Maharashtra.

8 Sagara has performed ninety-nine horse sacrifices, so this hundredth, achieved with the help of his sons, would make him the equal of Indra. The king of gods therefore steals the sacrificial horse to ensure that Sagara cannot complete the rite. Kapila is a sage (whom some Puranas identify as Vishnu) whose eyesight is so powerful that anything he gazes upon is reduced to ash.

9 The time period in many manuscripts is one thousand years.

10 When Vamana steps into heaven and punches a hole in its vault, the Ganga, which was previously flowing outside the universe, rushes in to pour over his foot. Brahma collects it in his water pot, and then pours it down so that it becomes the Ganga. See *Bhagavata Purana* 9.8–9.

11 Ashoka blossoms are bunches of orange, red and yellow flowers.

12 The red dye makes the diving birds mistake others in their flock for a different species.

13 In traditional lore, the water buffalo's milk flows when it thinks of its calf in the morning.

14 Verses 553–55 are absent from four manuscripts.

Beholding Mithila

1 The quarrel, which is held to intensify erotic desire, is critical to the Tamil literary depiction of sexuality, in which it increases the pleasure of subsequent lovemaking.

2 The women in the windows are the implicit object of comparison. Moon: face; spears: eyes, Kama's bow: brow; red pith: mouth; curl of sapphire: braid.

3 The courtesans' hearts are like mirrors because they reflect what their lovers want to see in them, rather than having any true romantic attachment. The second half of this verse closely approximates a verse ascribed to Vararuci: 'This one ball looks like three. Touching her palm, it's as red as red can be. On the ground, in the gleam of her toenails, it's white as white. In the space between, caught by her eyes, it's darker than the dark.' Narayana Rao and Shulman 1998: 43–44. My thanks to David Shulman for drawing these points to my attention.

4 Lotus: face; blue lily: eyes; red lily: mouth; creeper leaves: ears; blue lotus: braid; red sholapith: lower lip; waves: creases in the stomach; carp: eyes; murrel: shins.

5 The redness of the men's hair comes from them prostrating themselves at the women's feet, which are dyed with red lac.

6 The cruel serpent is Rahu, the headless asura said to swallow the moon during an eclipse. The simile involves the fresh, blooming flowers turning dark and disappearing as the moon does when swallowed by Rahu.

7 Rice reddened with turmeric and lime paste then soaked in water is whirled before a person said to be suffering from effects of the evil eye.

8 Southern breeze (tenral): a soft breeze said to be scented by flowers and sandalwood, delightfully cooling to the touch. For separated lovers, however, it burns like the harsh, hot northern wind.

9 Due to her lovesickness, things that would normally feel pleasurable—lake water, blossoms, the summer breeze—cause Sita so much pain she fears that she may die.

10 The krauncha (the sarus crane, or perhaps the red-naped ibis) is said to be inseparable from its mate, thus causing pain to separated lovers; see v. 5.

11 The ascetic practices Kaushika is performing (tapas) are held to increase internal heat and lead the advanced practitioner to glow. Indra's position as king of gods is not incontestable, and should a human being attain enough power through sacrifice or ascetic practice, he can be overthrown (see the myth of Sagara and his sons; vv. 502–30). Rambha is one of the apsaras, celestial dancing women renowned for their seductive beauty.

12 Ambarisha, son of Nabhaga, was a king of Ayodhya. The tale of Ambarisha's sacrifice of Shunahshepa is told in *Bhagavata Purana* 9.7.

13 Ricika's wife Satyavati is Kaushika's older sister (see v. 423). Shunahshepa is never explicitly named in Kampan's text, but is instead referred to as Kaushika's nephew.

14 The eagle, Garuda, is Vishnu's mount; Brahma's mount is a goose; and Shiva's mount is the bull Nandin.

15 The ida and pingala are said to be the right and left subtle channels, respectively, that flow in the human body. The ida is associated with lunar, feminine, blue, cool energy, while the pingala is associated with solar, masculine, red, hot energy.

16 'Guardians of the quarters': the cardinal directions are held to be safeguarded by gods, most prominently Indra in the east, Yama in the south, Varuna in the west and Kubera in the north.

17 When the primordial ocean is churned, two opposed liquids appear: the halahala poison, which is black, and the ambrosia of immortality (amrita), which is white.

18 Here Udayagiri, the eastern mountain behind which the sun is said to rise, is figured as Shiva, whose elephant cloak, a dappled hide that suggests stars twinkling in the sky, is compared to the enveloping darkness. The sun is Shiva's fiery third eye, emerging from his brow to fill the world with light.

The Noble Genealogy

1 The Cholas claim descent from the solar lineage, so the genealogy that Kampan presents in this chapter not only describes Rama's heritage, it aligns his Ramayana with the imperial rule under which Kampan wrote. As is common in Tamil genealogies, Kampan does not explicitly name each individual, preferring instead to identify them by their deeds. I add their names for the sake of clarity. Prithu is described in Puranic mythology (with variations on the theme) as the redeeming king who controls the earth goddess and forces her to feed the world's creatures. After the death of the evil king Vena, whose tyrannical, lawless rule led the world into famine, Prithu, mind-born from Brahma, hunts down the earth goddess Bhumidevi, who has taken the form of a cow. He compels her to release her

milk, which becomes all the world's vegetation necessary for sustenance, and thereby delivers all creatures from starvation.

2 The nine gems, associated with the nine planets of classical India and emblematic of royal power, are ruby, diamond, pearl, coral, hessonite garnet, blue sapphire, cat's eye, yellow sapphire and emerald. 'Pure Light': Narayana, Vishnu as the supreme being. Ikshvaku is said to have received Vishnu in his manifestation as Ranganatha as a boon from Brahma, and installed him in a shrine in Ayodhya. After his own royal consecration at the end of his war with Ravana, Rama gives Ranganatha to Vibhishana, who installs the god in the great temple complex Shrirangam, facing south so that he may always have Lanka in view.

3 The name of this king is not known, though some manuscripts give the name Nimi.

4 Mucukunda is said to have answered the petition of the gods and ascended to heaven, where he drove off the bellicose asuras and then ruled over the heavenly world in order to allow Indra, king of the gods, some respite. As U. Ve. Ca. notes, some hold that this king is Dilipa.

5 The meaning of the proverb 'like a [myrobalan] fruit in the palm of the hand' is that something is absolutely clear, hence the significance here is that the entire earth became transparently clear to this king, an object of complete understanding. The identity of this king is not known. U. Ve. Ca. notes that some identify him as Nahusha, while others identify him as Sudasa. The moon is said to bear the mark of a rabbit often described as a stain.

6 On Kuvalayashva (Dhundumara), see *Bhagavata Purana* 9.6.21–24. On the divine guardians of the quarters, see v. 686.

7 Vishwamitra is briefly retelling the tale of Rishyashringa given in vv. 215–72.

8 The twins Lakshmana and Shatrughna are said to be golden and silver, respectively, in hue.

The Bow

1 This verse is absent from several manuscripts.

2 The sixty thousand men (arupatinayirar) may also be taken as 'ten thousand cut in half', which matches the number given by Valmiki, who describes five thousand men wheeling the bow out in an eight-wheeled iron chest. See *Valmiki Ramayana* 1.66.1–5.

3 Meru, which Shiva also previously used as a bow to destroy the triple city, sees another vast bow lifted and is reminded of its own defeat.

4 Janaka levelling the bow on his own daughter means that mastery of the bow is her bride-price. If naccilai, 'fine bow', is taken as nacc' ilai, the phrase reads 'the king had no wish to level it on his daughter'.

5 Like Janaka facing this hostile band of kings, the owl, though alone, easily

attacks a group of crows at night without threat of harm due to its superior vision.

6 Snakes are said to fear lightning because it is attracted to the gemstones set in their heads.

7 The gods are said never to blink their eyes.

8 On the rabbit-shaped mark on the moon, see v. 721.

9 The ambrosia that grants the gods immortality is said to have arisen from the primordial ocean when it was churned by the gods and asuras; see vv. 491–95.

10 Golden spots (pacalai, temal) are said to spread over the breasts of a lovesick woman.

Setting Out

1 U. Ve. Ca. notes that emperors do not give their own wealth directly, but instead order their feudatories to pile up wealth, which is then given to a worthy recipient.

2 The drums will be played by a man of low status (a pariah, Kampan terms him 'Valluva') to announce a royal message that he will then proclaim.

3 In several manuscripts, the 'Karmukha Padalam' ('The Bow') ends with this verse, and the 'Ezhuccip Padalam' ('Setting Out') begins with v. 817.

4 Because the dark elephants are gathered so closely together and the rut pours in such quantity, the clouds (the banners held above the elephant troops) believe they are the ocean, and lie close as a result.

5 The jingling harnesses are here implicitly compared to the chittering sounds of the geese.

6 These are the eight elephants who, in Indian mythology, hold up the world at its cardinal points.

7 The 'cruel demons' (cur) are malevolent spirits that never directly touch the earth with their feet. Courtesans' bodies touch, but their minds remain apart.

8 The geese remind him of his lover's gait, while the lotuses remind him of her feet, face and hands.

9 The white insignia of kings under Dasharatha's command are so plentiful they look like whitecaps on a river as the procession moves forward. The conches and drums, moreover, echo the Ganga's roar.

10 The woman suffers because her waist is too thin to support her large breasts. The flowing rut may be compared to the sweat that pours down them as she struggles, and the jewellery she wears to the elephants' caparisons.

11 An unmarried woman, in this conservative social ethos, is not supposed to talk to men who are not family. Normally a person would have to call out in order to be saved from something like a river in flood, but the man here says that this woman's eyes are so expressive she has no need to speak with words.

12 Large eyes that 'reach back to the ears' are a standard of feminine beauty in Indic poetry.
13 Dwarves, U. Ve. Ca. notes, were employed as attendants in the palace harem, and are here depicted riding among their charges while the king's retinue is on the march. See *Civakacintamani* 631 for an extremely close textual parallel.
14 The horse is racing so fast its legs appear never to touch the ground, making it seem as though the horse is carrying the woman up to heaven. The elephant following it may be compared to Airavata, Indra's own mount, pursuing a woman so beautiful she could be a celestial dancer.
15 Walking on tiptoe to minimize contact with the ground, holding auspicious items demonstrative of status, and keeping noses blocked with the right hand are all prescribed ways to minimize ritual pollution. U. Ve. Ca. further notes that holding the nose would keep the scent of women's garlanded hair from affecting the brahmans' self-control.
16 In this extended comparison, the women are likened to geese because of their swaying gait; their jingling anklets to the geese's call; the diaphanous garments to the water's surface. The bees humming around the women's hair would swarm the lotuses in the pond, which themselves are implicitly compared to the women's faces, hands and feet.
17 The women are likely riding in palanquins veiled by thin white curtains (the 'wave-tossed milk sea').
18 The eyes in the third line might belong to men who are looking at the women's faces, or they may be the same joyful eyes of women referred to in the second line.
19 Elephants in musth discharge a secretion of temporin from ducts on their temples, which trickles down into their mouths.
20 Dark lilies: eyes; red lilies: mouths; red lotuses: hands.
21 Given the social dictate that an unaccompanied woman should have a man present to guide her, the men in this verse are trying to devise a stratagem to get the women out of a group and on their own.
22 The comparison between the bullocks and yogis involves a semantic shift in vocabulary when it is used in the philosophical genre. Patru, translated as 'burdens' in this verse, also means 'ego-bond', which yogis strive to eliminate. Paacam, the 'ropes', are also the karmic fetters that bind humans to continued death and rebirth. The bullocks free themselves of the burdens they carry, break the ropes that yoke them to the wagon carts, and end their own suffering. So too the yogis free themselves of ego-bonds, one after the other ('row by row'), and break the fetters (the 'ropes that bind them') in order to end their suffering and achieve liberation. Note as well that the women stand well clear of the freed bulls, just as yogis and women are supposed to remain apart.
23 Airavata is Indra's divine elephant, said to be pure white and to have five heads and ten tusks. On the comparison between an elephant's temples and women's breasts, see v. 1138.

24 The 'love in hardship' mode, naivalam, is a secondary mode of the paalaikurinji (the wasted mountain slope), well chosen for the trials Rama and Sita will endure after the crown prince is banished to the forest.
25 The roar of drums, chariots, elephants and cavalry evokes the sea, while the faces of the men and women suggest the full moon.
26 Conches played on auspicious occasions are kept wrapped in cloth when not in use. Kept in storage, the fan of yak hair that extends from their handles lies coiled like the spirals of a conch shell. Here, they are being brought out of their wraps to be ceremonially whisked.
27 Lakshmi is said to dwell on the chest or lap of a ruling lord.
28 Vishnu is identified in this verse as 'lord with the discus' (nemiyan). U. Ve. Ca. identifies him as Ranganatha, following the traditional tale of Brahma giving Ranganatha to Ikshvaku; see v. 713.
29 As the sun shines on the lotuses and causes them to blossom, so Dasharatha causes the lotuses in this verse (the women's faces and the worshipful hands of the lords he commands) to bloom as well.
30 As emperor, Dasharatha is said to support the entire earth, allowing the earth goddess to relax her back. Here, however, people note that his gathered army is so vast that it must certainly weigh her down, creating a paradox.
31 The Poṭiya Mountain is the mythic home of the sage Agastya where sandalwood trees grow in profusion. Their scent is said to be carried by the southern wind (tenral).

Seeing the Mountain

1 Chandrashaila is the mountain where Dasharatha's vast army and retinue stop and spend the night during their journey to Mithila.
2 'Renowned by the bowman Kama' (varicilai yanangan mel konda) may also be read as 'traced with designs made by a sugarcane pen'. 'They yearn for their lovers' heart' (avi vettana) may also be read as 'desiring fragrant incense'.
3 Because the elephant is unable to break the chain that shackles it to a shala tree, like a crafty political operative who destroys enemies through means other than open warfare, it employs strategy: grasping the base of the tree and ripping it out by the roots.
4 See close textual parallel in *Civakacintamani* v. 200.
5 The black kites, U. Ve. Ca. notes, may be following the smell of the elephant's rut, or the smell of flesh from all the animals the elephant has crushed as it races through the forest.
6 When in blossom, the saptaparni tree is said to smell like elephant rut. The elephant in this verse mistakes the tree for a rival and destroys it.
7 The women's girdles remind the peacocks of their own trains. Cochineals, red like a woman's lip or the ivy gourd, are a prime food source for peacocks during the rainy season.

8 'Arabs' (turukkar), literally 'Turks'. By the 11th century (see *Kalingattup Parani* v. 332), the word had come to mean Arab, or Western Asian. The earth goddess (Bhudevi) wears a necklace strung with nine different types of gems: ruby, diamond, pearl, coral, hessonite garnet, blue sapphire, cat's eye, yellow sapphire and emerald.

9 Curtains are like the ocean waves because they are white and diaphanous, and because they surround the women's quarters like the ocean surrounds the earth goddess as a belt or garment. Storehouses are like the seas because of all the valuables they contain; elephants are like the clouds due to their size and colour; and horses are like the wind because of their speed.

10 The foot of the mountain is here compared to the elephant's knee as it kneels so the rider can dismount.

11 Women's faces: reflections of the moon without its dark spot; silver sea: white tents in the women's quarters surrounded by white curtains; rolling waves: white banners (fluttering in the wind).

12 The 'open space' further signifies the liberation that wise people seek, and the 'three-stranded rope' refers to the three types of bonds that men striving for liberation aim to sever: desire for property (mannacai); lust for women (pennacai); and monetary greed (ponnacai). Alternatively, they are: egotism (anavam); delusion (mayai); and karmic bondage (kanman).

13 As the white sides of the tent (the waves) blow in the wind, the eyes of the women (glittering like fish) are briefly visible to the outside world, as are the molucca beans (the pearls in the waves) they throw as they play jacks.

14 This verse refers to the myth of the asuras Madhu and Kaitabha, who steal the Vedas from Brahma and deposit them deep inside the waters of the primeval ocean. At the behest of Brahma, Vishnu in his manifestation as Hayagriva searches the entire ocean, singing Vedic verses. Enchanted, the two asuras set the Vedas aside and come seeking the source of the song. Vishnu, meanwhile, retrieves the Vedas and gives them back to Brahma. Once they realize the Vedas are missing, Madhu and Kaitabha start churning the ocean to find them. They see Vishnu sleeping on his banyan leaf and believe him to be the culprit, so they announce they will confront him in battle. Vishnu tells them he will grant them a boon if they ask one of him; the asuras, however, are so haughty they tell the god that they will grant *him* a boon if he would like. Vishnu then asks them for the boon that they will both die by his hand, and so they do.

15 The fact that men and women are burning oudh, a luxury commodity used to manufacture oudh, to stoke their kitchen fires reflects their magnificent surroundings on the mountain slope.

16 When the kino tree blossoms on the mountain slopes and the local women smell its fragrance, tradition holds that it is the proper time to start harvesting fields of dry-cultivated millet. The women of the mountain tribe (kuravamakalir) are themselves said to be astrologers.

17 Given the singers' concentration, they do not cast the sidelong glances that would make their eyes reach to their ears.

18 Just as the spring water that flows over crystal rocks is dyed red by the kumkum on the bodies of women who bathe there, the toddy assumes a red hue from crystal cups inlaid with rubies.

19 The Ganga is held to begin in heaven as the Milky Way; its 'infinite pearls' are the stars. On Vishnu as the dwarf Vamana measuring out the worlds, see vv. 429–50.

20 This verse hinges on women's idealized innocence, one of the 'feminine qualities' (makaduu kunam) stipulated in poetic theory. They are: modesty (nanam); innocent naiveté (madam); timorousness (accam); and delicacy (payirppu).

21 At its simplest (many additional ingredients may be added), a betel chew consists of slices of areca nut wrapped in a betel leaf that has been smeared with a touch of slaked lime.

22 The glory lily's curvature and conical petal arrangement as it is budding makes it look somewhat like a cobra reared up with its hood spread.

23 Verses 944–52 are madakku verses, in which identical poetic feet repeated in each line yield a different meaning. Such verses in which the rhetorical device offers much of the aesthetic pleasure are hard to serve well in translation.

24 The drums and instruments are played to drive off wild forest beasts.

25 The dark clouds resemble Vishnu, while the golden garlands lying at the bottom of the mountain suggest Lakshmi.

26 Vishnu's 'display of the infinite', the vishwarupa (see *Bhagavad Gita* 11), is here likened to the mountain itself with its dazzling vistas, with its 'countless glittering peaks' suggesting the god's countless heads.

27 After Dasharatha slays the asura Shambara at the behest of Indra, the gods give him a celestial garland of mandara flowers to celebrate the time that Dasharatha ruled from the same throne as Indra himself. On Shambara, see v. 241.

28 After the jasmine garlands worn during the day have opened, yielded their fragrance and started to wither, the women put on new garlands for the evening and change into new clothes.

Picking Flowers

1 Asuras are dark in colour, hence the comparison between Hiranya and the night. This verse turns on an extended comparison between the narrated moment and a famed myth: in the first sense, the golden sun appears over the Udayagiri mountain, behind which it is said to rise, and then extends a thousand rays to conquer the night; in the second, mythic sense, Narasimha, the fourth avatar of Vishnu taken form as a being part lion and part human, bursts forth from a pillar and kills the asura Hiranya with his thousand arms.

2 'The geese try to follow' (annam otungum) may also be read as 'the geese leave them and go away'.

3 The extended comparison between women and creepers blooming on flowering boughs plays on the multiple meanings of the names for women's jewellery. Curul, 'rolled golden earrings', also means budding unfurled leaves, and kuzhai, earring, also means 'tender leaf'. The bees, moreover, would gather around both the flowering plants and the women's hair, which would be adorned with a flower garland.

4 Blossoming branches bend to the flowering creepers they bear as they grow, but this is nothing in comparison to the women's power in this verse, in which rocks (the men's shoulders) soften when touched by flowers (the women's hands).

5 The flowering creepers are the young women, the blossoming lotuses (in contrast to the closed lotuses in the rivers and ponds) are their mouths, and the blue lilies are their eyes. Since bees are held to seek newly blossomed flowers that are still filled with nectar, the young women provide all they could want: flowering creepers, lotuses and lilies.

6 Since the young men and women have been picking all the new flowers in the area, and the bees have already had their fill of the blossomed ones, they swarm to the women's hair, which—fragrant with flower pollen—will once more soon be adorned with garlands made from the new flowers.

7 The woman's face is the full moon; the loose hair covering her face are the clouds.

8 Although the woman's sulking is over, her pride insists that she find a way to make her lover end the quarrel, here (by suggesting through her words to the cuckoo) that he offer her a flower.

9 Who else apart from her, in other words, would be covering his eyes?

10 The bees swarming the elephant are implicitly compared to women's eyes as they gaze at the king.

11 She is miserable because she grows worried that, given her obstinate sulking, he will find another lover.

12 The madhavi creeper is used to construct shelters for lovers' secret assignations. As U. Ve. Ca. construes the verse, the man, sensing that his lover is distant from him because of some quarrel, asks the madhavi creepers he used to make their shelter to produce something miraculous, a celestial flower (mandara). In so doing, he asks his lover to forget her quarrel so they might make love.

13 Her heart wilts because her lover has not come to see her, and therefore will not see the mix of flowers on her garland that proves she had been earnestly searching for him.

14 Professional singers were recipients of a host's largesse, such as (in this case) jewellery.

15 In her simplicity (see v. 937), the woman notes that the goose walks as she does, and therefore treats it as though it were human.

16 The peacock is traditionally held to be a fierce enemy of snakes.
17 The woman's failure to understand that she can still be seen even if she herself cannot see gives a good sense of the naiveté the poetic tradition imposes on its female characters (see. v. 937).
18 The sun is traditionally pictured holding a lotus in his hand.
19 When evening falls, herdsmen bring in their cows with hand gestures and by playing flutes. Here, the hand gestures are implicitly likened to Kama lifting his arrows to his bow. U. Ve. Ca. notes, moreover, that herdsmen wear garlands around their wrists, further enriching the comparison with Kama's flower arrows.
20 The woman's brow is a bow of its own, which barely has to bend before men's passions are aroused. If Kama's bow is fully bent, the verse implies, they would stand no chance at all, even if they were mentally disciplined sages.
21 The man is so immersed in his love, he is not thinking correctly, and picks flower buds and tender leaves that are too immature for her to enjoy or wear.

Playing in the Water

1 On Durvasas cursing Indra, see vv. 482–95; *Sundarakandam* 659; *Tiruvempavai* 11.
2 Compare *Civakacintamani* v. 2659 for a close textual parallel.
3 Golden spots or streaks (pacalai, temal) are said to appear on women's breasts when they are suffering from unfulfilled desire; see v. 796.
4 Due to their shape, the carp (kayal) look like blinking eyes as they appear and disappear beneath the water's surface.
5 This verse is absent from several manuscripts.
6 As the sandalwood paste washes away, scratches made by lovers' sharpened nails are now clearly visible on the women's breasts, so the young men see that they have other lovers.
7 Compare *Civakacintamani* v. 1485 for a close textual parallel. The king in this verse subtly indicates that he desires the girl, and the girl, guided by the feminine quality of modesty (naanam; one of the makaduu kunam, see above v. 937) indicates to her friend that she is interested and wants the friend to act as her go-between, since she cannot speak to him directly.
8 On clothes scented with perfume, see *Civakacintamani* v. 71, *Perunkatai* v. 1.54.9–10.

Drinking and Playing

1 The full moon is Kama's parasol; its extension over the world asserts his dominion.
2 U. Ve. Ca. reads the verse differently, taking vellani, 'birthday festival',

as 'troops clad in white', in which case the last two lines would read 'the whole sea-girt world looked like troops clad in white / marching under Kama's sea-monster banner wielding swords as hard as diamond.'

3 The cup is made of translucent crystal.

4 As U. Ve. Ca. notes, *Tirukkural* v. 66 offers a close counterpart to the comparison of murmuring (mazhalai) with flutes and lutes: 'People who think the flute and lute sound sweet have never heard the murmuring of their own children.'

5 This verse is absent from some manuscripts.

6 The call of the krauncha (Tamil anril) is said to cause separated lovers great pain. As U. Ve. Ca. explains the verse, the parrot is calling the husband's name, so the woman implies that it is distressing her as much as a krauncha would; see vv. 5; 623.

7 In this pastime, a young woman closes her eyes and tries to draw a circle in the sand. If she successfully joins the circle, she will win the love of the man she desires.

8 'A woman holding a ball made beautiful by her fingers' (pantani viralinal) may also be read, 'a woman with beautiful fingers, their tips round as play balls'.

9 On the pleasure a man feels in this circumstance, see v. 142.

10 The woman's breasts, likened to ritual pots filled with sanctified water to be poured over warriors setting out for battle, will cool his burning skin.

11 The woman removes any article of clothing that will make a sound or catch light so that she can move in secret, but the moon still threatens to reveal her.

12 A woman in love is said to draw a picture of Kama and his wife Rati, and if the woman later glances at the drawn image of Kama, her friends and maidservants will know how much she is suffering.

13 Custom dictates that messages between lovers should be conducted through a go-between, usually a friend or maidservant of the woman, in order to preserve the lovers' secrecy.

14 The woman's lover is blameless, but her love-sickness has caused her great suffering, and her modesty prevents her from speaking earnestly to her friend. Strategies such as drawing a picture of Kama and Rati (see v. 1080) permit the woman to indicate her desire without the need to express it directly.

15 This verse is absent from some manuscripts.

16 Since the woman is intoxicated, she acts strangely when she comes upon her husband unexpectedly, treating him in an extraordinarily formal way. The husband grows fearful, wondering if she is angry or has heard something untoward about him.

17 The maidservant and mother are like the southern breeze and the nighttime, respectively, because even though they conventionally offer comfort, they cause separated lovers pain. The maidservant is like the southern wind

because in her capacity as go-between she moves back and forth like a breeze; the mother is like the nighttime because she never seems to leave the separated lover alone.

18 Due to her drunkenness, the woman is weary and her actions confused, so she is unable to tell her maidservant to act as a go-between. Instead, she simply raises her hands to her maid in silent reverence.

19 The jingling bells on the women's ornaments and waist chains announce the news of their secret trysts.

20 The woman, certain that her lover has fingernail scratches on his chest because he has been with another woman, is about to kick him while he is on his knees seeking forgiveness. The husband, for his part, knows that she will damage her delicate foot on his solid chest, so by covering it with his softer hands he is protecting her from harm.

21 Though the moon shines with cool light, it cannot equal the rays of the sun, so it retires even though it illuminates the world to a partial extent. The sun rising from the dark ocean is like the kaustubha jewel lying on top of the shrivatsa, the dark whorl of hair on Vishnu's chest.

The Welcoming Party

1 Dasharatha is born of the solar dynasty and Janaka the lunar dynasty; the respective brilliance of sun and moon indicates their relative status.

2 Indian mythology speaks of seven oceans. Here, Dasharatha's marshalled troops are likened to six of them joining together, while Janaka's army is likened to the seventh, the milk ocean from which Lakshmi emerged sitting on a red lotus.

3 The red and white colours of the various ceremonial regalia—white parasols with flower garlands, peacock parasols, round fans, chowries, etc.—are compared to red and white lotuses that bloom either in the day or at night, but here bloom together because the mass of royal parasols is turning day into night.

4 'A bow used to arrows' (evarun cilaiyinaan) may also be read with a long 'e' (e arun cilaiyinan), 'a bow that has never fired an arrow', to imply that Janaka is so powerful he has never had to resort to war. The ground, made dusty by all of Janaka's gathering troops, is covered with fine powders, gold dust and flower nectar because of all the body unguents, adornments and flower garlands they are wearing as they come to welcome Dasharatha.

5 Janaka's love is prompted by Dasharatha's innate noble qualities and the fact that Rama is now his son-in-law, bringing the kingdom of Mithila into marital alliance with Dasharatha's imperial realm.

6 On Indra's victory over the asura Shambara and his role in restoring Indra's heavenly rule, see v. 241. This verse is absent from some manuscripts.

7 His riches comprise sons, wives, army, retinue, counsellors, palace women, and his royal regalia and emblems such as the throne, white chowries, peacock fans, white parasol, etc.

8 This verse may also be read to refer to Rama's brothers rather than the soldiers.
9 Tamil poesis classifies women into seven stages of sexual maturity, a categorization that structures the poetic genre of ula that Kampan employs in the following chapter. See Wentworth 2011: 20–21; 105; 158.

The Procession

1 Note that, in associating Rama with Krishna, the seventh avatar of Vishnu is praised because he personifies the later, eighth avatar here portrayed as a familiar figure beloved by the audience watching him in procession.
2 The eyes are white, black and red due to the streaks of red (cevvari) held to be a standard of feminine beauty in Tamil poetry.
3 Snakes are said to fear thunderstorms because lightning is attracted to a jewel in their heads. See v. 776.
4 The ancestor is Shibi, who sacrificed his own flesh for the sake of a dove who had come to him for protection. See vv. 244; 718.
5 Anga: eastern Bihar; Avanti: western Madhya Pradesh; Vanga: central-southern Bengal; Malava: central Madhya Pradesh.
6 Magadha: southern Bihar; Macca: central India; Lata: southern Gujurat; Vidarbha: Berar; Panchala: western Uttar Pradesh.

Creating Beauty

1 'The girl lovely as Lakshmi' (ma iyal nokkinalai) may also be read as 'the girl with a doe's innocent gaze' or 'the girl with wide eyes'.
2 'Sparkling jewel strung on a golden chain' (netriccutti): a gem or ornament of inlaid gems that hangs down from a short chain to rest on the top centre of the brow. Raincloud: hair; tongue: brow ornament; moon: face.
3 A woman's neck is traditionally held to resemble a conch because of its creases; Sita's perfect neck compares to Vishnu's divine conch Panchajanya. 'Wedding cord' (mangalasutra): auspicious wedding cord, the adornment that beautifies all the other ornaments a woman wears, here considered to be Lakshmi herself. Even though Sita needs nothing to make her neck beautiful, for she is Lakshmi embodied, her maids place necklaces on her out of their fervent devotion.
4 Women's arms are traditionally compared to bamboo because of their perfect roundness and lustre. The comparison of Sita's arms adorned with many ornaments to bamboo set with rubies and pearls suggests that nothing in the real world can equal their beauty, only imagined possibilities.
5 Rama, scion of the solar lineage, offers the sunlight that will keep Sita's lotus hands from closing during the night as such lotuses would normally do. Bangles are held to protect a woman's virtue and chastity.
6 Just as Indian religious philosophies regularly describe the supreme being

as knowable only through inference, people infer that because Sita's upper and lower body are visible, she must have a waist that connects them.

7 Star: tilak; crescent moon: brow (the third day of the crescent moon is said to be the height of its beauty); lotus blossom: face; lilies: eyes.

8 These rituals are all performed to ensure that the marriage ceremony proceeds smoothly, to rid any influence of the evil eye, and to protect Sita from any potential harm.

9 The white fly-whisks swaying up and down on either side of Sita are implicitly compared to the white geese starting to take to the wing and then returning to the ground. The comparison of Sita to a peacock displaying its train is particularly fine, since one of the ornaments she is wearing, a girdle made of sixteen beaded strands, is 'the peacock's train' (kalaapam).

10 Geese: Sita's delicate stride; celestial dancers (apsaras): Sita's beauty; precious ambrosia: Sita's voice.

11 On naivalam, a secondary melody of the palaikurinji mode, see v. 868. Rama is not explicitly named in this verse; the 'delight of the world' may instead be taken to refer to Dasharatha.

12 Jambudvipa, the terrestrial world bounded by the sea in traditional Indian cosmology, is said to have eight mountain ranges. Rama broke one, Kailasa, in the form of Shiva's bow.

A Splendid Wedding

1 A thread is tied around the wrist for ritual protection or as a token of a vow to be fulfilled.

2 Unmarried women of high birth would be kept removed from men outside the family until they were married. In Tamil literature, they are often described as living in an upper floor of a multi-storeyed mansion (kannimadam), where they are served by a retinue of female maids and protected by guards.

3 In their preparatory festivities for the wedding, the people of the city are listening to musicians playing a wide variety of music, which for Sita is taking so long she feels as though it will never end.

4 'Rising up then falling down': conches rise and fall in the ocean, and conch bangles ride up and down Sita's arms because her lovesickness has made her so lean.

5 The clay pot filled with newly sprouted seeds (palikai) is used in a wide variety of rituals to demonstrate good fortune and ensure a favourable future.

6 'Please command us into service!' (pani pani yenalodum) may also be read as the words of Janaka's door-wardens saying to the kings, 'Come in, the king has orders to give you'.

7 Clouds: women's hair; bolts of lightning: their waists; stars: their eyes; gems: the ornaments worn by the onlookers; sun: Dasharatha, lord of the

solar lineage; moon: Janaka, lord of the lunar lineage. The imagery may also be taken literally, suggesting that the wedding canopy is so immense it soars above the heavens.

8 At the time of cosmic dissolution, Vishnu is said to swallow all the worlds within himself, and then lay down in meditative dreams on a banyan leaf floating on the primordial waters.

9 This verse makes clear that Dasharatha took a mobile image of the god with him to Mithila for prescribed daily ritual.

10 'Dark ocean surging with waves': Rama's black, curly hair; 'full moon': the circlet of sholapith and the ring around his topknot, with the strands of gold and flowers hanging from the topknot ornament over his brow the reflection of the moon on the ocean waters.

11 Rama's neck is the conch, the ring of pearls his discus.

12 The serpent is Vasuki, roped around Mount Mandara during the churning of the primordial ocean; see vv. 491–95.

13 The branches are implicitly compared to Rama's arms and hands, which like the wishing trees in Indra's heaven will offer gifts to those who appear before him.

14 On the necklace made of nine gems (navaratna) see v. 713. This necklace is the rainbow, the cloud is Rama's dark chest, and the stars are the pearls on his necklaces.

15 The sacred thread consists of three strands, here matched to the three lights of sun, moon and fire.

16 'Anklets and thick legbands' (cilampu nonkazhal) may also be read as 'thick legbands with jingling bells'.

17 Blossoming branch: Sita's body; full moon: face; two carp: eyes; two bows: eyebrows; jasmine buds: smiling teeth. 'Jasmine buds' (mulai) may instead be taken as 'breasts', in which case the phrase would read 'full breasts' instead of 'jasmine buds in blossom'. As before, Mount Meru is compared to the wedding canopy, with Sita implicitly compared to the moon just as Rama has been compared to the sun; see v. 1313.

18 As U. Ve. Ca. notes, because poison, war and dissociation were also produced from the churning of the primordial ocean, Vishnu's marriage to Lakshmi at that time was associated with disorder in a way Rama's marriage to Sita is not.

19 This ceremony, the saptapadi ('seven steps') is the most important rite in the wedding ceremony. Hands joined, the marrying couple walks clockwise around the fire (keeping the right sides of their body to it) seven times, declaring vows of union. Rama is here compared to the vital principle of life, while Sita is compared to the body, reflecting the ancient view that the patriline effects life and identity while the matriline represents the body in which a living being functions within the natural world.

20 Placing her foot upon the grindstone signifies a bride's dedication to the welfare of the home and faithfulness to the husband as solid and enduring as

rock. The husband then shows his new wife Arundhati, generally identified as the star Alcor (a faint star in the constellation Ursa Major). Arundhati, the wife of Vasishtha, is identified with constancy and faithfulness. Since Vasishtha is himself in attendance at Rama and Sita's wedding, Arundhati is presumably there as well, making Kampan's phrasing literally true.

21 Sita, the verse implies, is the emblematic kaustubha gem that Vishnu wears on his chest, just as Sita will embrace his chest closely in their love. On the kaustubha, see vv. 95; 1105.

22 The bride and groom consummate the marriage (samaveshanam) on the fourth night of the wedding ritual.

23 This fire sacrifice, the 'oblation of the remainder' (sheshahoma) occurs on the fifth day of the wedding and brings the ceremony to its end.

24 Janaka's other daughter Urmila marries Lakshmana. His younger brother Kushadhvaja is the father of Mandavi and Shrutakirti, who marry, respectively, Bharata and Shatrughna.

Parashu Rama

1 Surrounded by her dark-skinned husband and brothers-in-law, Sita's nearly invisible, radiant waist looks like lightning amid the clouds.

2 Omens of good fortune such as gathering peacocks, or the fleeing of ill omens like crows, result from the fact that the king is 'ever on the path of righteousness' (neri vantan). U. Ve. Ca. notes in his commentary that 'divination is a tradition of the ancients. In augury, when a pied wagtail, white-headed kite, rain quail, vulture, owl, Indian monitor lizard, mongoose, or monkey move counterclockwise, this is a good omen; when turning clockwise, the painted stork, kingfisher, crow, greater coucal, parrot, crane, peacock, chicken, iguana, spotted deer, civet, tiger, and fox are also good omens. When they travel in the opposite direction, they are ill omens'.

3 These are the five primal elements that compose the material world, which Shiva returns to their elemental state when he dances at the end of a cosmic age.

4 Kartavirya Arjuna, a king of the lunar dynasty, was a mighty thousand-armed fighter with a vast army who triumphed over all other kings. He is said to have defeated and jailed Ravana, and stolen the wishing cow (kamadhenu) from Parashu Rama's father Jamadagni. Parashu Rama retaliated by cutting off his thousand arms, beheading him, and laying waste to his army.

5 As U. Ve. Ca. narrates this myth, Parashu Rama and Murugan meet before Shiva to test their respective facility with weapons such as the bow. In order to test their power, Shiva points out Krauncha Mountain (Tamil Kurugupeyarkkundram), and commands them to pierce it with arrows. Murugan tries and fails, but Parashu Rama, filled with seething fury, succeeds. (A further myth states that Murugan then splits it with his spear.)

Many birds, moreover, live on the southern face of the mountain. When winter comes, killing the lotuses on the Himalayan slopes, they try to fly off to Lake Manasa, but the soaring Krauncha Mountain prevents them from doing so. After Parashu Rama pierces the mountain, however, they are given a clear path to the lake.

6 After Parashu Rama had conquered every king and claimed the earth for his own, his anger cooled, and he offered the earth to Kashyapa. Concerned that even this was not gift enough, he ascended Mount Sahya and hurled his axe into the sea. Due to the power of his austerities, the ocean dried up all the way out to his axe, forming an area known as Parashu Ramakshetra.

7 On the chest jewel as emblematic of a man's honour, see v. 346.

8 'The craftsman': Valmiki names him as Vishwakarman, others hold he is Maya. The circular orbit of the sun in his one-wheeled chariot resembles the radiant bows when they are bent fully back.

9 By extension, Brahma, grandfather of the gods, is through pretence asking an oft-repeated question of theistic factionalism: who is the mightier, Vishnu or Shiva? Compare *Valmiki Ramayana* 74.14–15.

10 Ricika is Parashu Rama's paternal grandfather, described in *Mahabharata* 3.115. Because Ricika marries Satyavati in the *Mahabharata* tradition, he is, therefore, Vishwamitra's brother-in-law.

11 As U. Ve. Ca. notes, Kampan here emphasizes that Parashu Rama is vastly different from an idealized brahman. Whereas his father Jamadagni was a peaceful, benevolent man, even though the bow imbued him with enormous power, his son displays the fiery wrath associated with kshatriyas.

12 Rama here intimates that Parashu Rama, even though he has been a killer, is in truth a proper brahman, for his father could recite all the Vedas, and Parashu Rama has performed innumerable austerities befitting a brahman sage.

13 Smelling the hair is, in Tamil culture, an intimate means of expressing great affection. Dasharatha's close embrace of his son and his pouring tears of joy presage the rite of Rama's royal coronation, consecrated by pouring sanctified water over the new ruler.

14 As U. Ve. Ca. notes, 'Not yet sixteen, Rama has killed Tataka, defeated rakshasas, returned Ahalya to human form, broken Shiva's bow, and triumphed over Parashu Rama. He is therefore Narayana, the basis of reality… Rama is a true avatar.'

15 On Kekaya, see above v. 269fn. Bharata's mother Kaikeyi is the daughter of its king.

16 Kampan ends the first book on a note of continuity: into the events of next book *Ayodhakandam*, as well as the karmic fruits of the gods ripening into action.

Bibliography

Editions and Translations

Kampan. *Śrī Kamparāmāyaṇam: Patavurai, Viḷakkavurai Mutaliyavaṟṟuṭaṉ*. Edited with commentary by U. Ve. Caminataiyar. Chennai: Makamakopatyaya Taktar U. Ve. Caminataiyar Nulnilaiyam, 1951–[1967].

——.*Kamparāmāyaṇam*. Commentary by Vai. Mu. Kopala Kirusnamacaryar. Chennai: Vai. Mu. Kopala Kirusnamacariyar Kampeni, 1962–1967.

——.*Kaviccakkaravartti Kampar Iyaṟṟiya Irāmāyaṇam*. Annamalainakar: Annamalaip Palkalaik Kalakam, 1956–1970.

Other Sources

Aiyar, V. V. S. 1950. *Kamba Ramayanam—A Study*. Madras: Delhi Tamil Sangam.

Arunachalam, M. 2005. *Tamiḻ Ilakkiya Varalāṟu*. Corrected edition. 14 vols. Chennai: T Parakkar.

——.1974. *An Introduction to the History of Tamil Literature*. Tiruchitrambalam: Gandhi Vidyalayam.

Blackburn, Stuart. 1996. *Inside the Drama-House: Rāma Stories and Shadow Puppets in South India*. Berkeley: University of California Press.

Bronner, Yigal and David Shulman. 2009. 'Self-Surrender' 'Peace' 'Compasssion' & 'The Mission of the Goose': Poems and Prayers from South India. New York: New York University Press.

Caminataiyar, U. Ve. 1997 [1950]. *Eṉ Carittiram*. 4th ed. Chennai: Makamakopatyaya Taktar U. Ve. Caminataiyar Nulnilaiyam.

Celvakkecavaraya Mutaliyar. 1974. *Kampa Nāṭar: Āyvu Nūl*. Tirunelveli: Tennintiya Caivacittanta Nurpatippuk Kalakam.

Cuppurettiyar, Na. 1996. *Paṇpāṭṭu Nōkkil Kampaṉ Kāviyam*. Chennai: Vanati Patippakam.

Emeneau, M. B. 1985. 'Kannaḍa Kampa, Tamil Kampaṉ: Two Proper Names'. *Journal of the American Oriental Society* vol. 105 no. 3 (Jul–Sep 1985), pp. 401–4.

Epigraphia Carnatica (EC). Edited by B. Lewis Rice and R. Narasimhacarya. Bangalore: Mysore Government Central Press, 1886–1919.

Epigraphia Indica (EI). vols. 1–42. Delhi: Archaeological Survey of India, 1892–1978.

Goldman, Robert P. 1984. *The Rāmāyaṇa of Vālmīki: An Epic of Ancient India. Vol I: Bālakāṇḍa*. Princeton: Princeton University Press.

Hardy, Friedhelm. 1983. *Viraha-bhakti: The Early History of Kṛṣṇa Devotion in South India*. Delhi: Oxford University Press.

Hart, George and Hank Heifetz. 1988. *The Forest Book of the* Rāmāyaṇa *of Kampaṉ*. Berkeley: University of California Press.

Iraṉaiyankar, Mu. 1938. *Ārāyccittokuti*. Madras: R.G. Press.

J.P. Fabricius's Tamil and English Dictionary: Based upon Johann Philip Fabricius's Malabar-English Dictionary. 4th ed. Tranquebar: Evangelical Lutheran Mission Pub. House, 1972.

Jesudasan, C. and Hepzibah Jesudasan. 1961. *A History of Tamil Literature.* Calcutta: Y.M.C.A. Publishing House.

Karuttiruman, P.G. 1963. *Kampar: Kāviyum Karuttum.* Chennai: Tamil Puttakalayam.

Kanapatiraman, Ca. 1970. *Kampar Vākkum, Nōkkum.* Tuttukkuti: Tirumakal Nulakam.

Kopalakirusnak Kon, I. Ma. 1922. *Kampar Carittiram.* Maturai: Pustaka Viyaparam.

Krishnaswami Aiyangar, S. 1933. 'The Tamil Śangam in a Pāṇḍyan Charter of the early Tenth Century A.D.' *Indian Historical Quarterly* vol. 9, pp. 63–75.

McCrea, Lawrence. 2011. 'Standards and Practices: Following, Making, and Breaking the Rules of *Śāstra*'. In *South Asian Texts in History: Critical Engagements with Sheldon Pollock.* Ann Arbor, MI: Association for Asian Studies, Inc.

Meenakshisundaram, T.P. 1961. *Prof. T.P. Meenakshisundaram Sixty-First Birthday Commemoration Volume: Collected Papers of Prof. T.P. Meenakshisundaram.* Annamalainagar: Annamalai University.

——.1965. *A History of Tamil Literature.* Annamalainagar: Annamalai University.

Monius, Anne E. 2000. 'Literary Theory and Moral Vision in Tamil Buddhist Literature'. *Journal of Indian Philosophy* vol. 28, pp. 195–223.

——.2001. *Imagining a Place for Buddhism: Literary Culture and Religious Community in Tamil-speaking South India.* New York: Oxford University Press.

Nagaswamy, R. 1980. 'Sri Ramayana in Tamilnadu in Art, Thought and Literature.' In *The Ramayana Tradition in Asia,* edited by V. Raghavan, pp. 409–429. New Delhi: Sahitya Akademi.

Namaccivaya Mutaliyar, Ka. 1914. *Kamparum Cōḻaṉum: Kalviyē Karuntaṉam.* Chennai: Si. Kumaracami Nayutu Sans.

Narayan, R.K. 2006. *The Ramayana: A Shortened Modern Prose Version of the Indian Epic.* New York: Penguin Books.

Narayana Rao, V. and David Shulman. 1999. *A Poem at the Right Moment: Remembered Verses from Premodern South India.* Delhi: Oxford University Press.

Narayanan, Vasudha. 2000. 'The Ramayana and its Muslim Interpreters.' In *Questioning Rāmāyaṇas: A South Asian Tradition.* ed. Paula Richman. New York: Oxford University Press.

——.1994. 'The Rāmāyaṇa in the Theology and Experience of the Srivaishnava Community'. *Journal of Vaisnava Studies,* vol. 2 no. 4 (Fall 1994), pp. 55–89.

Nilakanta Sastri, K.A. 2000 [1955]. *The Cōḻas.* 2nd ed. Madras: University o Madras.

——.1975. *A History of South India: From Prehistoric Times to the Fall of Vijayanaga* 4th ed. Delhi: Oxford University Press.

Peterson, Indira Viswanathan. 1991. *Poems to Śiva: The Hymns of the Tamil Sair* Delhi: Motilal Banarsidass Publishers.

Pollock, Sheldon. 2006. *The Language of the Gods in the World of Men: Sansl Culture, and Power in Premodern India.* Berkeley: University of California Pr

____,ed. 2003. *Literary Cultures in History: Reconstructions from South Asia*. Berkeley: University of California Press.

____.1998. 'The Cosmopolitan Vernacular'. *Journal of Asian Studies* vol. 57 no. 1 (Feb 1998), pp. 6–37.

____.1993. 'Rāmāyaṇa and Political Imagination in India'. *Journal of Asian Studies* 52 no. 2 (May 1993), pp. 261–297.

____.1984. 'The Divine King in the Indian Epic'. *Journal of the American Oriental Society* vol. 104 no. 3 (Jul-Sep 1984), pp. 505–528.

Puliyur Kecikan. 2001. *Kampaṉ Taṉip Pāṭalkaḷ*. Chennai: Mullai Nilaiyam.

Purnalingam Pillai, M.S. 1985 [1929]. *Tamil Literature*. Thanjavur: The Tamil University.

Raghavan, V. 1973. *The Rāmāyaṇa in Greater India*. Surat: South Gujurat University.

Rao, Ajay. 2015. *Re-figuring the Ramayana as Theology: A History of Reception in Premodern India*. New York: Routledge.

Richman, Paula, ed. *Many Rāmāyaṇas: The Diversity of a Narrative Tradition in South Asia*. Delhi: Oxford University Press.

Shulman, David. 2016. *Tamil: A Biography*. Cambridge, MA: Belknap Press of Harvard University Press.

____.2001. *The Wisdom of Poets: Studies in Tamil, Telugu, and Sanskrit*. New Delhi: Oxford University Press.

____.1985. *The King and the Clown in South Indian Myth and Poetry*. Princeton: Princeton University Press.

____.1979. 'Divine Order and Divine Evil in the Tamil Tale of Rama'. *Journal of Asian Studies* vol. 38 no. 4 (Aug 1979), pp. 651–669.

____.1978. 'The Cliché as Ritual and Instrument: Iconic Puns in Kampan's "Irāmāvatāram"'. *Numen* vol. 25 fasc. 2 (Aug 1978), pp. 135–155.

South Indian Inscriptions (SII). vols. 1–24. Madras: Archaeological Survey of India, 1890–1982.

Srinivasan, K.S. 1997. *Rāmāyaṇam as told by Vālmīki and Kamban*. New Delhi: Abhinav Publications.

Subramanian, A.V. 1993. *Literary Genres in Tamil: A Supplement to a Descriptive Catalogue of Palm-Leaf Manuscripts in Tamil*. Madras: Institute of Asian Studies.

Tamil Lexicon. 7 vols. Madras: University of Madras, 1924–1936.

Tiruttakkatevar. *Cīvakacintāmaṇi: The Hero Cīvakaṉ, The Gem That Fulfills All Wishes*. Translated with notes and introduction by James D. Ryan and G. Vijayavenugopal (vol. 2). 2 vols. Fremont, CA: Jain Publishing Company, 2005–2012.

Vaiyapuri Pillai, S. 1962. *Kampaṉ Kāviyam*. 3rd ed. Chennai: Pari Puttakalayam.

____.1959. *Tamiḻ Cuṭar Maṇikaḷ*. 3rd ed. Chennai: Pari Nilaiyam.

____.1938. *Kampan*. Madras: Kuppuswami Sastri Research Institute.

____.1956. *History of Tamil Language and Literature (Beginning to 1000 A.D.)* Madras: New Century Book House.

Veluthat, Kesavan. 1993. *The Political Structure of Early Medieval South India*. Hyderabad: Orient Longman.

Venkatachalapathy, A.R. 2012. *The Province of the Book: Scholars, Scribes, and Scribblers in Colonial Tamilnadu*. Ranikhet: Permanent Black.

Wentworth, Blake. 2011. *Yearning for a Dreamed Real: The Procession of the Lord in the Tamil Ulās*. PhD dissertation, University of Chicago.

Wilden, Eva. 2013. 'The ten stages of passion (*daśa kāmāvastāḥ*) and the eight types of marriage (*aṣṭavivāha*) in the *Tolkāppiyam*.' In *Bilingual Discourse and Cross-Cultural Fertilisation: Sanskrit and Tamil in Medieval India*. ed. Whitney Cox and Vincenzo Vergiani. Pondicherry: Institute Français de Pondichéry, École Française d'Extrême-Orient.

Zvelebil, Kamil. 1992. *Companion Studies to the History of Tamil Literature*. Leiden: E.J. Brill.

——.1973. *The Smile of Murugan on Tamil Literature of South India*. Leiden: E.J. Brill.

Acknowledgements

It has been a great pleasure to learn from the process of translating Kampan. I thank David Shulman for reviewing this translation, and bettering it with his elegant sense of style. Sheldon Pollock has from the beginning recognized the need for a translation of *Kamparamayanam*, and carefully reviewed the introductions to this work. Emily Silk read through the text with care and provided a wealth of editorial guidance. Ravi Singh and Radhika Shenoy of Speaking Tiger Books have worked diligently to ensure publication, and I am grateful for their efforts in bringing this text to an Indian audience. I spent many happy hours translating Kampan with my friend Bernard Bate, whose memory lasts in so many of the verses we enjoyed thinking through together. I would also like to thank Wendy Doniger for her enthusiasm for the project and her inspiring encouragement throughout.

ALSO FROM SPEAKING TIGER

GOD IS DEAD, THERE IS NO GOD

The Vachanas of Allama Prabhu

Translated by
Manu V. Devadevan

Twelfth-century saint-poet Allama Prabhu, along with Basavanna and Akka Mahadevi, was a founder of the Virashaiva or Lingayat movement in Karnataka. During a period of intense religious ferment, these Sharanas—protégés of Shiva—aimed to dismantle religious hierarchy and bigotry. They rebelled against exploitation based on class, caste and gender. And the form of expression they chose was the vachana—poetic compositions in everyday Kannada, which shook twelfth-century Karnataka out of slumber. Today, with their focus on devotion towards Shiva through love, labour and dedication, they form an integral part of the Bhakti tradition as well as India's cultural heritage.

The vachanas of Allama Prabhu symbolize his journey of freeing himself from worldly attachments and bondages. From gazing at Shiva from a distance, to uniting with Him, to declaring He doesn't exist and to finally realizing that He should be understood as a dynamic void: Allama covers a wide arc in his quest for spiritual enlightenment. Rooted firmly in the idea of experiential reality, his vachanas are passionate and filled with yearning; critical and brazen. Translated with great skill and fluidity by Manu Devadevan, *God Is Dead, There Is No God* is a treat for modern-day seekers as well as poetry lovers.

ALSO FROM SPEAKING TIGER

SWEET NOTHINGS

The Love Poems of Amaru

Translated from the Sanskrit by
Lee Siegel

Lee Siegel's English translation of the *Amarushataka,* an aristocratic collection of eighth-century amorous Sanskrit poems, is at once playful and erudite, amusing and poignant, carnal and sublime. The stanzas are little scenes from a panoramic comedy of erotic love.

The characters: Innocent girls and passionate ladies; devoted husbands and faithless rogues; female confidantes who help, console, or betray their friends.

The plot: First love, sexual union, separation (because of parents, friends, or the woman's jealous anger because the man has another mistress, or perhaps he must go on a journey), reunion, re-separation, re-reunion.

The theme is the delight of the game, the deliciousness of courtship, and the sweetness of sex.